D1604987

American Cooking:
Creole and Acadian

American Cooking:
Creole and Acadian

by

Peter S. Feibleman

and the Editors of

TIME-LIFE BOOKS

photographed by

Anthony Blake and Richard Jeffery

TIME-LIFE BOOKS, NEW YORK

THE AUTHOR: Peter S. Feibleman *(far left),* who was reared in New Orleans, based this book on boyhood memories and recent trips through South Louisiana. A novelist, playwright, film and television writer, he lived in Spain for 10 years and is the author of *The Cooking of Spain and Portugal* in the FOODS OF THE WORLD library. His fiction includes *Strangers and Graves, A Place without Twilight,* and *The Daughters of Necessity.* His play *Tiger Tiger Burning Bright* was produced on Broadway in 1962.

THE CONSULTANTS: James Beard *(center),* the leading authority on regional American foods, served as special consultant for this book. He has written *Delights and Prejudices* and *How to Eat Better for Less Money,* among many other books. The late Michael Field, who supervised the recipe writing as the library's consulting editor, was one of America's best-known culinary experts. His books include *Michael Field's Culinary Classics and Improvisations.*

THE STUDIO PHOTOGRAPHER: Richard Jeffery *(far left),* who made the studio pictures and the cover, has worked on a number of volumes in this series. Still-life material for his photographs was selected by Yvonne McHarg.

THE FIELD PHOTOGRAPHER: Anthony Blake *(center)* is one of Britain's most distinguished photographers. He did both field and studio photographs for *The Cooking of the British Isles* for the FOODS OF THE WORLD library.

THE LOCAL CONSULTANT: Marcelle Bienvenu, who assisted Mr. Blake in South Louisiana, was born in St. Martinville. A former feature writer for the New Orleans newspaper *The Times-Picayune,* she is now a public information assistant at Louisiana State University.

THE COVER: Superb shrimp, oysters and blue crabs abound in Louisiana's waters. Favorite shellfish accompaniments, for both Creole and Acadian cooks, are okra, fresh shallots (the local version of scallions) and dried red chilies.

TIME-LIFE BOOKS

EDITOR: Jerry Korn
Executive Editor: A. B. C. Whipple
Planning Director: Oliver E. Allen
Text Director: Martin Mann
Art Director: Sheldon Cotler
Chief of Research: Beatrice T. Dobie
Director of Photography: Melvin L. Scott
Associate Planning Director: Byron Dobell
Assistant Text Directors: Ogden Tanner, Diana Hirsh
Assistant Art Director: Arnold C. Holeywell
Assistant Chief of Research: Martha T. Goolrick

PUBLISHER: Joan D. Manley
General Manager: John D. McSweeney
Business Manager: John Steven Maxwell
Sales Director: Carl G. Jaeger
Promotion Director: Paul R. Stewart
Public Relations Director: Nicholas Benton

FOODS OF THE WORLD

SERIES EDITOR: Richard L. Williams
EDITORIAL STAFF FOR AMERICAN COOKING: CREOLE AND ACADIAN:
Associate Editor: William Frankel
Picture Editor: Kaye Neil
Designer: Albert Sherman
Staff Writer: Gerry Schremp
Chief Researcher: Sarah B. Brash
Researchers: Barbara Ensrud, Brenda Huff, Wendy Rieder, Timberlake Wertenbaker
Test Kitchen Chef: John W. Clancy
Test Kitchen Staff: Tina Cassel, Leola Spencer
Design Assistant: Anne B. Landry

EDITORIAL PRODUCTION
Production Editor: Douglas B. Graham
Quality Director: Robert L. Young
Assistant: James J. Cox
Copy Staff: Rosalind Stubenberg, Eleanore W. Karsten, Florence Keith
Picture Department: Dolores A. Littles, Joan Lynch

The text for this book was written by Peter Feibleman, recipe instructions by Michael Field and Gerry Schremp, other material by Charles Elliot and the staff. Valuable assistance was given by the following individuals and departments of Time Inc.: Editorial Production, Norman Airey, Margaret T. Fischer; Library, Peter Draz; Picture Collection, Doris O'Neil; Photographic Laboratory, George Karas; TIME-LIFE News Service, Murray J. Gart; Correspondent David Snyder (New Orleans).

Contents

The Recipe Booklet that accompanies this volume has been designed for use in the kitchen. It contains more than 130 recipes, including all of those printed in this book. It also has a wipe-clean cover and a spiral binding so that it can either stand up or lie flat when open.

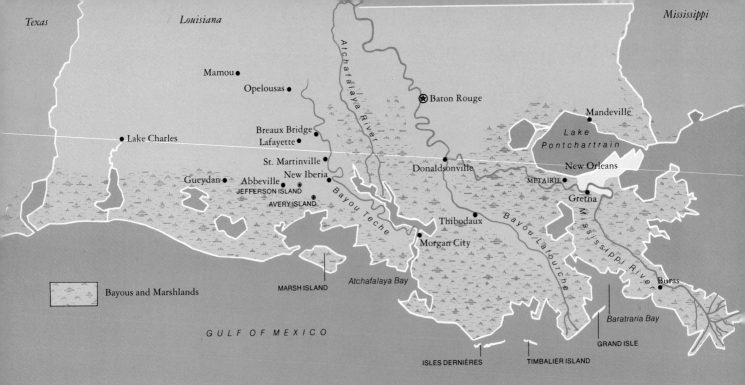

Texas

Louisiana

Mississippi

Mamou •

Opelousas •

⊛ Baton Rouge

Mandeville •

Lake Charles •

Breaux Bridge •
Lafayette •

St. Martinville •

Donaldsonville •

Lake
Pontchartrain

New Orleans

Gueydan •

Abbeville •
JEFFERSON ISLAND ⊛
AVERY ISLAND ⊛

New Iberia •

METAIRIE •

Gretna •

Thibodaux •

Bayou Teche

Morgan City •

Bayou Lafourche

Mississippi River

Buras •

Bayous and Marshlands

MARSH ISLAND

Atchafalaya Bay

Baratraria Bay

GRAND ISLE

GULF OF MEXICO

ISLES DERNIÈRES

TIMBALIER ISLAND

The Creole and Acadian Country

The French Quarter of New Orleans

Introduction: That Luscious Louisiana Larder

There is a saying in New Orleans: "He who tastes of Mississippi water, he'll be back someday." Meaning: He who has ever savored crawfish bisque (or shrimp jambalaya or redfish courtbouillon), he'll be back the first chance God gives him. One way to tell whether the speaker is a native or adopted Louisianian is his pronunciation of the name of the small lobsterlike crustacean that rises out of the wet soils around the Gulf of Mexico. Most outlanders say "crayfish," but to the native this betrays ignorance; the only permissible pronunciation is "crawfish."

To be sure, outlanders can appreciate Creole and Acadian food. Mark Twain once lowered a knife and fork into a plate of steaming pompano from Louisiana's waters and let out a long breath. The dish, he remarked, was as "delicious as the less criminal forms of sin." And a knowing Illinoisan once told me, "You folks down here not only swallow and digest your food with a wonderful enjoyment, but you pleasure yourselves talking and arguing about it, from the ideal combination of herbs to the finest way to mix meats and fish with everything else imaginable."

Obviously, food is important to the city Creole and the country Cajun. The story is told of a French-Spanish Creole (a descendant of early settlers) who entered Heaven and waved his hand with typical aplomb toward St. Peter: "Comment ça va, M'sieu?" Then, with no less ebullience, he tugged at the wing of an angel beside him and asked, "Where's the nearest pot of jambalaya?"—that vigorously original Louisiana mixture of rice, shrimp, oysters, tomatoes, onion, garlic, various peppers, chicken, sausage, thyme and parsley, among other ingredients. When he found that, for some preposterous reason, the kitchen of the Good Place had overlooked this masterpiece, he shook his head, accosted the next angel and learned that he could get it down below. Without a word he leaped from Paradise—proving, if proof were needed, that a real Louisianian will gladly go to Hell for a dish of jambalaya.

Anyone inclined to consider that tale an exaggeration is simply not of Louisiana. In travels on every continent and many countries, I have rarely found a region in which food is so thoroughly or so warmly appreciated—and so often the subject of conversations, ranging from the loudly argumentative to the dreamily reminiscent.

Peter Feibleman is strikingly qualified to write of Creole-Acadian food, of its origins, of its best practitioners and of its philosophers, for he has understood and appreciated it from birth. I first met him just after a superlative meal at his father's home in New Orleans. Peter, a rather plump little boy, came into the dining room briefly to be introduced to me. Since then I have visited with him on many occasions, and learned to respect and admire him as a man of rare capacity.

He has lived in many parts of the world. He has written perceptive books dealing with many phases of American life; he has had plays produced on Broadway, written for and appeared on national television, and lived as a literary celebrity. But he has never lost his identification with Louisiana, which has brought him back to the state again and again. In this volume he has stressed the way in which Creole and Acadian homes produce food of a quality that equals or exceeds that of the celebrated public places; and as only a native could, he has noted the cuisine's wonderful amalgamation of Latin, Negro, Indian and something else, perhaps best summarized as "of the lowest Mississippi."

He has also woven into his passages the flavorful personalities who figure in the Creole-Acadian world of food, past and present. Not the least of these for me, was the original Madame Begué, whose unique establishment flourished near the French Market. She did superbly resourceful things with meat—I have known Creoles whose moustaches quivered at the recollection—but liver was her *specialité*. As one old customer assured me, "What that lady did with her liver, no woman on earth ever did." Similarly, what the Creoles and Acadians have done with their food, few people on any continent have ever matched.

—*Harnett T. Kane, author of "Queen New Orleans," "The Bayous of Louisiana" and "Plantation Parade"*

South Louisiana (top map) reflects the influence of Creole and Acadian settlers on its place names, customs and cuisines. The detail map (bottom) provides a guide to one of the oldest centers of these customs and cuisines: New Orleans' French Quarter, or Vieux Carré, with its landmarks and famous restaurants.

POINTS OF INTEREST:
1 *French Market*
2 *Jackson Square*
3 *St. Louis Cathedral*
4 *Pontalba Buildings*
5 *Cabildo*
6 *Old Absinthe House*
7 *House of Madame Lalaurie*
8 *Old French Opera House*
9 *St. Louis Cemetery No. 1*

RESTAURANTS:
10 *Acme Oyster House*
11 *Antoine's*
12 *Brennan's*
13 *Felix's*
14 *Galatoire's*
15 *The Gumbo Shop*
16 *Café du Monde*
17 *Morning Call*
18 *Tujague's*

I

Two Aspects of a Great Cuisine

A late afternoon sun strikes the spires of New Orleans' St. Louis Cathedral, casting long, dark shadows across Jackson Square and silhouetting the delicate tracery of a balcony on which *café au lait* and cheesecake await late-afternoon guests. Here at the ancient hub of the city are elements that have shaped Creole culture: the Catholic faith, a complex past (in the building at left, in 1803, Louisiana was formally transferred from Spain to France and then, soon afterward, sold to the United States), and an abiding joy in the special delights of a distinctive cuisine.

On a late spring evening in one of the more elegant homes of New Orleans' French Quarter, Madame X is overseeing the preparation of a Creole meal. She expects 11 guests to arrive between 7:30 and 8 o'clock —the time when the shadows of the crape myrtle and the long white jasmine, now in violent bloom, will begin to blend softly on the dark red-brick walls of the patio. There will be cocktails on the patio, accompanied by pungent hot baked mushrooms stuffed with finely chopped seeded tomatoes, pimientos, black and green olives, anchovies and capers, and covered with bread crumbs. There will be a second hors d'oeuvre of shrimp —very small, very pink, very sweet river shrimp, fresh from the Mississippi, that already have been boiled in a pot of herb-filled water and are now waiting on the sideboard to be served hot with a tangy greenish dip of butter and watercress.

Having finished with the shrimp for the moment, Madame X's cook is organizing the rest of the meal under her mistress' watchful but unnecessary eye. The first course will be a *daube glacé:* chopped sliced meats, cooked with herbs, covered with a delicate brown gelatin extracted from knuckles and bones—*not* from a packet—and set to chill in individual molds the day before. This will be followed by a *bisque d'écrevisses,* a crawfish bisque, the thick and noble soup made from the frail, ignoble "mudbug" of the southern Louisiana swamps, which is now at the height of its season. The soup is ready in a black iron kettle, not quite simmering, just keeping warm on the back of the stove. After these two courses, served with a chilled dry Pouilly-Fumé that will appear midway

8

through the first, the dishes will be cleared and a silver platter will be passed, containing thin sautéed fillets of Gulf pompano, crisp and brown on the outside, juicy and gleaming white on the inside.

The pompano will be the last of the white-wine courses. After it, Madame X will observe an old Creole custom: she and her guests will pause for some 15 minutes for a *coup de milieu,* an alcoholic beverage served between the middle courses of a meal; in this case, it will be a small glass of the strong apple brandy called Calvados, hard and smooth and gold. Madame would tell you that the *coup* serves to lighten digestion and to make the meal relaxed and leisurely, like the Creoles themselves; her husband may add that the practical Creoles use the bite of the Calvados to "put a hole in your stomach so there will be room for more food." In any case it will give the dinner party a chance to breathe and to prepare itself for the next course, whole roasted quail served exquisitely in woven baskets of fried potatoes on beds of long-grain and wild rice mixed with green onions and diced ham. This main course, accompanied by a fragrant dark Beaujolais, will be followed successively by a *salade Napoléon,* crisp pieces of romaine lettuce and slices of cucumber in a peppery vinegar dressing; a plate of assorted cheeses; and icy champagne and some small *gâteaux aux fraises,* fresh light strawberry cakes. The dinner will end with a cup of dark aromatic *café brûlot*—black coffee that has been laced with brandy (and possibly one or two liqueurs) and heated with strips of clove-studded orange peel.

If the weather holds and there is no rain, the diners at the long formal table on the brick patio will be stroked by the end of their meal with the black Mississippi River air, soft and heavy in the spring, with the first gentle hint of summer like a secret long-held breath that aches for release. The air will come like a touch of balm after the fullness of the long, carefully planned meal; indeed, it might almost seem a separate last course, ordered by Madame X for the comfort and pleasure of her guests.

A hundred miles or so to the southwest, the same night air is just beginning to flow, equally gentle but thick with the night-blooming heaviness of the swamp. Another dinner is in preparation—an Acadian dinner in the country kitchen of Madame Y. She does her own cooking, methodically and magnificently, as if she were born with the talent (which she was) and as if she were as used to cooking as to breathing (which she is). Madame Y expects a few cousins "from downstream" who have gone hunting in the marshes with her husband. The party for dinner, she tells us, "could be five cousins, but, *mon cher,* it could also be ten." It could, in fact, be almost any reasonable number. Some guests may bring their wives, others may not. What is more, some will bring in game and some, who have decided to fish instead, will bring a string of *sacalait* (white crappie) or a basket of live blue crabs. If children have gone along to explore the marsh's muddy shores, there surely will be crawfish.

Actually, it will not matter much to this meal what food there is or isn't —how many people come or do not come—whether it rains or doesn't rain. Madame Y is as used to coping with unexpected guests as with expected hurricanes. Back in the French Quarter a last-minute cancellation might do serious damage to Madame X's seating arrangement, and the last-minute addition of a single guest would be almost unthinkable. Here in the country, Madame Y couldn't care less—she'll manage, and manage very well, whatever happens; she is, in fact, almost a lesson in how to manage skillfully without ever making it look as if anything out of the ordinary has occurred. Thus, though she pays fully as much attention to food as any Creole cook, the attention is paid in a different way. Richness, yes; careful combinations, yes; strength, yes; spiciness, yes indeed —but an exact number of servings, no.

At this point in her preparations, a huge black iron pot is simmering on Madame Y's stove—a pot of seafood gumbo, with crabs and shrimp and okra and spices—and the sharp smell of the gumbo pervades the kitchen. Next to the kettle is a large pan of rice waiting to be cooked to a cotton-cloud white. Below that, in the oven, are two wild ducks from an earlier hunting trip; they have been stuffed with herbed rice and basted in low heat until they are crisp and juicy. From the open kitchen window, Madame Y can see the people when they arrive; and if there are more than two ducks' worth of guests, there will be a third duck in the oven by the time she has opened enough beer for everybody and said hello. She won't count on the game and fish that her guests are bringing; except for shellfish, which might spoil, those are for another day. She will count only on her own possessions—her pantry and her skills.

Like Acadian women of all classes, Madame Y is a queen of "le make-do"—but nobody thinks of her cookery as "making do," partly because it doesn't look it, and partly because most people who come to her house can make do, too. You don't survive in these marshes unless you can. Nothing that moves by the house on all fours—or even on its belly—will be looked at without an eye to what it might be like if it were cooked. "I could make thees jus' like my *étouffée d'écrevisses, moi,*" Madame Y will tell you thoughtfully, very much like a woman standing in a market and adding new ingredients to old recipes in her mind. Only she is standing on the bank of a bayou, and what she is looking at is an alligator.

Obviously, both the Creoles and the Acadians take food—its presence, its freshness, its preparations—as seriously as they take anything on earth, and more seriously than they take most things. In the heart of the swamps or in the heart of town, there is style and wit and grace "in the pot." What, then, is the difference between the terms Creole and Acadian as applied to food? Most authorities will start with a simple answer: they will tell you that it is the difference between city French cooking and country French cooking. But then the reservations and qualifications begin. Both Creole and Acadian cooking are *Louisiana* French in style, of course —which (the authorities will add) isn't really French at all. Is that clear? No? Well, Acadian cooking is a little spicier than Creole—sometimes, not always. Acadians like a lot of rice—well, of course, the Creoles like a lot of rice, too. Acadian cooks are likely to put all the ingredients for a course into one big pot, while Creoles like these ingredients separate. Yes, that's true—at least, *most* Creoles like them separate. "Look [the authorities will finally say], maybe you'd better just taste it. . . ."

Tasting these foods is certainly the most pleasant way of studying them, but knowing something about the two kinds of people who cook

The 19th Century Creole breakfast re-created here is not entirely a thing of the past. One long-honored feature of the meal is now nearly forgotten: piping-hot rice cakes called calas *(center)*, traditionally served with cane syrup *(Recipe Index)*. But ripe strawberries with bowls of rich Creole cream cheese *(right)* are still popular today, and the basic breakfast beverage remains *café au lait*—half hot coffee, half warm milk.

them will help, too. In fact, you don't need to know a great deal about the history of this part of the world to know what Creole and Acadian truly mean—and what they do not mean.

Some Northerners seem to think that the word Creole means anything from mulatto to part Mexican. The fact is, it simply denotes French or Spanish colonists and their descendants, particularly those who maintain some of the customs and language of their mother country. Here in southern Louisiana the original colonists were the French, who began to arrive as early as 1699. They were followed by settlers who were Spaniards, Africans, Germans, Italians and English. Modern Creole cooking reflects nearly all of these—and some other—influences.

Even before they were inundated by water and wars and other cultures, the wives of the first lonely French newcomers found themselves at a loss for the traditional ingredients to which they were accustomed. The spices and herbs, the vegetables, the meats of their homeland were not available. Indian herbs and native ingredients were soon combined with French cooking skills, forming the foundation of what has come to be known as Creole cooking. Down through the years it has been greatly enriched by the Spanish style; by African cooks; by West Indian peppers and allspice, by such West Indian vegetables and dishes as mirliton (a type of squash) and *moussa* (cornmeal mush) and sugar cane (along with the rum made from it); by bitters and brandy and the smoke-pit cooking of Haiti; by trade with Mexico and Cuba. The long, slow evolution resulted in a new culinary form, a whole that was not only greater than the sum of its parts, but better.

But local ingredients here in Louisiana were also provided by yet another culture, another influence. In the mid-18th Century, a group of settlers were living in Canada, in what is now called Nova Scotia but was then known as Acadie. These settlers, the Acadians, had been coming over from France since the early 17th Century. They were a hardy people who lived off the land and the sea, who bothered nobody, and who still spoke French as it had been spoken when they left France. When the English took over Canada, the Acadians refused to swear allegiance to the English flag; they refused to stop speaking French or to give up Catholicism. In 1755, suspicious of this alien ethnic group in their midst, the English routed them out, separated the women and children from the men, and deported the entire settlement—cruelly sending them off in every direction with total disregard of family ties.

For 10 years and more the Acadians wandered, searching for each other and for a new home in the New World. Some were never to meet again: mothers lost their children, husbands their wives. Some died, some simply disappeared. Finally, the survivors found a place and a people that would accept them. The place was southern Louisiana; the people, the French and Spanish Catholics who lived there. The Acadians came to rest in the swamps and waterways west and south of New Orleans.

Life in the marshes was not easy; there were all sorts of strangeness here. There were people, for example, who couldn't say "Acadian" properly and corrupted the word into "Cajun." There were hurricanes and quicksand and snakes; malaria and yellow fever lurked in the mosquito-

On the bank of Bayou Teche, 170 miles west of New Orleans, Miss Grace Broussard, a retired schoolteacher, makes her weekly batch of Creole cream cheese. A day or so earlier, Miss Broussard dropped half a rennet tablet into two quarts of raw milk from the family cow, and let the milk clabber; at this point in the process, she is straining the clabbered milk through cheesecloth. She will let the curds drain for a day, then add some fresh cream to make the final product, ready to eat plain or with sugar, salt and pepper, or fruit. Curiously, Creole cream cheese has proved difficult to make in other parts of the country, possibly because of the absence of certain unidentified but essential bacteria in either the milk or the air.

ridden swamps or were brought via refugees from New Orleans. And there was also malnutrition. The place was not quite the new Eden the Acadians had hoped it might be. But they made do. In cooking, they taught the Creoles certain techniques they had learned in their travels, and they received other secrets in return.

Gradually, all the cooking of southern Louisiana developed and changed. The process can be followed if you trace the evolution of almost any of the dishes the settlers started with. Take the French dish called bouillabaisse, fish stew. When the first Frenchmen came to Louisiana they brought a great love for bouillabaisse to a place that had none of the ingredients necessary for making it. There was no *rascasse*—a Mediterranean fish—in southern Louisiana; there were no eels or lobsters. But the Frenchmen (Creoles, by then) found that they could get crabs from Lake Pontchartrain, and oysters, shrimp, red snapper and pompano from the Gulf of Mexico. They could still make a fish and shellfish stew even if they had to use different raw materials. After a while, the Acadians showed the Creoles that they didn't really need any fish at all—they could make a fine stew with crabs and shrimp alone. Spanish settlers made their own contribution of red peppers (which, it was later discovered, would grow profusely on Avery Island, west of New Orleans);

At dawn, in the Atchafalaya Spillway, Acadians Willis Broussard, his wife Regina and her son Darel check a fish trap—and find they haven't much of a catch. On good days a long open-ended trap like this one, baited with chunks of fish, may contain up to 150 pounds of bream, catfish, gaspergou and carp.

the Africans brought okra; the Indians of the region taught the use of filé powder, or ground sassafras leaves.

After about a century, the colonists' stew was no longer even recognizable as bouillabaisse. What they had instead was an extraordinary new dish known as gumbo. The essential story of Creole and Acadian cooking is told in the dish: in gumbo, something that started as second best became, for many tastes, better than the original. Just as the strict limitations of meter and rhyme can force a true poet into great flights of language and insight, so the limitations of the ingredients available in southern Louisiana forced culinary genius out of a people who otherwise might never have discovered that they had it.

Despite their interdependent histories, what basic culinary differences remain between the Creole and Acadian? As the authorities insist, the answer is perfectly simple. Many Creoles were rich planters who led a life of relative luxury. The Creole kitchen aspires to *grande cuisine;* it is a kitchen of delicate blends, of subtle combinations and separate sauces. Its earliest recipes came directly from Europe, because many of the French and Spanish aristocrats who settled New Orleans were sophisticates who had lived high in the Old World and had brought their chefs along with them. On the other hand, the Acadians, a strong people used to living under strenuous conditions, tend to serve strong country food. Theirs is still a food of the people—pungent, peppery, the ingredients cooked together in one pot, sometimes fiercely spiced but almost always gentled by a bed of taste-calming white rice, and always good. Only in their most delicate dishes do the Acadians approach *grande cuisine,* and here the two kitchens, Creole and Acadian, become practically interchangeable.

But in a way they are *always* interchangeable, for most of the characteristic dishes and foods of the region appear in both Creole and Acadian kitchens. Rice is a staple of both, and is often served three times a day. It has been said that a Louisianian consumes as much rice in one year as any other American eats in five. You find rice in gumbo, in the shrimp-and-ham dish known as jambalaya, in a dish of rice with red beans, in rice cakes for dessert—in almost any way at all except as a cold cereal for breakfast. Both Creole and Acadian cooks usually start a dish by making a *roux* of butter or oil and flour. Basic shellfish from the sea, the lakes and the swamps—crab, river shrimp, lake shrimp, oyster, crawfish—appear and reappear in both kitchens like refrains in a song. So does an enormous variety of fresh-water and salt-water fish. So, in a lesser way, do squirrels, wild turkeys, ducks, frogs, turtles, pork, homemade sausages, beans of many kinds, tomatoes, okra, yams, pecans and oranges.

Both the food and the water tie the region together, and southern Louisiana is a land spider-webbed by waterways. The flat earth is sliced by rivers, spotted by lakes, crisscrossed and interlaced by smaller streams and by those maverick water lanes, halfway between river and stream, called bayous. Travel in the swamps was almost impossible until the invention of the pirogue, a hollowed-out cypress log that, the Acadians say, can "ride on a heavy dew." Travel on the big rivers like the Mississippi was impossible without the steamboat, which brought everything from oysters to people to the big plantation houses in the interior. (The great Creole balls could never have flowed with champagne all night if the champagne had not been floated up the river the night before.)

If the Creoles lived in luxury in New Orleans, along the Mississippi and on a few of the bayous, while the Acadians were settling the swamps and the back country, the two groups met at least long enough to agree on one paradoxical rule in all matters of food. The rule was, and is, that there is no rule—no one way of doing things. There are likely to be dozens of different recipes for gumbos within an area of one square mile; a hundred jambalayas, a hundred turtle soups. It couldn't matter less—nobody is wrong, because everybody is right. Only for tourists in the big cities do Creole and Acadian cooks label their dishes the "original" this or the "genuine" that. Privately, they know that everything they cook is genuine, if only because they cook it. Everything is original, for the evolution that brought the dishes into being is still going on. In the best sense, both Creole and Acadian kitchens are the kitchens of ad lib. Their cooks are wildly experimental and always have been. If you can't get a fish, get a crab; if you prefer not to thicken a soup with okra, use filé; if you don't care for this sauce, try that one; if this vegetable won't grow, that one will and does—throw it in the pot and see what happens.

The biggest pot of all, the bayou country itself, is a superb mixture of cultures, a blending of different peoples on the same lush, glistening flatland. To sense what they are and what they cook, you must sense the land itself, and what it feels like to live on it. Enough books have been written about plantation life and the "romantic old Creoles" of the last century to sink a ship. If the ship hasn't sunk, it is perhaps because the Creole cooks have kept it afloat; they never were as romantic as they were pragmatic. Those who wish to understand them should not confuse romanticism with fine food—they aren't the same thing.

This book, then, will present not so much the shape of things that were, as the taste of things that are. But we will find that the products of modern Creole and Acadian kitchens retain within them all of the time and talent that went into their devising. A taste of the past continues to tingle on the tongue like a rare spice. And so does a taste of the future—for these freewheeling kitchens, past, present and future are all one. If you ask a Creole cook about the nature of her cuisine, she will sit you down and serve you something from it. If you ask an Acadian cook she will answer, like the Dodo in *Alice in Wonderland,* who tried to give the rules for the Caucus Race: "The best way to explain it is to do it."

The best and simplest way to get at the essence and texture of Creole and Acadian cooking is, of course, to grow up with it. In the next chapter we will see how this cooking can become a part of life for a child in New Orleans—as it did for me—before he even knows what the terms Creole and Acadian mean. Then we will see what life is like today in New Orleans, and travel on into the Acadian country—the bayous, the marshlands and the Delta. We will taste as we go, and watch and listen and smell and touch as we taste; for in this land of extremes, of wind and of water, of sudden bloom and sudden decay, all the senses must be open. To know what cooking is like here you must know what the life is like. To know what the life is like, you must live it, if only vicariously.

Live oaks hung with Spanish moss break the sunlight and give Shadows-on-the-Teche its name. This façade faces the bayou.

A Mansion That Survives as a Painter's Living Work of Art

"Mellow as a great tree," in Henry Miller's phrase, the mansion called Shadows-on-the-Teche rises above rich moist lawns on the edge of Bayou Teche in New Iberia, Louisiana. Built in 1830 by a planter named David Weeks, it survives as one of the most splendid examples of antebellum architecture—partly because of the devotion of an eccentric descendant of the original owner. Weeks Hall was trained as a painter and lived the artist's life in post-World War I Paris before returning to the near-derelict Shadows in 1922. For the next 36 years, virtually without interruption and often under financial strain, Hall dealt with the old mansion as with a work of art —studying it, restoring it and above all enjoying it. At his death he willed the house and its contents to the National Trust for Historic Preservation. A famous host and gourmet, Weeks Hall would surely have enjoyed the elegant Creole banquet shown on these pages in the rooms of his beloved mansion.

A dinner at Shadows-on-the-Teche begins with cocktails and hors d'oeuvre served in the cool shade of the back gallery. Bottles and ice are set out on a portable butler's table; in the foreground, assembled on a silver tray, a cold collation includes *daube glacé (left; Recipe Index)* and a plate of Roquefort and Stilton cheeses.

20

After cocktails on the back gallery, the guests at Shadows-on-the-Teche move downstairs to the dining room, situated on the first floor convenient to the outside kitchen (generally, the more elegant rooms are on the second floor, to take full advantage of the cooler, drier breezes). Laid out on the table and ready for serving is the main course: roast Muscovy duck, with a "dirty-rice dressing" (in the bowl at right, and so-called from its appearance; *Recipe Index*); candied yams; stuffed eggplant and artichokes with vinaigrette sauce.

Coffee is served in the second-floor drawing room from a silver service, a Weeks family heirloom. Brandy and cordials will complete the meal. Like the rest of Shadows, this room was restored on the basis of over 200,000 documents accumulated in the house over the course of years —memoranda, bills and receipts dating as far back as the 1790s.

To make two 9-by-5-by-3-inch
   loaves

6 tablespoons vegetable oil
4 pounds beef shinbones, sawed
   into 1-inch lengths
4 pounds veal shinbones, sawed into
   1-inch lengths
3 medium-sized onions, peeled and
   coarsely chopped
2 medium-sized celery stalks,
   including the green leaves,
   trimmed and coarsely chopped
2 large carrots, scraped and coarsely
   chopped, plus 3 medium-sized
   carrots, scraped and coarsely
   grated
2 pounds fresh pigs' feet
3 sprigs fresh parsley
5 quarts water
5 pounds bottom round beef,
   trimmed of excess fat and cut into
   3 equal pieces
2 teaspoons finely chopped garlic
1 teaspoon ground hot red pepper
   (cayenne) or 1 teaspoon freshly
   ground black pepper
2 teaspoons salt
1 lemon, sliced crosswise into 6 thin
   rounds

Daube Glacé
MOLDED JELLIED BEEF

In a heavy 12-inch skillet, heat 4 tablespoons of the oil over moderate heat until a light haze forms above it. Brown the beef and veal bones in the hot oil, eight or nine pieces at a time, turning them frequently with tongs and regulating the heat so that the bones color deeply and evenly on all sides without burning. As they brown, transfer the bones to a heavy 10- to 12-quart stock pot.

Pour off all but about 2 tablespoons of the fat remaining in the skillet and in its place add the onions, celery and chopped carrots. Stirring frequently, cook over moderate heat for 8 to 10 minutes, or until the vegetables are soft and delicately brown. Scrape the vegetable mixture into the stock pot and drop in the pigs' feet and parsley. Add the water, bring to a boil over high heat, reduce the heat to low, and simmer partially covered for 4 hours.

With a slotted spoon, remove and discard the bones and pigs' feet. Strain the stock through a fine sieve into a large bowl, pressing down hard on the vegetables with the back of a spoon to extract all their juices before discarding the pulp. Set the stock aside.

Set the 12-inch skillet over moderate heat again and heat the remaining 2 tablespoons of oil. Brown the beef, one piece at a time, turning it with tongs and regulating the heat so that the meat colors richly and evenly on all sides without burning. As the pieces of beef brown, transfer them to a heavy 8- to 10-quart casserole.

Pour the reserved stock over the beef. The stock should cover the beef completely; add water if necessary. Bring to a boil over high heat, reduce the heat to low and cover the pot tightly. Simmer the beef for 3 to 3½ hours, or until it is very tender and shreds easily with a fork. Transfer the beef to a cutting board and strain the stock remaining in the casserole through a fine sieve lined with four layers of dampened cheesecloth and set over a large bowl.

When the beef is cool enough to handle, cut it into strips about ¼ inch wide and 2 inches long or, with the aid of two forks, pull the beef into 2-inch-long shreds. Drop the beef into a bowl, add the grated carrots, garlic, red or black pepper, and salt, and toss the ingredients together thoroughly with a fork. Refrigerate the beef mixture until you are ready to use it.

With a large spoon, skim the fat from the surface of the stock. Pour the stock into a 4- to 5-quart saucepan, cool to room temperature and refrigerate for at least 2 hours, or until the surface is covered with a layer of congealed fat. Carefully lift off the fat and discard it. Warm the stock over low heat and, when it liquefies, pour a ¼-inch layer of the stock into the bottoms of two 9-by-5-by-3-inch loaf pans. Refrigerate the pans until the stock has jelled and is firm to the touch.

(Keep the remaining stock at room temperature so that it remains liquid and ready to use. If it begins to set at any time, warm the stock briefly over low heat to soften it.)

Dip the lemon slices into the liquid stock and, when they are coated, arrange three of the slices in the bottom of each loaf pan. Chill until the lemon slices are anchored firmly.

Pour all the remaining liquid stock over the beef and mix well. Then ladle the mixture into the loaf pans, dividing it equally between them. Refrigerate the daube for at least 12 hours before serving.

Before unmolding the daube, scrape off any fat that has floated to the surface. Run a knife around the sides of one mold at a time and dip the bottom in hot water for a few seconds. Wipe the mold dry, place an inverted plate over it and, grasping plate and mold together firmly, turn them over. Rap the plate sharply on a table and the jellied beef should slide out easily. Refrigerate the *daube glacé* until ready to serve.

Calas
DEEP-FRIED RICE BALLS

Before the turn of the century, the cala woman vending "Belle cala! Tout chaud!" ("Nice cala! Piping hot!") was a familiar sight along the streets of the French Quarter of New Orleans. The cala women have disappeared, but these unique deep-fried rice balls are still available, fresh and hot, at Maxcy's Coffee Pot Restaurant in the heart of the Quarter.

To make 6 balls

1½ cups water
⅔ cup uncooked white rice, not the converted variety
1½ cups unsifted flour
1½ teaspoons double-acting baking powder
1 teaspoon ground cinnamon
1 teaspoon ground nutmeg, preferably freshly grated
¼ teaspoon salt
2 eggs
2 tablespoons sugar
Vegetable oil for deep frying

Bring the water to a boil in a small heavy saucepan set over high heat. Pour in the rice in a slow, thin stream, stir two or three times, then cover the pan tightly. Reduce the heat to low and simmer for 15 minutes, or until the rice has absorbed all of the liquid in the pan and the grains are plump and tender. Spread out the rice in a large shallow pan and let it cool to room temperature.

Meanwhile, combine the flour, baking powder, cinnamon, nutmeg and salt, sift them together into a bowl, and set aside.

In a deep bowl, beat the eggs and sugar for 2 or 3 minutes with a wire whisk or a rotary or electric beater. Add the cooled rice and stir briskly with a spoon until the grains are separated and evenly coated with the egg-and-sugar mixture. Add the flour mixture ½ cup at a time, stirring the dough well after each addition.

Divide the rice dough into six equal portions and, moistening your hands frequently with cold water, pat and shape each portion into a ball about 2½ inches in diameter. As you proceed, place the balls side by side on wax paper.

Pour the vegetable oil into a deep fryer or large heavy saucepan to a depth of about 3 inches and heat the oil until it reaches a temperature of 350° on a deep-frying thermometer.

Deep-fry the rice balls, two or three at a time, turning them about with a slotted spoon for about 8 minutes, or until they are golden brown and crusty. As they brown, transfer the rice balls to paper towels to drain while you deep-fry the rest.

Arrange the calas attractively on a heated platter and serve them while they are still hot. Calas are traditionally served at breakfast, accompanied by cane syrup or jelly or sprinkled with a little confectioners' sugar or a mixture of granulated sugar and cinnamon.

Shrimp-and-Ham Jambalaya

Bring the water and 1 teaspoon of the salt to a boil in a small saucepan set over high heat. Add the rice, stir once or twice, and immediately cover the pan. Reduce the heat to low and simmer for about 20 minutes, or until the rice is tender and the grains have absorbed all of the liquid in the pan. Fluff the rice with a fork, cover, and set it aside.

Meanwhile, shell the shrimp. Devein them by making a shallow incision down their backs with a small sharp knife and lifting out the black or white intestinal vein with the point of the knife. Wash the shrimp briefly in a colander set under cold running water. Drop the shrimp into enough boiling salted water to cover them completely and cook briskly, uncovered, for 4 to 5 minutes, or until they are pink and firm. With a slotted spoon, transfer the shrimp to a bowl and set aside.

In a heavy 5- to 6-quart casserole, melt the butter over moderate heat. When the foam begins to subside, add the onions and garlic and, stirring frequently, cook for about 5 minutes, or until they are soft and translucent but not brown. Add the tomatoes, the tomato liquid and the tomato paste, and stir over moderate heat for 5 minutes. Then add the celery, green pepper, parsley, cloves, thyme, red pepper, black pepper and the remaining teaspoon of salt. Stirring frequently, cook uncovered over moderate heat until the vegetables are tender and the mixture is thick enough to hold its shape lightly in the spoon.

Add the ham and, stirring frequently, cook for 5 minutes. Then stir in the shrimp and, when they are heated through, add the reserved rice. Stir over moderate heat until the mixture is hot and the rice has absorbed any liquid in the pan.

Taste for seasoning and serve the shrimp-and-ham jambalaya at once, directly from the casserole or mounded in a heated bowl.

Leeks Vinaigrette

With a sharp knife, cut off the roots of the leeks and strip away any withered leaves. Line up the leeks in a row and cut off enough of their green tops to make each leek 6 or 7 inches long. Then slit the green parts in half lengthwise, stopping within about ½ inch of the root ends. Carefully spread the leaves apart and wash the leeks under cold running water to rid them of all sand.

Lay the leeks in one or two layers in a heavy stainless-steel or enameled skillet or casserole just large enough to hold them flat. Pour in enough cold water to cover them by about 1 inch and bring to a boil over high heat. Reduce the heat to low, cover the pan partially, and simmer for 10 minutes, or until the leeks show only the slightest resistance when their bases are pierced with a fork.

With tongs or a slotted spoon, transfer the leeks to a double thickness of paper towels and let them drain for a minute or two. Arrange the leeks attractively in a serving dish or deep platter and pour the Creole vinaigrette sauce over them. Cool to room temperature, then refrigerate the leeks for at least 1 hour to chill them thoroughly before serving.

To serve 6 to 8

2 cups water
2 teaspoons salt
1 cup broken white rice *(see Glossary, page 198)* or 1 cup short-grain white rice
2 pounds uncooked medium-sized shrimp (about 20 to 24 to the pound)
6 tablespoons butter
1½ cups finely chopped onions
2 tablespoons finely chopped garlic
A 1-pound can tomatoes, drained and finely chopped, with all their liquid
3 tablespoons canned tomato paste
½ cup finely chopped celery
¼ cup finely chopped green pepper
1 tablespoon finely chopped fresh parsley, preferably the flat-leaf Italian variety
3 whole cloves, pulverized with a mortar and pestle or finely crushed with a kitchen mallet or the flat of a heavy cleaver
½ teaspoon crumbled dried thyme
½ teaspoon ground hot red pepper (cayenne)
¼ teaspoon freshly ground black pepper
1 pound cooked lean smoked ham, trimmed of excess fat and cut into ½-inch cubes

To serve 4 as a salad

8 firm fresh leeks, each 1 to 1½ inches in diameter
½ cup Creole vinaigrette sauce *(page 31)*

Shrimp-and-ham jambalaya, alluringly accented with onions, garlic, chopped tomatoes, spices and herbs, is complemented here by tangy leeks vinaigrette.

To serve 4

2 medium-sized eggplants (each
  about 1 pound)
⅓ cup olive oil
8 tablespoons butter, cut into
  ½-inch bits, plus 4 teaspoons
  butter, melted
½ cup finely chopped onions
½ cup finely chopped scallions,
  including 3 inches of the green
  tops
1½ teaspoons finely chopped
  garlic
1 cup coarsely chopped drained
  canned tomatoes
1 teaspoon crumbled dried thyme
½ teaspoon ground hot red pepper
  (cayenne)
¼ teaspoon freshly ground black
  pepper
½ teaspoon salt
½ pound lean smoked ham, finely
  ground
2¼ cups soft fresh crumbs made
  from French- or Italian-type
  white bread, trimmed of all crusts
  and pulverized in a blender
¼ cup finely chopped fresh
  parsley, preferably the flat-leaf
  Italian variety

To serve 6

1½ pounds fresh okra
3 large firm ripe tomatoes
½ pound sliced bacon, cut
  crosswise into halves
1½ cups coarsely chopped onions
1 cup coarsely chopped green
  peppers
3 dried hot red chilies, each about
  2 inches long, washed, stemmed,
  seeded and coarsely crumbled
  *(caution: see note, Recipe
  Booklet)*
1 teaspoon salt

Ham-stuffed Eggplant

Cut the eggplants in half lengthwise and, with a spoon, hollow out the center of each half to make a boatlike shell about ¼ inch thick. Finely chop the eggplant pulp and set it aside.

In a heavy 12-inch skillet, heat the olive oil over moderate heat until a light haze forms above it. Add the eggplant shells and turn them about with tongs or a spoon until they are moistened on all sides. Then cover the skillet tightly and cook over moderate heat for 5 or 6 minutes. Turn the shells over and continue to cook, still tightly covered, for 5 minutes longer, or until they are somewhat soft to the touch. Invert the shells on paper towels to drain briefly and arrange them cut side up in a baking dish large enough to hold them snugly in one layer.

Preheat the oven to 400°. Drain off the oil remaining in the skillet, add the 8 tablespoons of butter bits and melt them over moderate heat. When the foam subsides, add the onions, scallions and garlic and, stirring frequently, cook for 5 minutes, or until they are soft but not brown.

Add the reserved chopped eggplant pulp, the tomatoes, thyme, red and black pepper, and salt and, stirring frequently, cook briskly until most of the liquid in the pan evaporates and the mixture is thick enough to hold its shape almost solidly in a spoon. Remove the skillet from the heat and stir in the ground ham, 2 cups of the bread crumbs and the parsley. Taste for seasoning.

Spoon the filling into the eggplant shells, dividing it equally among them and mounding it slightly in the centers. Sprinkle each shell with 1 tablespoon of the remaining bread crumbs and dribble 1 teaspoon of the melted butter on top. Bake in the middle of the oven for 15 minutes, or until the shells are tender and the filling lightly browned. Arrange the ham-stuffed eggplant attractively on a large heated platter or individual plates and serve at once.

Spiced Stewed Okra

Wash the okra under cold running water and, with a small sharp knife, scrape the skin lightly to remove any surface fuzz. Cut off the stems and slice each pod crosswise into ½-inch rounds.

Drop the tomatoes into boiling water and remove them after 15 seconds. Run them under cold water and, with a small sharp knife, peel them, cut out the stems, then slice the tomatoes in half crosswise. Squeeze the halves gently to remove the seeds and juice, and chop the pulp coarsely.

Fry the bacon in a heavy 12-inch skillet set over moderate heat, turning the slices frequently with tongs until they are crisp and brown and have rendered all their fat. Transfer the bacon to paper towels to drain.

Pour off all but about ¼ cup of the fat remaining in the skillet and add the onions and green peppers. Stirring frequently, cook over moderate heat for 5 minutes, or until the vegetables are soft but not brown.

Add the okra and, still stirring from time to time, cook uncovered for about 15 minutes. When the okra is tender, add the tomatoes, chilies and salt, reduce the heat to low, and simmer, tightly covered, for 10 minutes.

Taste for seasoning, then mound the okra in a heated serving bowl and sprinkle the bacon slices on top. Serve at once.

Dirty Rice

The term dirty rice may be a jocular reference to the appearance of the finished dish, since the bits of chicken gizzard and liver that are tossed with the rice give it a brown, or "dirty," look.

Put the chicken gizzards, chicken livers, onions, green pepper and celery through the finest blade of a food grinder. In a heavy 4- to 5-quart casserole, heat the olive oil over moderate heat until a light haze forms above it. Add the ground chicken mixture, stir in the salt and black pepper, and reduce the heat to low. Stirring occasionally, cook uncovered for about 1 hour, or until the bits of chicken are richly browned.

Meanwhile, place the rice in a heavy 1-quart pot, stir in the water and bring to a boil over high heat. Reduce the heat to low, cover tightly, and simmer for 20 to 25 minutes, or until the rice has absorbed all the liquid in the pan and the grains are tender. Remove the pan from the heat and let the rice rest, still tightly covered, for 10 minutes or so.

When the chicken mixture has cooked its allotted time, fluff the rice with a fork and add it to the casserole. With the fork, toss the rice and the chicken mixture together gently but thoroughly.

Taste for seasoning and stir in the parsley. Mound the dirty rice on a heated platter or in a heated serving bowl and serve at once.

To serve 6 to 8

½ pound chicken gizzards, thoroughly defrosted if frozen, trimmed of excess fat and coarsely chopped
½ pound chicken livers, thoroughly defrosted if frozen, and coarsely chopped
2 medium-sized onions, peeled and coarsely chopped
1 large green pepper, stemmed, seeded, deribbed and coarsely chopped
½ cup coarsely chopped celery
2 tablespoons olive oil
1½ teaspoons salt
½ teaspoon freshly ground black pepper
1 cup uncooked long-grain white rice, not the converted variety
2 cups water
½ cup finely chopped fresh parsley

Pecan Pralines

With a pastry brush, spread the softened butter on the bottom of two large baking sheets or jelly-roll pans. Set them aside.

Warm the light cream or evaporated milk over low heat in a small saucepan. When bubbles begin to form around the edges of the pan, remove the pan from the heat and cover it tightly to keep the cream or evaporated milk warm.

Combine the granulated sugar and water in a 10-inch cast-iron or enameled-iron skillet about 2 inches deep and bring to a boil over high heat, stirring until the sugar dissolves. Reduce the heat to moderate and, gripping a pot holder in each hand, tip the pan back and forth gently until the syrup turns a rich, golden brown. This may take 10 minutes or more.

As soon as the syrup reaches the correct color, remove the skillet from the heat and, with a wooden spoon, stir in the brown sugar and salt. Stirring constantly, pour in the warm cream or evaporated milk in a slow, thin stream. Add the vanilla extract, and then stir in the pecans.

To form each praline, ladle about 4 teaspoons of the pecan mixture onto a buttered baking sheet. As you proceed, space the pralines about 3 inches apart to allow room for them to spread into 2½-inch rounds. When the pralines have cooled to room temperature, transfer them to a serving plate with a wide metal spatula.

NOTE: To make benne pralines, substitute ½ cup of sesame (or benne) seeds for the 2 cups of pecans. Before warming the cream or milk, place the seeds in a heavy ungreased 8-inch skillet and, stirring constantly, toast them over moderate heat for about 5 minutes, or until they are a delicate golden color. Then prepare the pralines as described above, adding the benne seeds after the vanilla extract is incorporated into the candy.

To make about 2 dozen 2½-inch round candies

2 tablespoons butter, softened
¼ cup light cream or evaporated milk
2 cups granulated sugar
½ cup water
⅓ cup light brown sugar
⅛ teaspoon salt
1 teaspoon vanilla extract
2 cups (about ½ pound) coarsely chopped pecans

The flavors of garden-fresh celery, onions, tomatoes, green pepper and garlic are sharpened by paprika and red pepper to produce the rich red sauce for shrimp Creole. In this sauce plump shrimp are simmered to pink perfection. Traditionally, the dish is served with white rice that has been boiled or steamed in a separate pot.

To serve 6

12 medium-sized firm ripe tomatoes
   or 4 cups coarsely chopped
   drained canned tomatoes
3 pounds uncooked medium-sized
   shrimp (about 20 to 24 to the
   pound)
½ cup vegetable oil
2 cups coarsely chopped onions
1 cup coarsely chopped green
   peppers
1 cup coarsely chopped celery
2 teaspoons finely chopped garlic
1 cup water
2 medium-sized bay leaves
1 tablespoon paprika
½ teaspoon ground hot red pepper
   (cayenne)
1 tablespoon salt
2 tablespoons cornstarch mixed with
   ¼ cup cold water
6 to 8 cups freshly cooked long-
   grain white rice

Shrimp Creole

If you are using fresh tomatoes, drop them three or four at a time into a pan of boiling water and remove them after 15 seconds. Run cold water over them and peel them with a small sharp knife. Cut out the stems, then slice the tomatoes in half crosswise, and squeeze the halves gently to remove the seeds and juice. Chop the tomatoes coarsely. (Canned tomatoes need only be thoroughly drained and chopped.)

Shell the shrimp. Devein them by making a shallow incision down the back with a small sharp knife and lifting out the black or white intestinal vein with the point of the knife. Wash the shrimp in a colander set under cold running water and spread them on paper towels to drain.

In a heavy 4- to 5-quart casserole, heat the oil over moderate heat until a light haze forms above it. Add the onions, green peppers, celery and garlic and, stirring frequently, cook for about 5 minutes, or until the vegetables are soft and translucent but not brown.

Stir in the tomatoes, water, bay leaves, paprika, red pepper and salt, and bring to a boil over high heat. Reduce the heat to low, cover the casserole partially and, stirring occasionally, simmer the mixture for 20 to 25 minutes, or until it is thick enough to hold its shape almost solidly in a

spoon. Stir in the shrimp and continue to simmer, partially covered, for about 5 minutes longer, or until they are pink and firm to the touch.

Stir the cornstarch-and-water mixture once or twice to recombine it, and pour it into the casserole. Stir over low heat for 2 or 3 minutes, until the sauce thickens slightly. Pick out and discard the bay leaves, then taste the sauce for seasoning.

Serve the shrimp Creole at once, directly from the casserole, accompanied by the rice in a separate bowl. Or, if you prefer, mound the rice on a deep heated platter and ladle the shrimp Creole around it.

Creole Vinaigrette Sauce

Combine the vinegar, paprika, mustard, red pepper and salt in a deep bowl and beat vigorously with a wire whisk to dissolve the salt. Whisking constantly, dribble in the oil a few drops at a time until no more oil is absorbed. When the sauce is thick and smooth, taste for seasoning.

Creole vinaigrette may be served immediately or, if you prefer, cover the bowl tightly with foil or plastic wrap, and set the sauce aside at room temperature until you are ready to use it.

To make about ½ cup

2 tablespoons tarragon vinegar
1 teaspoon paprika
½ teaspoon Creole mustard *(see Glossary, page 198)*
¼ teaspoon ground hot red pepper (cayenne)
½ teaspoon salt
6 to 8 tablespoons olive oil

31

II

Coming of Age in Louisiana

Mrs. Carrie Dean of New Orleans, shown here at an angle that emphasizes her cooking hand, prepares a brown *roux (Recipe Index),* the starting point for many Creole and Acadian dishes. Basically, the *roux* is a mixture of flour and fat, blended and browned over gentle heat, but the kind of fat and the proportions are decided by the cook. As a Louisiana proverb has it, *chakin connin ça kapé bouilli dans so chodière—*"each cook knows his own pot best."

The best way to know New Orleans cooking is to be raised there. You should start, as a child, by tasting the New Orleans air. Breathe it; eat in it; venture out in it to discover the foods most commonly found in the city —crabs, shrimp, oysters, crawfish—in their simplest forms. These foods become the accents of your day, but they are part of New Orleans, too. This is a city caught in a bend of the Mississippi River, touched by a wide lake, surrounded by swamps—and its foods are closely related to the breath and texture of the land where they are eaten.

Like all cuisines, this one begins early in the morning. There is the hooting of a boat on the river, the chugging of a train somewhere near the river. Silence . . . then, as you stir and your senses open, you become aware of the odor of magnolia buds, the gentleness in the dew that rises in the humid breeze, the salad of smells mixed by the sour weed and wild flowers in the empty lot next door. Your nose is already enjoying itself when a clatter from the kitchen informs you that there is good reason to get out of bed. Well before the sun is up you're hungry.

I remember a Saturday morning like that when I was 10 years old. I dressed and ran down the back stairs into a siege of smells even more varied and tempting than those outside my window. The steam of rich black chicory coffee mingled with the fragrance of hominy grits. Better yet, the gravy scent hovering over a black iron skillet told me that my breakfast this day was going to include a dish of Creole fame—grillades *(Recipe Index).*

I remember sitting by the sideboard, still waking up, and watching the

Keith Stamps *(left)* and his friend Tom Staub perch on some rocks along the New Orleans riverfront to consume "po' boys" stuffed with ham, Swiss cheese, lettuce and tomatoes. The po' boy (for poor boy) is often described as New Orleans' version of the hero or submarine sandwich, but the comparison is inadequate. Po' boys may contain an extraordinary variety of substances, from potatoes (one of the cheapest) to oysters (for boys with money to spend).

first step in the preparation of my grillades—the making of a *roux*. The *roux (Recipe Index)* is the basis of all Creole and Acadian cooking and yet more than that: it is the embodiment of a tradition. It was in the *roux* that the great French sauces became great Creole gravies, cooked with the food rather than apart. Any South Louisiana cook will tell you that if you can't make a good *roux,* you had better not cook at all. Yet a *roux* is little more than a heated mixture of flour and fat, often with stock added. Its color is the acid test. Ideally, a *roux* should have something like the color of deep honey, brown but not quite brown, a color that comes into being in a moment and lasts for only a few seconds before it turns too dark and must be thrown out. The most obstreperous child will behave himself while it is in preparation, for if the cook must take time out for him then, he will end up being punished twice—once for what he did in the first place, and once for causing the *roux* to burn.

I sat quietly that morning while chopped onion and minced garlic browned slowly in shortening. As our cook Thelma added the flour, she turned to sprinkle salt and pepper and cayenne over the steak, which had already been cut into grillades about three inches square. The air over the frying pan changed and sharpened as Thelma added juicy sliced tomatoes; then the odor was suddenly enhanced as the grillades themselves were laid upon the mixture. When the meat had browned, the calm black hands added a dash of vinegar and a splash of water and briefly stirred the whole together. Finally, the skillet was covered and pushed to the back of the stove to simmer gently for half an hour. By the time the grillades were ready, my first feelings of hunger had deepened to a conviction that I was starving.

Grillades can be eaten in several ways—most often, perhaps, over rice or over red or white beans. I had them that morning, though, over grits, and I thought I would never taste anything so good. There was a sparkle in the rich, tender meat, and the pungent dark gravy sank into the grits and produced soft tentacles of steam that enveloped me as I ate. An accompanying *café au lait*—in my case, a glass of hot milk with only a tangy splash of chicory-bitter coffee in it—seemed to warm the way for the food. By the time I finished, I was ready for another plateful, for it is one of the characteristics of Creole cooking that the more it satisfies, the more it sharpens the taste buds and spurs the desire for more food. Finally Thelma chased me out of the kitchen so that I could get started on the business of my day—and she could get started with lunch.

The early mist had lifted by now, and the reflection of the white morning light on two or three mud-rimmed crawfish holes in our back yard reminded me that there was more to life than just breathing and eating. The season was spring, and in the spring crawfishing and crabbing are two primary occupations of small boys in South Louisiana. I decided on crabbing at Lake Pontchartrain (more accessible by streetcar than the crawfish-filled marshes) and telephoned my friend Richard, who lived in the French Quarter of New Orleans, on the other side of town from my house. We met halfway between, on the road that led out to the lake, took the streetcar there, and rode in rattling comfort over glistening ground beneath mossy trees.

Richard had brought a round crab net and I had brought the bait, some beef scraps I had wheedled from our butcher. The sun was strong and the day humid; the flat earth seemed to swim with vapors. It was the kind of day when you can almost sniff things growing. A few blocks from the lake we got off and walked to a small counter-restaurant owned by a Spanish Creole family—a dark, hot but utterly clean place run by a little old woman with white braids and gold earrings. For a nickel, she produced a long catfish po' boy—or more formally, a poor-boy sandwich—that we could split for lunch.

There is nothing, I think, quite like sitting on a cement ledge at Lake Pontchartrain with a baited net sunk into the lapping lukewarm lake water and a poor-boy sandwich at hand. Poor boys were traditional in New Orleans long before the rest of the country knew what they were, and fried fillets of fresh catfish make what is to my mind the best poor boy of all. A whole long loaf of crisp French bread had been hollowed out and filled with the fish, topped by a layer of sliced tomatoes, young lettuce and a dark yellow mayonnaise with a hard bite. The faint oily sweetness of the deep-fried fish combined with the lightly acid taste of the tomatoes and the tang of hot pepper in the rich Creole mayonnaise. All of those tastes, crumbled into the mouth with the crusty sun-warmed bread and savored along with the breeze that brought the scents of fish and shellfish from the lake, made a perfect lunch.

Below us, from time to time, we could see a blue crab feel its way gingerly into the net toward the beef scraps tied by a string to the center. When a crab reached the bait, one of us raised the net quickly while the other flipped the victim into a wicker basket. By late afternoon we had caught 18 or 20 crabs and were hungry again. Nearby there was another small restaurant. We went in and swapped six of our crabs for a second po' boy—this one made with meatballs and *chaurice (Recipe Index),* a peppery Creole pork sausage that may have had its origin in Spain as *chorizo.* We had just completed the transaction and were walking back to the lake when a storm came up.

Heavy squalls gather over the swampland around New Orleans faster than anyone would believe; and they are as much a part of life here as the marsh smells or gray-bearded trees. One moment the sun is out—then a sudden cessation of the breeze makes you look up at the motionless moss and, beyond it, to a small dark cloud on the horizon. The next moment, the sky is black and the wet wind whips you with rain, sometimes so hard it can practically knock you down. It is a good idea, really, to carry food with you as we were doing—for you never know when you'll be trapped somewhere in a storm.

Children in New Orleans believe that the only thing better than eating outdoors in the sun is eating outdoors in the rain. Richard and I ran under a moss-laden oak tree to wait for the squall to pass. The water lashed us, soaking the live crabs and everything else except our new poor boy—which we protected from the rain simply by swallowing it. The hot gravy of the meatballs, flecked with red pepper and rich with the taste of onion and thyme, had soaked into the bread and fused there with the taste of the garlic pork *chaurice;* the good French bread and its contents were as warm in my throat as the rain on the back of my neck. Maybe there *are* finer ways of eating hot food than in a subtropical squall—but I don't know them. Afterward, Richard and I walked by the lake in the sun, now burning again, till our clothes had dried.

On the way home with our catch we checked by phone to learn which of "our" cooks—the one who worked for Richard's family or the one who worked for mine—would be able to make a crab gumbo the next day, Sunday. My cook won (his was getting Sunday off) and we took the crabs to my house. Almost immediately we were sent back out to market for some other gumbo ingredients—shrimp and ham and fresh thyme. The evening market on the outskirts of town was filled with people picking up last-minute ingredients for Sunday meals. The scent of fresh red snapper met with the briny scent of oysters, the sunny smell of Creole tomatoes, the green, hard odor of sweet peppers; tendrils of the smells mingled and followed us into the first scent of jasmine that announced the coming of nightfall. As we walked back to my house, we passed the odors of simmering *roux,* changing from house to house like so many invitations to supper.

Supper at my house that night—Richard stayed, of course—consisted of some of the shrimp we had bought, first parboiled, then cooked in a *sauce piquante* of tomatoes, green peppers and onions, seasoned with bay leaf and a sprig of thyme and a light whiplash of red-pepper-soaked

Opposite: Gumbo, perhaps the most famous of all Louisiana dishes, is a happy marriage of cooking techniques and ingredients used by white settlers, Negro slaves and American Indians. Thus, the crab, shrimp and okra gumbo *(Recipe Index)* combines North American, African and European elements: it features Louisiana seafood thickened by an African vegetable, okra, and made with brown *roux,* a rich sauce base with French antecedents. The finished dish is a savory stew, traditionally served with a mound of freshly cooked rice.

vinegar, then the whole served over rice. The sauce, a rich red gravy, was Spanish with a French flair, yet too sharp to be either. Distinct tastes of sea and earth clashed like sparks in it and flamed alive, but the rice held them together with a blandness that smoothed them into one.

The dish was a usual Saturday night supper at my home, one I liked very much then and still do. Years after I left New Orleans I found it in a restaurant in Paris under the title shrimp Creole. But as a boy I had no name for it. I knew it simply as one of the best ways to eat not only sea-food but chicken and veal as well. Both in New Orleans and in the Acadian countryside *sauce piquante* heightens the flavor of almost any food that is cooked in it. But it is especially good, I think, the way we ate it that Saturday night. We followed it with homemade pecan ice cream, frozen the old-fashioned way in a bucket of dry ice, with bits of pecan streaked through it. This made a glorious finish to a budding spring day that had existed more than anything else as an excuse to eat.

The next day, Sunday, Richard returned to collect his portion of Saturday's loot—a bowl of gumbo. As you will have gathered by now, good food is taken seriously even by children in New Orleans, and though fine dishes may be found at the nearest street corner, a good gumbo is still worth a trip from one end of town to the other, for gumbo is the classic Creole and Acadian dish—perhaps the greatest achievement of all South Louisiana kitchens. While the *roux* for the gumbo was being prepared, Richard and I played ball in the back yard. Suddenly from the kitchen the sound of an impending disaster brought us running in to witness a battle I still vividly remember.

It was a battle that grew out of an important, though often forgotten, rule of New Orleans cooking. The rule is simply this: there is no one way to do anything—or, to put it differently, there are at least 200 ways to do everything. A gumbo is a gumbo in much the way that a snowflake is a snowflake or a fingerprint a fingerprint. All gumbos look alike until you get close to them; then you find that no two are the same. South Louisiana cooking is inventive—it had to be, or it wouldn't have invented itself. New combinations of ingredients are always being tried by good Creole and Acadian cooks, and made to come out right by a sprig of this or a spoonful of that. Louisiana recipes, in fact, are only as good as the cooks who use them—and few Louisiana cooks ever consult anything in writing. They believe that you either know how to make a dish or you don't— and if you do, your neighbors won't agree with you anyway; so why write it down? Be polite about the cooking next door and they will be polite about yours. Be rude about it, and you invite open warfare.

What Richard and I had heard from the back yard was the first volley. Our cook, Thelma, had been chatting in the kitchen with her sister-in-law Ruby. Now Ruby was also a fine cook. This did not distinguish her; most New Orleans women are fine cooks, whether they happen to make their living at it or not. What did distinguish Ruby was that she had a preference for okra gumbo—and Thelma had just gone on record as believing that okra gumbo was made only by fools and other idiot types who have never learned that filé gumbo is far superior. Ruby, who had stopped by on her way home to make lunch for Thelma's brother, took her hat off, put her purse on the kitchen counter, smiled patronizingly and settled down for a battle royal.

To understand the clash between those women, you must know that there are two distinct categories of gumbo worshipers: those who believe that a gumbo should be thickened with fresh okra, and those who prefer it thickened with a substance called filé powder—a product originally made by the Choctaw Indians of Louisiana from the young leaves of the sassafras tree. The leaves were dried, pounded to a powder and pressed through a sieve; the result was then brought to New Orleans to be sold at the French Market. Early on, Creole cooks found that filé powder made an excellent thickener that gave their gumbos a new taste. But the filé can only be used at the last minute, just before the dish is served—otherwise the gumbo becomes stringy. Okra, on the other hand, can be put in at the beginning; simmered right along with the gumbo, it subtly alters the flavor. But—and this is the catch—you can't use both of them together: in combination, filé and okra overthicken the dish and lose their own flavors. So you must choose, and the choice on this Sunday was stark. Thelma slammed a black iron pot down on the left side of the stove; Ruby got another out of the cabinet and set it on the right burner. Both a filé gumbo *and* an okra gumbo were to be made, and Richard and I were to decide which was better. It was all very simple.

That is, it was simple until Ruby saw that Thelma was going to put chicken and ham into her gumbo along with the crabs. That procedure, according to Ruby, could only be followed by a woman ignorant enough not to know that a Creole crab gumbo was originally a "maigre" dish—a dish for a fast day—and should never contain meat. This information greatly amused Thelma. Between belly laughs, she explained to all and sundry (Richard and me) that she had never before met anyone so misguided as to confuse crab gumbo with an oyster or shrimp gumbo, which are true Lenten foods. She saw clearly that her brother must have married Ruby for some reason other than Ruby's abilities in the kitchen.

Now in other cultures and in other lands it may not be insulting for one woman to suggest that another woman's greatest talent lies outside the domain of the kitchen. In New Orleans it is about the worst thing you can say. Even women of ill fame are supposed to know how to cook. All great ladies know how to cook, though they usually have someone to cook for them. In fact, to *be* a woman in South Louisiana is to know how to cook, and you are a lot safer in casting aspersions on a woman's intelligence or even her appearance than you are in questioning her right to stand at a stove. I don't recall what words passed between Ruby and Thelma after that, but it didn't really matter—they were shouting too loud to hear each other anyway. I do recall that each stood facing the other, that neither of them seemed to look at the stove for the next hour—and that neither stopped cooking for an instant. By the end of the hour I had learned a great many new and gorgeously unrespectable words, and was ready to enjoy two totally different kinds of gumbo.

While Ruby and Thelma cried and made up, Richard and I enjoyed the spoils of war. Ruby's gumbo was composed of crabs, shrimp, onions, okra, chilies, bay leaf, thyme, Tabasco, water, salt and a touch of cayenne.

> ### *Filé Powder: An Indian Legacy*
>
> *Filé powder, made from the dried leaves of sassafras trees that grow wild along the Gulf Coast, was discovered and used by the Choctaw Indians long before the Acadians reached Louisiana. When used in a gumbo, it imparts a delicate flavor somewhat similar to that of thyme, and a spoonful or so thickens stock into the kind of rich gravy that a genuine gumbo must have. But the cook must be careful: filé powder will become stringy if it is allowed to boil (the word filé may in fact derive from the French word for "thread") and should be added only at the last possible minute.*

In Louisiana, Monday is red-beans-and-rice day. The beans, often simmered with the ham bone left over from Sunday dinner, come in one pot and the rice in another; at the table, the beans are ladled over the rice and sprinkled with scallions. Beer and a green salad round out the combination.

It was a gumbo of the lake and the earth: rich and dark, yet smelling somehow of the purity of wind-blown water. When you put your face over it —as you should with all gumbos—and let the steam cloud hold you for a moment before you tasted it, you knew what the essence of shellfish smelled like. Then, when you put a spoonful in your mouth, the word pungent could never again hold the same meaning for you. You could not have imagined a pungency combined with sweetness and the taste of herbs, not to mention the sting of red pepper on the tongue, and the deep taste of crab. In its simplicity the dish was a marvel.

By contrast, Thelma's gumbo was less simple and pure, but fuller and rounder. In her anger at Ruby she had dismissed the crabs entirely and produced instead a gumbo based on chicken, ham and two dozen oysters that she had been saving to fry for dinner. The dish was prepared in about the same way as Ruby's, but without okra, with oyster liquor instead of water, and with a generous measure of filé powder spread over the top just before the gumbo was served. Richard and I happily ate bowlfuls of both gumbos, each with two spoonfuls of white rice at the center of the dark liquid to add substance and softness to the spicy meal. Gumbo is exactly that—a meal; it isn't really a soup and it isn't a solid. As we drank the liquid off, we ate the chicken and ham and the pieces of crab and the shrunken oysters and shrimp that lay at the bottoms of the bowls.

There are other good gumbos, made from turkey or rabbit or even squirrel. There is a pure shrimp gumbo (best with filé), a pure chicken gumbo and a pure oyster one. There is cabbage gumbo, and even a gumbo made with herbs and greens alone, called *gumbo aux herbes* or *gumbo z'herbes (Recipe Index);* it is said to have been originated by the superstitious Creoles especially for Good Friday when, it was believed, you would have good luck for the coming year if you ate seven greens and met seven people during the day. In the bayous there are muskrat gumbos, and if you were to transplant an Acadian family to Maine there would doubtless be a lobster gumbo. In short, a gumbo can contain whatever you get your hands on—if your hands can cook. It is indeed the all-containing dish; as the Creoles put it, "Gumbo, c'est bon—c'est tout" —or, in English, "It's plain good, it's everything."

I recall other Sundays and other meals from those years—meals that move in my memory like the slow pour of dark cane syrup onto French bread. Things are not done in a hurry in New Orleans; even growing up seems to take an extraordinarily long time. Cooking itself is done in the way everything else is, with a kind of endless but easy energy, and people seem to move through the heavy air as if in a dream; nothing but a flare of temper or a sudden turn in the weather can make a person hurry. Waxy leaves wait in the lush quiet green; dogs often stare at cats rather than chase them; dropped bay leaves seem to drift down into waiting pots. Unless a child brings something home that must be cooked on Sunday, as Richard and I brought those crabs, the day is usually left free for church and social gatherings. A ham, baked the previous day, is left on the sideboard with a dish of sliced sweet Creole tomatoes in a tart French dressing, and people help themselves when they get hungry. And on Monday, of course, the cook knows exactly what to do with the ham bone. Nothing is wasted in Creole or Acadian kitchens; if you can't concoct something magnificent with the most meager leftovers, you might as well go North, where (it is whispered) people actually throw leftovers away.

In New Orleans a ham bone is considered the whole point of the ham. Without it, you could hardly live through Monday, for on that day, as everyone knows, you need it to get a lyrical taste into what sounds at first like the drabbest of all local recipes—the classic Monday dish of red beans and rice *(Recipe Index)*. The idea of starch cooked with starch makes some non-Louisianians stare unbelievingly at the restaurant menus on which this dish appears every Monday. Yet it is a great way to face a week's work; every Tuesday morning, even though I have not lived in New Orleans for 20 years, I still find myself wondering just what I missed in my meals the day before.

Both Creole and Acadian cooks do something to a plain red bean that changes its taste and texture. Soaking is not the secret, though the beans must be soaked. Thyme sometimes flavors the beans, and so do onions and occasionally garlic, but you can use those ingredients and more and still not achieve the smooth, dark, almost creamy quality of the finished dish. The secret is known to you, though, if you've sat as a child in a New Orleans kitchen on a Monday and seen the cook either crack the ham bone or make sure that one end of it is open. The red beans will taste like well-seasoned pellets of carbohydrate if the bone isn't cracked or open. But if it is, the thick marrow from the bone leaks into the simmering beans, coats them, cooks slowly with them, seems to drain them of starch, and produces a silky food that is more like incredibly tender meat than like a vegetable. Bits of the ham flow through the mixture, and the thick, dark beans-and-gravy triumph is ladled over fluffy rice that soaks it up and gives it even more body.

People in New Orleans have any number of good ways to eat this dish. Classically it is served at lunch with a green salad that has a good sharp tarragon-vinegar dressing to complement the rich marrow-soaked beans. But if you are a boy of 10 or so and if you live next door to an empty lot, you wait until early evening, take a plate of beans and rice and another of salad and go out and sit in a tangle of honeysuckle and blackberry bushes while the crickets chirp the last of day into night. There in the breathtaking scent of the flowers, with the sun descending, you sit with one plate in your lap and the other next to you, and you alternate forkfuls of the hot beans and rice with the sour crisp cold lettuce until both plates are half gone. Then you empty a bit of vinegar from the salad into the beans, stir it around, and finish with a combined taste—smooth and sharp, sour and sweet together—that makes you wonder why anybody in the world ever bothered cooking anything else.

The old Creoles had great elegance. Their table settings were impeccable, their choices of wines superb. But good Creole food, whether prepared with *grande cuisine* finesse or with peasant plainness, tastes best to me not when it is sealed indoors but when it is eaten out on the flat land that produced it, amid smells and sounds and slow air that become parts of the meal itself. And in the summertime, for a growing boy, the joy is complete when he ends the meal with a walk to the nearest seller of snow-

balls—cups of shaved ice and fresh fruit syrup, derived from the original Creole sherbets. The quicksilver crunch of the ice blends with the thick fruit taste, thinning it and turning it alive in the mouth as if the fruit were ripening on the tongue.

The long, soft summer of New Orleans—the wet air and violent heat, the mornings of fierce sunshine and the afternoons of sudden warm rain —finally ends in a cooling off, followed by a brief spell of really cold weather. This period of ice and frost surprises everybody, because it isn't ever supposed to happen. Though there is no formal autumn, and even less a formal spring, New Orleans does have a winter, otherwise known as February. It is a time when people are busy preparing for the carnival called Mardi Gras—and it is a time when splendid dishes are prepared and eaten, along with simpler, body-warming foods.

For youthful eyes, it is more fun to be where things are prepared than where they are presented. On his own, away from his family, a boy can relax; and he will learn a lot more from kitchens and back alleys than anyone in a living room would believe. He can, for instance, wander through the French Quarter toward evening, when the chill winter sky hangs heavy and gray over the grillwork balconies. If he manages to look forlorn enough, a family friend is sure to take him in for a cup of hot milk and a slice of marble cake made with cane syrup—the cake so fine and sweet that it makes his teeth ache, the milk smooth and warm to his stomach. There, too, he can watch the Mardi Gras costumes being sewn: the ball gowns and chain mail and harlequin suits and mad court clothes that will be worn before Lent. People have been making their costumes all year, ever since the last Lent ended. Now, with the new Mardi Gras only a little way off, preparations take on a tempo of fury. Sequins and lace, velvet and feathers fly from one room to the next. In the kitchen, off the courtyard, someone will be making a bowl of orange cream from fresh orange juice, sugar, sweet milk and eggs. It will be cooked, then frozen, and finally served with a dash of brandy to give people the tingling energy they need to get through the last days before carnival begins.

I remember walking through the French Quarter one evening when I was about 12. Properly called the Vieux Carré, the Old Square, the neighborhood was originally French, but it was rebuilt twice—after the fires of 1788 and 1794—when New Orleans was under Spanish rule. The old streets, with their enclosed plant-lined patios, look more like an Andalusian city than anything in France. That evening the streets were full of the aromas of Creole cookery. The scents of thyme and bay leaf, garlic and onion seeped from baked fish; the ever-present fresh shellfish smell seemed to rust like iron on the air; steam rose from opulent dark soups and bisques. The cold, shadowy alleys rang with the echoes of jazz from Bourbon Street; elegant restaurants and cheap jive joints flung their sounds and smells at each other; and all this cacophony was, for me, like an end to childhood and a prelude to the music of the adult world. I stopped at a friend's house for a taste of a strange, little-known French Quarter combination—a cup of vanilla ice cream with a light sprinkle of cayenne over it. The sweet-and-spice-hot mixture, with its blend of cold and a touch of burning, made me feel that my insides were melting. I

Opposite: Kings' cake, like the French *gâteau des Rois* that inspired it, is served on Twelfth Night, at the start of the carnival season. Made of rich yeast dough and citron, the regal ring is decorated with sugar tinted in the classic carnival colors. Inside is a single bean or pecan half; whoever finds this treasure in his portion is declared King or Queen of the Twelfth Night celebration. Cups of champagne punch, enriched by fresh strawberries, accompany the cake. The coins are souvenir "doubloons" tossed at carnival spectators by participants in the floats. *(The cake and punch recipes are listed in the Recipe Index.)*

Continued on page 53

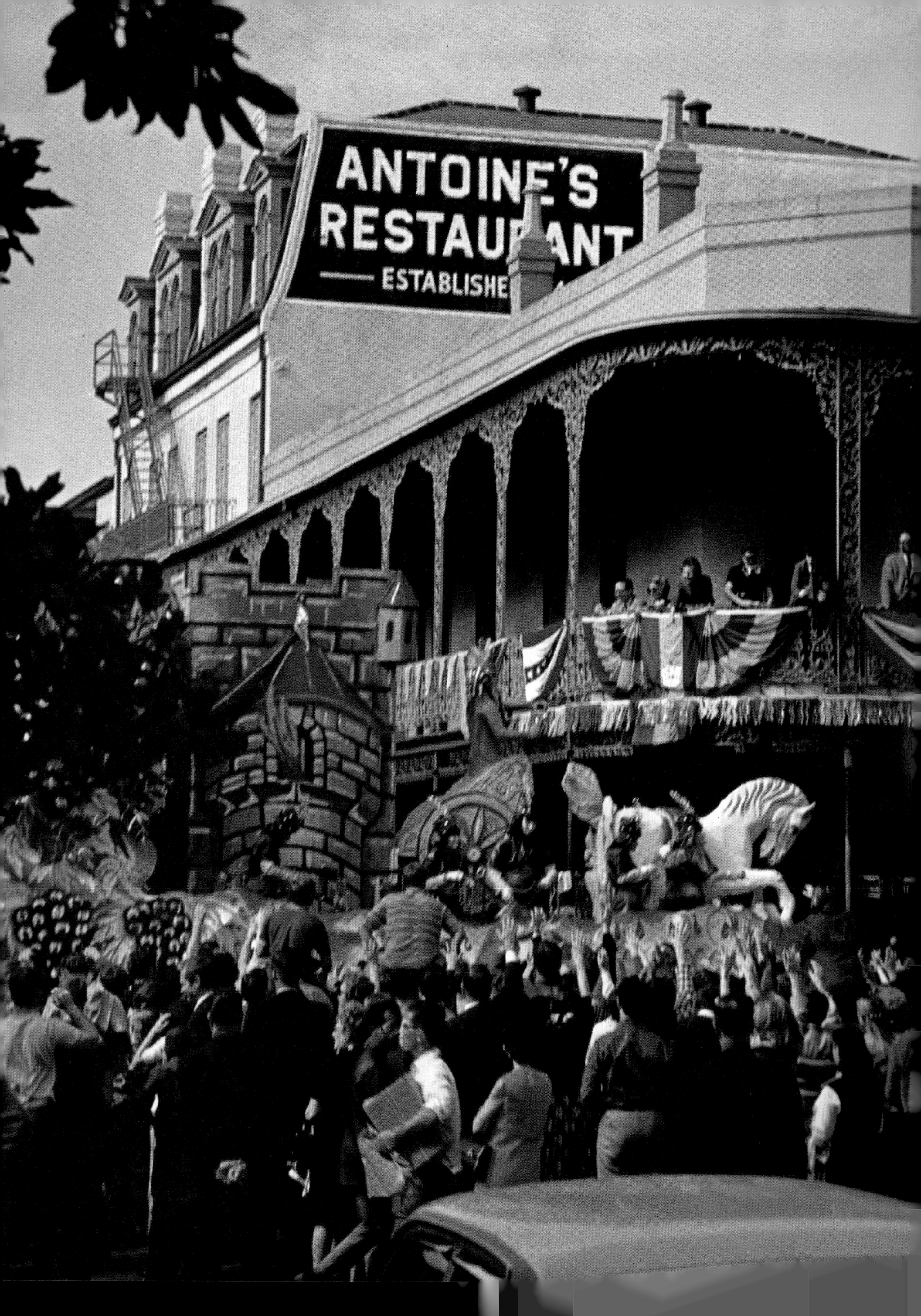
ANTOINE'S
RESTAU ANT
ESTABLISHE

"Fat Tuesday" – the New Orleans Festival That Began on a Mississippi Mud Bank

Guests at Antoine's interrupt their lunch to watch the parade of the Krewe of Iris pass down Royal Street. This krewe is made up solely of women —one of the few so constituted. The Krewe of Iris holds its own ball, at which women, rather than men, are masked—and the men must wait for women to ask them to dance.

The word carnival means, literally, "farewell to meat"; it comes from the Latin. *Mardi Gras* is French for "fat Tuesday." Together, the three words describe with admirable precision the magnificent New Orleans hullabaloo that annually anticipates the rigors of Lent. Tomorrow, the words say, will be a time of fasting; today will be given over to meat and to merriment.

It seems probable that the first Mardi Gras was celebrated in 1699, before New Orleans even existed, by some melancholy French colonists in a temporary camp pitched on a mud bank 30 miles above the mouth of the Mississippi. By the mid-18th Century the custom was apparently well established in the city itself—but mainly as an excuse for licentious frolic. Not until 1857 did the festivities begin to take on their modern character. In that year, some socially prominent young blades, irked by the ill-bred antics of the Mardi Gras celebrants, formed a secret society called the Mistick Krewe of Comus, staging a splendid parade, with floats and costumes, and a ball to which only the best people were invited. Today the "krewes," the parades and the balls have proliferated, and Mardi Gras and New Orleans are inseparable.

At the Comus Ball, the stellar social event of Mardi Gras, members of the Krewe of Comus are masked and theoretically incognito.

Much of the charm of Mardi Gras is ad lib and
unexpected. The clowns at left, for example, created
their own costumes and their own vertical parade.
The celebrant above is a member of the gloriously
bedecked Indians, a somewhat secretive group
of New Orleans Negroes who do not parade
formally, preferring to wander freely through the city.

Theme of the Rex Parade, the biggest of all, was Classics and Comics. The tale of the fox and grapes is seen here.

Aboard his regal float, Rex himself waves majestically. He is usually a leading businessman, his queen a debutante.

During the afternoon of
Mardi Gras, guests still
clad in their parade
costumes assemble for a
late buffet lunch at the
home of Judge and Mrs.
John Minor Wisdom. At
left, a tureen of gumbo filé
stands on a table decorated
with flowers in the
traditional Mardi Gras
colors of green, gold and
purple, symbolizing Faith,
Power and Justice,
respectively. At the other
end of the table *(above)*
is a ham *à l'orange*. And
as a final elegant touch, a
lace-covered sideboard
(right) offers iced
champagne and three
desserts: coffee mousse,
*bâtons de noisettes (Recipe
Index)* and pecan crisps.

The King and Queen of Comus reign over their ball. The queen is debutante Lynn Howard; the king's identity is traditionally secret.

remember going home as I ate, leaving behind the Quarter and the lights that flickered from places I would soon be old enough to enter—the siren world that waited in the night.

I also remember a day in late winter, just before Mardi Gras began. I was sitting at a dock on the Mississippi where the flat barges called oyster luggers stopped on their way upstream. I joined the dock workers as they pried open a few of the fresh cold oysters, which are at their best this time of year. No sauces, no fork—nothing but a knife to open the oysters, wielded by a man who knew exactly where to pierce each tight-shut shell and flip it open to reveal the glistening, quartz-colored, charcoal-edged object inside. As each shell was opened, he made a slit under the oyster's "eye" to separate it from the shell, then passed it along. A chill breeze blew in from the river, bringing with it the deep-water smell from the vast mound of oysters lying like fallen leaves on the barge. We ate the oysters with only the air for sauce, swallowing the oyster liquor after them to hold and extend the flavor. If you once eat them that way, you will know for the rest of your life that all the great dishes made around oysters could not improve on that first salt-sweet natural taste, any more than great perfumes can improve on the fragrance of fresh flowers.

The winter quiet came to an end as Mardi Gras approached. Lights and flares turned the air to brilliance over the city, and the season of parties was launched, unfolding in full the style and luxury of the old Creoles as night began and people gathered at one house or another. I was able to glimpse this stunning spectacle one evening as I sat in the kitchen of a friend who lived in the Garden District. Through the kitchen doorway we watched as lace-shouldered women and dinner-jacketed men were seated at a long gleaming table. The table was lit by candles alone; dozens more lined the room, their deep yellow light picked up by the polished silver and crystal. An oyster soup seethed in a silver tureen; I could imagine its taste on the tongue. The candlelight flickered, voices grew mellow over the wine, and stuffed crabs were served in their shells—crabmeat mixed with butter, salt, cayenne, eggs and parsley, brushed with white of egg, sprinkled with bread crumbs and baked to a high gold color. It tasted sweet and hot, rich and yet easy to digest.

The *coup de milieu,* the customary pause in mid-meal, came next, a frozen punch made of champagne, oranges, kirsch, pineapple syrup, lemon juice and strawberries, the icy sweetness and the alcohol combining to make way for the remaining courses. There was a platter of spiced beef cooked with tomatoes and carrots and onions, cloves and allspice, with a taste that surely soothed as it sparkled. Accompanying the beef was an eggplant soufflé *(Recipe Index)* that turned this heaviest of vegetables into the lightest froth. Then a huge tossed salad was brought to the table, dressed with garlic and paprika and Worcestershire and Tabasco along with vinegar and oil; the greens looked as if they were growing in the bowl. A platter of cheeses followed, and then dessert. . . .

The dessert was a dish that is apt to turn all children into adults, and vice versa. Crêpes—paper-thin pancakes—had been rolled up to enclose a smooth dab of orange paste. As the crêpes were served, brandy and curaçao and several other liqueurs were flamed in sugar over the silver platter, illuminating the room with blue flame and small orange flares, brighter even than the candles. There was probably too much variety in the sweet liqueurs and too dark a bitter taste in the orange paste for this dish to be properly called by its French name, crêpes suzette—crêpes Creole would be a more accurate term.

These, in turn, were followed by a great bowl of flaming black *café brûlot (Recipe Index)*. Three of the same ingredients figured here as in the crêpes—brandy and curaçao and sugar—but they were flavored differently, with cinnamon, cloves, orange peel and strong black coffee. *Café brûlot* and its counterpart *café diable* (traditionally, the difference between them is simply that the latter contains only lemon peel) seem to fuse one's taste buds so that one's tongue retains the meal's bouquet for the rest of the evening. In my friend's kitchen, I too had a taste of *café brûlot* after dinner. It melted the bright edges of my vision until the guests who rose from the table and passed through the distant doorway dissolved into dream figures that floated and finally faded.

When I woke the next morning it was Mardi Gras—"Fat Tuesday" (Shrove Tuesday). New Orleans had given itself over to Rex, King of the city for a day, as it had done every year since 1872. The costumes and allegorical floats that had been in preparation for a year burst into the streets like a flight of insanely colored pigeons. Private clubs had given their dinners and galas for a week now, and today they sent their floats out into the city, each float gaily decorated and wildly populated by people wearing every color of silk and satin, velvet and lace. Costumed crowds, shoulder to shoulder in the old streets and alleys of the Quarter, preceded the floats in cheering waves. This was one day when things did *not* move slowly in New Orleans. Clanking steel armor careened behind a flush of purple feathers; dark ran beside light; sequins flashed like silver needles thrown into the swift-flowing mass.

I started the day with Richard, my friend in the Quarter, by seeing to our food supply: a good hamburger apiece, Creole style, cooked with oregano and thyme and smothered in *sauce piquante,* and to go with it, thick slices of Mardi Gras cake. Louise, the handsome woman who cooked for Richard's family, had done the honors for this occasion. She wrapped the food for us in wax paper, and we took it into the crush of the streets, flattening ourselves against buildings while people and floats roared by. Someone, we knew, would have a bottle of pop or a thermos of iced tea we could sip to wash down the fine spicy hamburger; after that we would take a crumbling bite out of the moist cake, filled with nuts, candied fruits and bits of sticky fruit peel. As the floats passed, we scrambled over the pavements with the rest of the onlookers for the strings of bugle beads, "gold" coins, wrapped chocolates and whistles thrown by Rex and his courtiers and costumed friends, seated high above us on swaying papier-mâché scenes of royalty and piracy and other bits of history.

As the evening came on, Richard and I went to a corner stand for a cup of hot chocolate and a warm *beignet (Recipe Index),* a Creole pastry of sweetened fried dough with a sprinkling of powdered sugar like white lace over the top. The light, chewy *beignet* went perfectly with the heavy, steaming chocolate. The Creoles say that the combination is like dunking, but in the mouth rather than in the cup. It gave us energy to play out the rest of the evening, as the crowds slowed and lingered in the streets and the stars rose above the Old Square. Afterward, as we walked home through the sifting streamers and leftover glitter, we talked and thought about the many carnivals that we would see before we managed to grow up—but we were deluded, for we were to grow up before we knew it.

The moss in the trees moves endlessly, soundlessly, the river slides by, dark and thick, and then one day you are 16. How it happens, you can't quite tell, but it does: instead of going to visit boys your own age, you discover that girls have a certain interesting quality all their own. The trouble is, girls your age are apt to date men a lot older than you are— unless you can find a way to hold their interest, which is difficult when the competition so unfairly comes up with things like sports cars and dance parlors. Of course, you can always invite a girl out to the lakefront at night. But how do you get her to go there? Easily. Don't talk about late evening strolls among the May flowers—that's movie talk, and it won't work in New Orleans. Instead, double-date and take her to one of the inexpensive picnic-type restaurants that line Lake Pontchartrain's west end. More specifically, ask her if she wants to share a platter of crab boil. There isn't a girl in South Louisiana who can turn that down.

You take her along with another couple and you sit at a square table. The sun has set over the flat water and the pier you are on juts out over the lake, supported by pilings. The water laps gently beneath you as the waitress sets down an enormous platter heaped with orange hard-shell crabs and whole pink river shrimp in a bed of crushed ice. Nothing is peeled; the crabs are fully clawed and uncracked, the shrimp all have their heads. The shellfish have merely been lowered briefly into bubbling-hot water flavored with a Creole combination of herbs and spices. You wouldn't think that anything cooked so easily could taste so good, but it took years to put these spices and herbs together in just the right proportions to intensify the flavor of shellfish. The four people at your table "square off" like boxers; the sight of the food has changed two demure Southern girls and their escorts into four hungry adolescents with a will. The waitress brings four ice-cold beers, everybody literally digs in—and the heaping pile of shellfish begins to disappear.

People say you can tell a person who comes from New Orleans by watching him peel boiled shellfish, and it's true. Nothing moves but the fingers—and you can hardly see them, just as you can hardly see a hummingbird's wings. Visitors to New Orleans always look as if they were fighting the shellfish rather than eating them; they struggle visibly with the shells and legs and feelers and heads and claws. New Orleans folk are deft—they have to be, or they'd have starved through their adolescence. In the time it takes to think about it, a tiny river shrimp can be broken in two, the juicy head sucked, the feet and tail removed, the body peeled and popped into the mouth. River shrimp, only about a third the size of lake shrimp, are far more subtle in flavor, and the herbs and spices enhance their flavor to a single exquisite edge. Then you take a crab, break it in two crosswise, break each half in two again, and pick out the lumps of sweet white meat from inside. Don't let the crabmeat flake, for

Continued on page 60

55

A Picnic on a Favorite Lakefront

Some New Orleans families picnic on the banks of Lake Pontchartrain nearly every Sunday of the year, except in the rare cold spells. But the Brennan clan must look to more than the thermometer for a day when all of them can get together, for they own two of the best restaurants in New Orleans, and these keep them busy. When they do find time, they have an advantage: the food for their picnic can be prepared the day before in the restaurants' kitchens. The Brennan women welcome this assistance because a typical Brennan picnic involves the consumption of some 30 pounds of crawfish and eight dozen crabs boiled with spices and peppers, plus a couple of dozen ears of fresh corn (not to mention such extras as beer, soft drinks and watermelon).

On the occasion shown here, there were 13 hungry participants in the Brennan picnic party: Dick Brennan and his wife Lynne with their two children, Dick's nephew Owen Brennan Jr. and his wife Barbara with their four children, plus Dick's two nephews, his niece and a friend. The park on the shores of Pontchartrain is just 10 minutes' drive from the center of the city, but the Brennans had to walk only a little way from their parking spot to reach a fairly secluded stretch of the lakefront. After the young fry had a ball game (won by the girls, as usual) while the grownups set the picnic cloth with cold boiled crabs, crawfish and corn, the entire party fell to the main business of eating *(right)*, with varying degrees of expertise. Shannon Brennan, 10, had not quite mastered the technique of eating crab *(left)*, and managed to get through only three. She made up for it by eating what she described as "a whole lot" of crawfish—"they are easier to get at and you can eat more of them."

Lavishing extra care on seeds, the girls round off the meal with watermelon.

it is better when eaten in lumps. Don't use cocktail sauce, for it drowns the first fresh taste of the crab. The two, crab and shrimp, make a double seafood taste, and together with a good light bitter beer, they fill the senses as they fill the stomach.

Very soon the big platter is empty and four people are left sitting with four plates piled high with empty shells in front of them. Best to wash your hands now, and maybe have another beer. Then the girls will change back into girls and the boys into boys; you can pair off and walk along the darkened lakefront under the green summer moon.

But if it is a special date, there is another ending to the meal in the little outdoor restaurant. I remember a Fourth of July when the cook at one of those inexpensive eating places produced a dessert that was both elegant and luscious. There is a simple dessert called ambrosia, which consists of orange slices covered with grated coconut. On that summer night, ambrosia was improved on; a wonderfully new dessert was concocted for our party of eight people. The cook sliced a ripe watermelon lengthwise and hollowed it out. The flesh of the melon was scooped into small round balls, along with the flesh of other melons—pale green ones, orange ones, opaque yellow ones. One of the empty watermelon shells was lined with a layer of sliced oranges and another of fresh grated coconut. Over this the cook put a thick layer of the variously colored melon balls; then the three layers—orange, coconut, melon—were repeated again and again, until a heaping rainbow mound rose out of the long hollow shell. That cooled in the refrigerator during our meal. Then, just before the dessert was served, a bottle of iced champagne was opened and poured over the whole thing so that the wine fizzed and bubbled and seeped its way down through the fruit as people helped themselves. The variety of sweet tastes, the fresh coconut, the bubbling champagne combined to effect a brilliance like the Fourth of July fireworks that were bursting in the night sky. In New Orleans a dessert alone can make a celebration.

Early one morning you are yet another year older. It is late spring again, and you know that you will leave New Orleans soon, for schooling in the North. Alone now, you buy a paper cone full of boiled crawfish, and walk along the river. You climb from the river road up the levee above New Orleans and sit in the morning mist over the Mississippi. The river below you is as brown as *café au lait*. You peel and eat the crimson crawfish the same way you do shrimp. Their flavor is loud by comparison, their shells are harder, but they too have been boiled in herb-filled water, and there is something about their taste that reminds you of the gentle moss in the trees and the violent skies and waves of air from the swamps.

You may be going away from New Orleans, but you will never really leave it. Other places will always seem a little bland by comparison, just as all other cooking will seem pale and faint, no matter how good it is. You have grown up with the ingredients of a cuisine that has an explosion of tastes built into it; you will never stop wanting to try the bisques and daubes and baked dishes that are themselves the grown-up products of those ingredients.

So, if you must go now, you stand up and go readily. For you will surely come back another year.

Opposite: Grillades and grits *(Recipe Index)* are a breakfast dish as basic to New Orleans as ham and eggs to other parts of the United States. Grillades are round steaks of veal (or sometimes beef) braised in a sauce of onions, green peppers, celery, tomatoes and garlic. The accompanying white or yellow hominy grits soak up the sauce and take on its full, zesty flavor.

CHAPTER **II** RECIPES

To make one 12-inch ring

CAKE

½ cup lukewarm water (110° to
   115°)
2 packages active dry yeast
2 teaspoons plus ½ cup granulated
   sugar
3½ to 4½ cups unsifted flour
1 teaspoon ground nutmeg,
   preferably freshly grated
2 teaspoons salt
1 teaspoon finely grated fresh lemon
   peel
½ cup lukewarm milk (110° to
   115°)
5 egg yolks
8 tablespoons butter (1 quarter-
   pound stick), cut into ½-inch
   bits and softened, plus
   2 tablespoons butter, softened
½ cup finely chopped candied
   citron
1 shelled pecan half or uncooked
   dried bean
1 egg, lightly beaten with
   1 tablespoon milk

SUGARS

Green, purple and yellow food-
   coloring pastes
12 tablespoons granulated sugar

ICING

3 cups confectioners' sugar
¼ cup strained fresh lemon juice
3 to 6 tablespoons water
2 candied cherries, cut lengthwise
   into halves

Kings' Cake

The New Orleans carnival season begins on January 6, or Twelfth Night, and ends with the revel of Mardi Gras, on the day before Lent begins. Kings' cake is baked for Twelfth Night celebrations—and the lucky person who finds the pecan or bean in his slice of cake is "king or queen for a day." Traditionally, the cake is decorated with sugar tinted in the classic carnival colors: green, purple and yellow.

To make the cake, pour the lukewarm water into a small shallow bowl and sprinkle the yeast and 2 teaspoons of the granulated sugar over it. Let the yeast and sugar rest for 2 to 3 minutes, then stir to mix the ingredients well. Set in a warm, draft-free place (such as an unlighted oven) for about 10 minutes, or until the yeast bubbles up and the mixture almost doubles in volume.

Combine 3½ cups of flour, the remaining ½ cup of granulated sugar, the nutmeg and the salt, and sift them into a deep mixing bowl. Stir in the lemon peel, then make a well in the center and into it pour the yeast mixture and the milk.

Add the egg yolks and, with a large wooden spoon, gradually incorporate the dry ingredients into the liquid ones. When the mixture is smooth, beat in the 8 tablespoons of butter bits, a tablespoonful at a time. Continue to beat for about 2 minutes longer, or until the dough can be gathered into a medium-soft ball.

Place the ball on a lightly floured surface and knead, pushing the dough down with the heels of your hands, pressing it forward and folding it back on itself. As you knead, incorporate up to 1 cup more flour, sprinkling it over the ball by the tablespoonful. When the dough is no longer sticky, knead it for about 10 minutes longer, or until it is smooth, shiny and elastic.

With a pastry brush, spread 1 tablespoon of softened butter evenly over the inside of a large bowl. Set the dough in the bowl and turn it about to butter the entire surface. Drape the bowl with a kitchen towel and put it in the draft-free place for 1½ hours, or until the dough doubles in volume.

Brush a large baking sheet with the remaining tablespoon of softened butter. Punch the dough down with a blow of your fist and place it on a lightly floured surface. Scatter the citron over the top, knead the dough until the citron is well distributed, then pat and shape it into a cylinder about 14 inches long. Loop the cylinder onto the buttered baking sheet and pinch the ends together to form a ring.

Press the pecan half or dried bean gently into the ring so that it is completely hidden by the dough. Drape the dough with the towel again and set it in the draft-free place to rise for about 45 minutes, or until the ring doubles in volume.

Preheat the oven to 375°. (If you have used the oven to let the dough rise, transfer the ring to another warm place to rest while the oven heats.) Brush the top and sides of the ring with the egg-and-milk mixture and bake the Kings' cake in the middle of the oven for 25 to 30 minutes, or until it is golden brown.

Slide the cake onto a wire rack to cool to room temperature.

Meanwhile, prepare the colored sugars. Squeeze a dot of green coloring paste onto the center of the palm of one hand. Sprinkle 2 tablespoons of granulated sugar over the paste and rub your palms together briskly until the sugar is evenly green. Add more paste if the color is too light and rub the sugar a few minutes longer. Place the green sugar on a saucer or piece of wax paper and repeat the entire procedure again to color 2 more tablespoons of the sugar.

Wash your hands, squeeze a blob of purple food coloring paste on one palm and in a similar fashion color 4 tablespoons of the granulated sugar purple. Wash your hands again and, using the yellow food coloring paste, tint the remaining 4 tablespoons of granulated sugar yellow. Set the green, purple and yellow sugars aside.

When the cake has cooled, prepare the icing. Combine the confectioners' sugar, lemon juice and 3 tablespoons of the water in a deep bowl and stir until the icing mixture is smooth. If the icing is too stiff to spread easily, beat in up to 3 tablespoons more water, 1 teaspoonful at a time. With a small metal spatula, spread the icing over the top of the cake, allowing it to run irregularly down the sides.

Sprinkle the colored sugars over the icing immediately, forming a row of purple, yellow and green strips, each about 2 inches wide, on both sides of the ring as shown in the photograph on page 44. Arrange two cherry halves at each end of the cake, pressing them gently into the icing.

NOTE: Food coloring pastes are available at bakers' supply stores or by mail *(see Shopping Guide, page 199)*. Do not use liquid food coloring, which makes the sugar dissolve and clump and does not color the granules evenly.

Bâtons de Noisettes
NUT STICKS

To make about thirty 2½-inch-
long sticks

1 tablespoon plus ½ pound
  unsalted butter, softened
¼ cup granulated sugar
¼ teaspoon salt
2 cups unsifted flour
2 teaspoons vanilla extract
1 cup finely chopped walnuts or
  filberts
1 cup confectioners' sugar

Preheat the oven to 350°. With a pastry brush, spread the tablespoon of softened butter evenly over a large baking sheet and set it aside.

In a deep bowl, cream the remaining ½ pound of the softened butter with the granulated sugar by beating and mashing them against the sides of the bowl with the back of a large spoon until light and fluffy. Sprinkle the salt over the flour and add the flour mixture to the butter about ½ cup at a time, beating well after each addition. Beat in the vanilla extract and the chopped walnuts or filberts.

To shape each *bâton,* cut off a heaping tablespoon of the dough and roll it with your hands into a cylinder about 2½ inches long and ½ inch in diameter. Arrange the *bâtons* 1 inch apart on the buttered baking sheet and bake them in the middle of the oven for 10 to 12 minutes, or until they are a delicate golden color.

With a wide metal spatula, transfer the *bâtons* to wire racks. When they are completely cool, roll each cookie in the confectioners' sugar to coat it evenly on all sides. In a tightly covered jar or tin, *bâtons de noisettes* can safely be kept for several weeks.

To serve 2

1 pint medium-sized shucked oysters
    (about 12 oysters)
¼ teaspoon ground hot red pepper
    (cayenne)
¼ teaspoon freshly ground black
    pepper
2 eggs
½ cup evaporated milk
⅛ teaspoon salt
1 cup unsifted corn flour *(see
    Glossary, page,198)* or 1 cup all-
    purpose flour
1½ cups soft fresh crumbs made
    from French- or Italian-type
    white bread, pulverized in a
    blender
1 loaf French- or Italian-type bread
    about 15 inches long and 3 inches
    wide
4 tablespoons butter, melted
Vegetable oil for deep frying
½ cup Creole tartar sauce *(Recipe
    Booklet)*
1½ cups finely shredded lettuce
1 large tomato, washed, stemmed
    and cut crosswise into ¼-inch-
    thick slices

To serve 4 to 6

6 cups water
1 pound dried small red beans *(see
    Glossary, page 198)* or 1 pound
    dried red kidney beans
4 tablespoons butter
1 cup finely chopped scallions,
    including 3 inches of the green
    tops
½ cup finely chopped onions
1 teaspoon finely chopped garlic
2 one-pound smoked ham hocks
1 teaspoon salt
½ teaspoon freshly ground black
    pepper
6 to 8 cups freshly cooked long-
    grain rice

Peacemaker
OYSTER LOAF SANDWICH

In the 19th Century, according to tradition, a New Orleans husband who had spent the night in the French Quarter saloons brought this oyster loaf sandwich home to his wife as a médiatrice, or peacemaker. Called a "poor boy" in New Orleans, this kind of sandwich is known in other sections of the United States as a hero, a grinder or a submarine.

Pat the oysters completely dry with paper towels and season them on all sides with the red and black pepper. In a shallow bowl, beat the eggs to a froth with a wire whisk or fork, add the evaporated milk and salt, and mix well. Spread the corn flour or all-purpose flour on one piece of wax paper and the bread crumbs on another piece.

Roll one oyster at a time in the flour and, when it is evenly covered, immerse it in the egg mixture. Then turn the oyster about in the crumbs to coat it on all sides. Arrange the oysters in one layer on a plate and refrigerate them while you prepare the bread.

Preheat the oven to 350°. With a large sharp knife, slice the loaf of bread horizontally in half. Pull out all the white doughy crumbs from both the top and bottom to create two boatlike shells of the crusts. With a pastry brush, spread the melted butter evenly inside both halves of the loaf. Place the shells on a baking sheet and bake in the middle of the oven for about 15 minutes, or until they are crisp and lightly brown.

Meanwhile, pour vegetable oil into a deep fryer or large heavy saucepan to a depth of about 3 inches and heat the oil until it reaches a temperature of 375°. Deep-fry the oysters, six at a time, turning them with a slotted spoon for 2 to 3 minutes, or until the coating is crisp and golden brown. As they brown, transfer them to paper towels to drain.

To assemble the peacemaker, spread the tartar sauce inside both the bottom and top parts of the loaf. Scatter the shredded lettuce on the bottom half of the loaf and arrange the tomato slices and finally the oysters over it. Set the top part of the loaf in place, slice the loaf crosswise into four portions and serve at once.

NOTE: If you prefer, you may omit the sliced tomatoes from the sandwich and instead of using the Creole tartar sauce spread the inside top and bottom of the loaf with a mixture of ½ cup of bottled chili sauce, 2 tablespoons of prepared horseradish, 2 teaspoons of strained fresh lemon juice and ¼ teaspoon of Worcestershire sauce.

Red Beans and Rice

In a heavy 3- to 4-quart saucepan, bring the water to a boil over high heat. Drop in the beans and boil briskly, uncovered, for 2 minutes. Then turn off the heat and let the beans soak for 1 hour. Drain the beans in a sieve set over a large bowl; measure the soaking liquid and, if necessary, add more water to make 4 cups. Set the beans and liquid aside.

Melt the butter in a heavy 4- to 5-quart casserole set over moderate heat. When the foam begins to subside, add ½ cup of the scallions, the onions and the garlic and, stirring frequently, cook for about 5 minutes, or until they are soft and translucent but not brown.

The peacemaker, New Orleans' apotheosis of the hero sandwich, contains fried oysters, tomato, lettuce and nippy tartar sauce.

Stir in the beans and their liquid, the ham hocks, salt and pepper. Bring the mixture to a boil over high heat, reduce the heat to low and simmer partially covered for about 3 hours, or until the beans are very soft. Check the pot from time to time and, if the beans seem dry, add up to 1 cup more water, a few tablespoonfuls at a time. During the last 30 minutes or so of cooking, stir frequently and mash the softest beans against the sides of the pan to form a thick sauce for the remaining beans.

With tongs or a slotted spoon, transfer the ham hocks to a plate. Cut the meat away from the bones and remove and discard the skin, fat and gristle. Cut the meat into ¼-inch dice and return it to the beans.

Taste the red beans for seasoning and serve at once, directly from the casserole or from a large heated tureen. Place the rice and the remaining ½ cup of scallions in separate bowls and present them with the beans.

NOTE: In Louisiana, red beans and rice are traditionally made with a leftover ham bone, and you may substitute a ham bone for the ham hocks in this recipe. Without trimming off the meat, cut the bone into 2- or 3-inch pieces with a hacksaw, so that the marrow inside the pieces will melt and flavor the beans. Add the pieces of bone to the soaked bean mixture and pour in enough additional water to cover them completely. When the beans are cooked, remove the bones from the pot, trim off and dice the meat, and return it to the beans. Discard the bones.

1 pound uncooked medium-sized shrimp (about 20 to 24 to the pound)

7 quarts water

5 dried hot red chilies, each about 2 inches long *(caution: see note, Recipe Booklet)*

1 lemon, cut crosswise into ¼-inch-thick slices

3 large bay leaves

1½ teaspoons crumbled, dried thyme

1 tablespoon plus 1 teaspoon salt

10 live blue crabs, each about 8 ounces

4 tablespoons brown *roux (below)*

½ cup coarsely chopped onions

1½ teaspoons finely chopped garlic

½ pound fresh okra, trimmed, washed and cut into 1-inch chunks

¾ cup coarsely chopped green pepper

1 teaspoon ground hot red pepper (cayenne)

½ teaspoon Tabasco sauce

4 to 6 cups freshly cooked long-grain white rice

Crab, Shrimp and Okra Gumbo

Shell the shrimp. Devein them by making a shallow incision down their backs with a small knife and lifting out the intestinal vein with the point of the knife. Wash the shrimp briefly and set them aside.

In a 10- to 12-quart pot, bring the water, chilies, lemon slices, 2 bay leaves, 1 teaspoon of thyme and 1 tablespoon of salt to a boil over high heat. Drop in the crabs and boil briskly, uncovered, for 5 minutes. Remove the crabs from the stock with tongs, and set them aside to cool.

Drop the shrimp into the stock remaining in the pot and cook uncovered for 3 to 5 minutes, or until they are pink and firm to the touch. With tongs, transfer the shrimp to a plate. Then boil the stock, uncovered, until it is reduced to 3 quarts. Strain the stock through a fine sieve set over a large pot, and discard the seasonings. Cover the pot to keep the stock warm until you are ready to use it.

When the crabs are cool enough to handle, shell them in the following fashion: Grasping the body of the crab firmly in one hand, break off the large claws and legs close to the body. With the point of a small sharp knife, pry off the pointed shell, or apron, and loosen the large bottom shell from around the meat and cartilage, cutting near the edges where the legs are joined to the shell. Lift the body of the crab, break it in half lengthwise, then with the knife pick out the firm white pieces of meat. Discard the gray featherlike gills and tough bits of cartilage but save the morsels of yellow liver and "fat" as well as any pieces of orange roe. Leave the large claws in their shells, but crack the legs lengthwise with a cleaver and pick out the meat. Reserve the meat, claws and roe (if any).

In a heavy 5- to 6-quart casserole, warm the *roux* over low heat, stirring constantly. Add the onions and garlic and stir for about 5 minutes, or until they are soft. Add the okra and green peppers and mix well.

Stirring constantly, pour in the reserved warm stock in a slow, thin stream and bring to a boil over high heat. (If the stock has cooled, reheat before adding it.) Add the red pepper, Tabasco, the remaining bay leaf, ½ teaspoon of thyme and 1 teaspoon of salt. Stir in the crabmeat and claws, reduce the heat to low and simmer, partially covered, for 1 hour.

Add the shrimp and simmer a few minutes longer, then taste for seasoning. The gumbo may require more Tabasco or red pepper.

Ladle the gumbo into a heated tureen and serve at once, accompanied by the rice in a separate bowl. Traditionally, a cupful of rice is mounded in a heated soup plate and the gumbo spooned around it. Give each diner a nutcracker so that the claws can be cracked easily at the table.

8 tablespoons unsifted all-purpose flour

8 tablespoons vegetable oil

Brown Roux

Although the term roux is familiar in French cooking, the kind of brown roux used in Louisiana is unique. Flour and fat (usually vegetable oil) are cooked slowly until the mixture is brown and has a nutlike aroma and taste. This brown roux then serves as the base and thickening agent for bisques, gumbos and other soups, as well as for gravies and stews.

Combine the flour and oil in a heavy 10-inch skillet (preferably cast-iron or enameled iron) and, with a large metal spatula, stir them to a smooth paste. Place the skillet over the lowest possible heat and, stirring constantly, simmer the *roux* slowly for 45 minutes to an hour.

After 5 minutes or so the mixture will begin to foam and this foaming may continue for as long as 10 minutes. After about half an hour, the *roux* will begin to darken and have a faintly nutty aroma. Continue to cook slowly, stirring with the spatula, until the *roux* is a dark rich brown. (During the last 5 minutes or so of cooking, the *roux* darkens quickly and you may want to lift the pan from the heat periodically to let it cool. Should the *roux* burn, discard it and make another batch.)

Immediately scrape the contents of the skillet into a small bowl. Let the *roux* cool to room temperature, then cover with foil or plastic wrap and refrigerate it until ready to use. (It can safely be kept for weeks.)

When it cools the *roux* will separate and the fat will rise to the surface. Before using the *roux,* stir it briefly to recombine it. Measure the desired amount into the pan and warm the *roux* slowly over low heat, stirring constantly. Whether added immediately or not, any liquid that is to be incorporated with the brown *roux* must be at least lukewarm or the mixture may separate. If it does, beat it together again with a whisk.

Grillades and Grits
BRAISED VEAL STEAKS WITH HOMINY GRITS

To serve 4

Pat the veal steaks completely dry with paper towels and season them with 1 teaspoon of the salt and the black pepper. One at a time, dip the steaks in the flour to coat them evenly. Then shake off the excess flour.

In a heavy 12-inch skillet, melt the lard over moderate heat until it is very hot but not smoking. Brown the veal steaks, two at a time, turning them with tongs and regulating the heat so that they color richly on both sides without burning. As they brown, transfer the steak to a plate.

Pour off the fat remaining in the skillet, add the butter, and melt it over moderate heat. When the foam begins to subside, add the onions, green peppers, celery and garlic and, stirring frequently, cook for about 5 minutes, or until the vegetables are soft but not brown. Stir in the stock, tomatoes and bay leaf, and bring to a boil over high heat. Reduce the heat to low, partially cover the skillet, and simmer for 20 minutes.

Return the steaks and the liquid that has accumulated around them to the skillet and turn to coat them with the vegetable mixture. Simmer partially covered for about 1 hour, or until the veal is tender and shows no resistance when pierced with the point of a small sharp knife. Pour the cornstarch-and-water mixture over the simmering veal and stir for 2 or 3 minutes, until the gravy thickens slightly. Taste for seasoning.

About half an hour before the veal is done, bring the water and the remaining teaspoon of salt to a boil in a heavy 1½- to 2-quart saucepan. Pour in the hominy grits slowly enough so that the boiling continues at a rapid rate, stirring all the while with a wooden spoon to keep the mixture smooth. Reduce the heat to low and, stirring occasionally, simmer the grits tightly covered for 30 minutes.

Mound the grits on heated individual plates or a deep platter and place the veal steaks on the top. Pour the gravy over the grits and steaks and serve at once. (If allowed to cool, the grits will be undesirably firm.)

Four 5- to 6-ounce boneless veal round steaks, sliced ½ inch thick and trimmed of excess fat
2 teaspoons salt
¼ teaspoon freshly ground black pepper
½ cup flour
3 tablespoons lard
4 tablespoons butter
2 large onions, peeled and coarsely chopped
1½ cups coarsely chopped green peppers
½ cup coarsely chopped celery
1 tablespoon finely chopped garlic
2 cups chicken stock, fresh or canned
1½ cups coarsely chopped drained canned tomatoes
1 medium-sized bay leaf
1 tablespoon cornstarch combined with 1 tablespoon cold water
5 cups water
1 cup regular yellow or white hominy grits, not the quick-cooking variety

III

Dining Out
in New Orleans

Shrimp-stuffed artichoke, displayed here in its most elegant form, is actually a plebeian dish by New Orleans standards and appears on the menus of some of the city's humblest restaurants. The boiled artichoke is packed with a shrimp-and-bread-crumb mixture, made pungent by the addition of garlic, grated cheese, parsley and lemon peel. Leaves and stuffing are eaten together, then the last morsels of artichoke bottom are dipped in a spicy Creole vinaigrette sauce. *(For details, see the Recipe Index.)*

For anyone who has lived in New Orleans, returning there in the dead of winter, as I did not long ago, is a plunge into a nostalgic mingling of tastes, smells and textures that spread like a haze on the heavy cold air. For me, the haze cleared and old memories came into sharp focus at certain splendid meals. In the end, I stayed on month after month until late spring, reliving old experiences and acquiring enough new ones to fill —and more than fill—both this chapter and the one that follows it. Hardly a moment of my time, I think, was poorly spent, for good food is a way of life in this city, and almost every restaurant, every home, presents some facet of the basic cuisine that is unique and superior.

There are so many good restaurants in New Orleans that it is pointless to name them all, and they serve so many fine Creole dishes that a complete listing would be as rambling as a reading from the telephone directory. You may go to the same grand restaurant five times for five entirely different banquets, or you may prefer to eat at an anonymous snack bar on the river, patronized by New Orleans people; you are at liberty to choose. That is in the local tradition. The city has been bred and groomed to tantalize its own citizens before it turns to strangers, in the sure knowledge that you can only please someone else after you've taken the trouble to please yourself.

For natives there are many gourmet seasons in the year, but only two basic changes of climate. These are defined, by those who dislike the heat, as "February" and "midsummer." I happen to like subtropical weather, but I also like to visit the city while it is still cold and awaiting the heat that is to come. But whatever one's views on the seasons, the food is great all year round.

The winter I first went back to the city as an adult, I was amazed by the varied ways of preparing the same basic foods, simple and complicated, plain and fancy, that had seemed to me so natural and commonplace as a child; I had forgotten the spangling of tastes, and the wide array of restaurants. Take Antoine's, for instance, the oldest and most famous restaurant in the city, celebrated for its cooking since 1840.

A visit to Antoine's is always a treat for someone born in New Orleans, because it contradicts almost every cliché you have ever heard about fine eating places. It is *not* kept going just to cater to tourists; indeed, all the good restaurants of the city cater first to hometown and regular customers. If you are known in New Orleans, you can always get a table at Antoine's, no matter what the hour or how crowded it is. If you are *really* known, which is to say if you are a senior citizen, you can get your own private table and your own waiter. Indeed, a great many New Orleans people, including my Great-uncle Max, in his nineties, would not think of sitting at any table other than the one they have always sat at, or being served by anyone other than the old familiar friend who has served them through the years and who knows his customers' special likes and dislikes. At the dinner hour, summer or winter, you will always find a long line of out-of-towners standing outside Antoine's, waiting up to an hour to be allowed in. Local citizens don't wait; they elbow politely through the line, knock on the front door, and present their faces to the nearest waiter, whose job it is to open the door and to know them at a glance. For those oldtimers who prefer not to crash the line, there is even a secret entrance.

Once in—however you get in—the excitement begins. Antoine's has a consciously plain décor: white-tiled floor, big bony-looking hatracks, Victorian brass chandeliers, large white-covered tables, lit in winter by the original gas mantles. All this forms a sharp contrast to the wild blends and intricate subtleties of the aromas that fill the place. But not all are exotic. Ignoring for a moment the scents of hot fish and shellfish, spices and sauces, I don't know of any other restaurant in the United States where you are so aware of the smell of plain bread when you enter. There is something about hot, crusty French bread, fresh from the oven, that affects the salivary glands more powerfully than any other aroma, and all Creole chefs know it. You walk through that smell to your table; you sit down peacefully, knowing that you can take as long about your meal as you want, and won't be rushed off to make way for the next customer. The table is yours for the evening if you choose, and the menu, printed in French, lists enough dishes to keep you munching contentedly, with pauses between courses, until the dawn.

While you have a cocktail the waiter will bring you long loaves of French bread, very hot, and a plate of butter. You break off a piece of a loaf and find the white fluffy inside steaming and too hot to touch—the way it should be, so that the butter will melt instantly (though, to my taste, bread this good goes as well without butter as with). Antoine's bread is so crusty that eating it leaves a mess of crumbs on the tablecloth; its taste makes you think you have never eaten real bread before.

Along with the bread, have the waiter bring a basket woven of fried potato strips and filled with soufflé potatoes. These are little tan-colored finger-shaped bubbles of the thinnest potato film—thinner than potato chips, crisp as the bread crust—and they taste like potato petals melting on the tongue, salty and barely singed, or like weightless bites of fried air. The story goes that the founder of the restaurant, Antoine Alciatore, learned how to make them from the great French chef Collinet—who invented them by accident. One day in the 1830s, King Louis Philippe of France was given a dinner to celebrate the completion of the first railroad in his country. Mistrusting the railroad, he arrived late, by horse carriage. The French fried potatoes for his dinner had been removed from the fat half cooked; returned to the fat when His Majesty finally arrived, the potatoes surprised the chef and entranced the King by bubbling up like blowfish into little sacs of air.

But don't eat too many of these potatoes and don't down more than two loaves of the hot French bread, for there is much more to come. Order a bottle of dry white wine, and have a small cup of turtle soup to begin with. Creole turtle soup, not watery but dark brown and very thick, is one of the most wonderful concoctions that any kitchen has ever produced. Fresh turtle meat, onions, celery, garlic, tomato sauce, beef extract, bay leaves, cloves, thyme and parsley, with a dash of this and a dash of that added, are simmered together for hours to produce a smooth, pungent, elegant potage—heavy in the spoon, yet light in the mouth, and producing a great stinging warmth that opens the stomach for the rest of the meal. The soup has sherry in it, too, added just before serving, and a thin slice of lemon; if you are lucky and they are available, there will be little round yellow crumbly turtle eggs floating in it. The whole magic of the Creole kitchen is contained in a single spoonful of this thick soup, which manages to taste spicy and calm, lemony and bland, prickly and smooth all at the same time. Cut the taste with an occasional sip of the chilled white wine and you will have launched yourself on the long Creole road to good eating.

Now take a pause, and have half a dozen baked oysters Rockefeller, a specialty of Antoine's. The dish was first concocted by the founder's son Jules Alciatore as an alternative to snails *bourguignon*. There are 18 ingredients in Antoine's oysters Rockefeller, and the recipe has been so well guarded that other New Orleans restaurants cannot ever quite get it the same (they use spinach, for instance, to produce the desired green color and fresh texture that Antoine's wondrously achieves by other means). The baked oysters are served on the half shell, lying on a bed of rock salt that retains enough heat to keep them sizzling at the table. If there are any out-of-towners at your table, keep an eye on them as you eat, for there is no telling what an out-of-towner will do. I once yelled just in time to prevent a visiting New Yorker from happily eating a forkful of blistering-hot rock salt, which would have put him in the hospital and the waiter in a quiet rest home.

Over each oyster is spread a green sauce so rich that the dish was named for the richest man its inventor could think of: John D. Rockefeller Sr. Let the sauce cool a little—but only a little—then take a bit of

the green topping on your fork and get its piercing spicy taste. When it is cool enough, eat the remaining green sauce with the oyster, kept steaming by the rock salt. The sweetness of the oyster and the fierceness of the sauce make a combination that justifies oysters Rockefeller's claim to be one of the best of all Creole creations—though other oyster dishes in other restaurants give it competition.

Next have an order of—let's see—chicken Rochambeau. (One of the hallmarks of Antoine's is that its meat and poultry are just as good as its seafood.) Order the house salad with the chicken, and while the food is coming, wander around: into the Rex Room, devoted to Mardi Gras pictures and memories; into a larger room filled with photographs of guests who have dined at Antoine's, many of them world-renowned (this room is called the Mystery Room, because a painting once disappeared from it); into the 1840 Room, lined with old menus and other Alciatore family souvenirs; and on and on. Each room, public or private, gives you a sense of the seriousness with which Creole food is approached: the restaurant is everywhere comfortable, but nowhere do you find that excessive plushness by which expensive restaurants in some cities try to give customers the feeling that they are getting their money's worth. Here, as in all Creole eating places, the cooking is what matters, and nothing is permitted that might disguise or detract from it.

Now go back to your own table for your next course; the waiter won't bring it until you're comfortably seated again. The chicken Rochambeau will come to you brown and steaming, and with it, the tossed green salad. The chicken is served on a Holland rusk that has been covered first with a slice of ham, then with a sweet, spicy sauce containing (among other ingredients) green onions or shallots, topped by the sautéed chicken itself, and finally covered with a gleaming lemony béarnaise sauce. The saltiness of the ham, the sweet sautéed chicken, the rusk and the two quite different sauces combine to give a faintly tart, full richness to this dish, a taste that lingers on the tongue. The salad, made of four feathery mixed greens and dressed with a light vinaigrette sauce, is a bright green complement to the tender fowl.

You will want to take another pause before having brandy, coffee and maybe a few French pancakes *à la gelée*—crisp crêpes that have been browned, spread with red currant jelly, rolled, sprinkled with powdered sugar and glazed under a broiler. The dish is not one of the famous flamed desserts that keep the electricity flickering at Antoine's (all lights in the front room are turned out to show the blue flame that floats like ghostly fire over crêpes suzette or cherries jubilee), but it is fruity tasting, bright as a laugh, a good end to a good meal. If you enjoy the crêpes tell the waiter—such compliments are in the local tradition. But if you plan on returning to Antoine's for another visit, don't tell the waiter that you have formed a special liking for a dish unless you really have. The last time I went there with my great-uncle I ordered another kind of crêpes for his dessert. The waiter (who has known him for more than 40 years) stared me down and said in a flat, toneless voice, "Mr. Max prefers them *à la gelée.*" He waited for an answer. When I didn't come up with one, he added, "And he likes the edges burnt."

Opposite: Chicken Rochambeau, a dish to try a cook's mettle, occupies a place of honor on the menus of fine New Orleans restaurants—but it can also be prepared at home (*Recipe Index*). The base of this splendid composition is a toasted Holland rusk, overlaid with a slice of ham and mushroom sauce. The superstructure is a boned, butter-fried chicken breast blanketed with tarragon-flavored béarnaise sauce.

Few meals in New Orleans are as elegant or formal as a dinner at Antoine's. But you can eat Creole food just as well sitting on a park bench or at a cheap restaurant or in the humblest home, for elegance, as a Creole cook once told me, is "in the wrist of the chef," not in the quality of the serving dish. And if you stay up as late as you generally do after a full dinner, you will want eventually to go to one of the coffeehouses at the old French Market. There, at any time from midnight until dawn (or, for that matter, at any time at all), you find people sitting quietly at tables next to the levee of the Mississippi River, sipping *café au lait* and munching quietly on *beignets,* the Creole version of doughnuts.

Coffee with milk is a New Orleans institution, and a French Market coffeehouse is really the only place to drink it. The coffee may be drunk with chicory, which makes it stronger and thicker, and adds a bitter flavor. Chicory was first used in New Orleans during the Civil War, when coffee was not easy to come by, and its presence in coffee has been known to scare a stranger into thinking that a survivor of the poison-prone Borgia clan has been at his cup. Even without chicory, New Orleans coffee is a powerful brew, often double-dripped from a much darker roast than you will generally find elsewhere in the United States. Mixed with hot milk in equal parts, the resulting *café au lait* steams down through the body, and within minutes seems to do something odd to your chemistry—something that can only be corrected by swallowing a little more, or possibly swallowing something else. To give you that something else to swallow, the *beignets* are served. They are fluffy squares of dough, brown on the outside, and they are sprinkled with powdered sugar by the waiter or by yourself, depending on the coffeehouse you go to.

There is something gracious about ending a night in this way, with the aroma of the steaming coffee mixed with the full raw smell of the river moving invisibly on the other side of the levee. A sense of the old Creole ways of doing things seems to be carried in the air. Afterward, you can walk along the French Market, past tiers and pyramids of fresh fruit and vegetables, gleaming like iridescent bubbles of red and yellow and green and orange. Here, long ago, old women walked every day wearing striped scarves, called *tignons,* on their heads, carrying baskets to shop with. They walked past stalls of fresh Creole cabbages and shallots and tomatoes, and other stalls where thousands of fish hung glintingly over baskets of blue and green crabs, their feelers and legs moving back and forth, next to other baskets of gray translucent shrimp and oysters and wriggling crawfish. In those days, too, coffee was drunk with *beignets,* as a kind of respite between bouts of marketing, with the loud calls of street sellers resounding like echoes out of the old city.

After that experience—and after a nap, perhaps—you may decide to eat a light meal standing up. A few raw oysters at one of the French Quarter oyster bars make a good midmorning snack, especially on a crisp, cold, wet December morning, when the sky is rolling with gray clouds like weightless whales. Walk along Iberville Street and stop in Felix's or the Acme Oyster House for a dozen fresh oysters on the half shell. The room at the Acme is spacious and bare; there is a bar and there are tables, but almost no decoration. At the bar, you take a paper cup from a stack at the end of the counter and mix your own sauce from the ingredients lined up before you. You may like the full treatment—a little tomato sauce thinned with lemon or vinegar, fired with enough Tabasco to make you gasp for breath, and thickened with enough hot horseradish to keep your sinuses clear for a full day. Or you may be a comparative purist, and take your oysters with lemon juice alone or just a few drops of hot peppery vinegar. You may be a *real* purist and revert to your childhood habits by taking nothing with the oysters but the natural oyster liquor, or you may grind a little fresh pepper over them.

With a turn of the wrist, the man behind the marble-topped bar will flick open an oyster, scoop under it and slide it toward you on the marble. Your height at the bar is a good measure of your age. I remember being so short that I couldn't reach up to the bar (my father had to hand the oysters down to me), then growing tall enough to stand at eye level with them. When I went back to the city as an adult and found myself actually looking down at the oyster bar from above, it seemed (and was) a completely new and refreshing angle. To my left and right were other people of varying sizes on friendly terms with their oysters.

There may be four customers at the bar, and each may have ordered a dozen oysters. The oyster shucker will manage to keep all four happy, and will know, with a quick glance, who is ready for another oyster and who has just swallowed one but wants to wait a bit. Have a cold New Orleans beer—Jax or Dixie—and let the gold, not-too-bubbly liquid wash down the fresh yet brackish taste of the shellfish. If you are a connoisseur of raw oysters, you will tip the barman a little extra and let him know whether you prefer the smaller flat ones with the dark curling smoke-colored edges or the fatter white ones that rise like pearls from their shells. Wash the last of them down with the beer, and go for a walk in some part of the Quarter to work up an appetite for lunch. Don't try to walk through all of it in one day—that would be like trying to taste all of Creole cooking in one week. Just take a ramble down this street or that and keep your eyes open. . . .

Over you in the narrow streets are the buildings where the old Creole balls and great banquets took place. Imagine those rooms full of the movement of long skirts, as Creole belles whirled away from their chaperons with young beaux. Imagine the men, so formally dressed that they looked as if in uniform, with long coats of bright colors, fancy boots and *colichemardes,* or sword canes, wide at the hilt and tapering down to a vicious rapier blade. The men often quarreled over this or that belle, and such quarrels often ended in duels; there were bloody deaths under the oaks that still twist high in the air, only a short carriage ride from the Quarter. Now the buildings stand high and silent every wet December—some of them hotels, some apartment houses, only a few still private homes—but red brick and black iron grillwork still glint in the sunlight.

Walk along to one of the Quarter's haunted houses—say Madame Lalaurie's, where, not so long ago, no child would walk after dark for fear of hearing the groans and screams of the ghosts. The story behind it is said to be a true one. The most elegant and grandest of all the 19th Century hostesses of New Orleans was Madame Lalaurie. Nobody who was

Overleaf: An 1881 newspaper illustration shows the dock area of New Orleans—the famed levee—as a vast open-air warehouse palisaded by the tall smokestacks of river steamers and ocean-going vessels. By that year Louisiana had recovered from the worst effects of the Civil War and was enjoying a boom. Huge quantities of such native agricultural products as sugar and molasses were shipped from here, while from abroad all manner of culinary delicacies flowed in for the delight of Creole gourmets—South American coffee, West Indian bananas, French liqueurs and French and German wines, the waters of Vichy, the sardines of Bordeaux and the capers and olives of Marseilles.

anybody gave a dinner party without checking with her first, and she dominated the social life of the city for two decades. Her own dinners were famous; her canapés and gumbos and bisques and daubes and pastries were insuperable, her wines of the best vintage, her crêpes of the utmost delicacy. Then, one day, a fire broke out in the first floor of the house—a fire set on purpose, they say, by Madame's own cook—and in the raging flames a secret room was revealed. The room was filled with slaves, helpless men and women bound in chains, and the entire Quarter rose in outrage at the disclosure. The citizens of New Orleans came to kill Madame Lalaurie, but she made a dramatic escape in a coach-and-four to the bayous, and thence, they say, to France, leaving behind her a legend and another haunted house for the city to shudder at.

Even in Madame Lalaurie's time there were already many hauntings in New Orleans—it has in fact been called the Haunted City—for there was cruelty here as well as luxury. The ghost of Jean Laffite, the pirate, once haunted no fewer than seven French Quarter houses at the same time —a full schedule, even for a ghost. Observe the Lalaurie house today and you will see only a pleasant-looking old apartment building, but tenants occasionally complain of strange cries, of objects that move mysteriously and—strangest of all—of sudden delicious smells of banquet dishes in the night. (Where but in the French Quarter of New Orleans would you ever find a house that is haunted by food?) Double back down another street and you will find a cluster of little shops where apothecary jars once lined the windows, offering herbs and spices that were used both for cooking intricate dishes and for curing the people who were going to eat them. Then walk away from the old elegance for a bit, just a few blocks toward the river, turn left and you will find yourself at Messina's, an inexpensive Creole restaurant with an Italian flair.

Stop here for a simple lunch (simple by Creole standards, anyway): a beer or a glass of wine, a few cold boiled shrimp and then a stuffed artichoke *(Recipe Index)*—which, correctly prepared, is one of the minor wonders of the vegetable world. Messina's is a very small place, lined with jars of its own Italian salad (called a "Wop salad" in New Orleans by the Italians themselves, who print the term proudly on their menus, to the horror of some visitors); the tables are tiny and the place is usually crowded. The chef makes an artichoke stuffing of shrimp that have been cooked with bread crumbs, onion, garlic, thyme, other herbs and vegetables and sometimes other shellfish. He stuffs the boiled artichoke not only in the center, but painstakingly behind each single leaf. The dish is a meal in itself, and one of the best lunches I know. It arrives at the table so hot that you must sip your beer or wine for a while before you can touch it. Then you peel off a leaf and the flat layer of stuffing that comes with it. The bit of tender gray-green artichoke heart that clings to the leaf is exactly suited to the full-tasting, slightly pungent stuffing.

There is no vegetable known to man that Creole cooks can't improve on by stuffing it; an artichoke is among the best proofs of this because it is one of the most difficult to stuff. In less capable hands, the iron aftertaste of this vegetable might well kill the flavor of the stuffing, but the Creole cook makes her dish as delicately balanced as the scales of justice.

Seafood, vegetable and herbs are blended in a new flavor that satisfies as it fills—and it does fill. If you can get through a whole stuffed artichoke by yourself, you will think you will never be interested in food again.

You won't be, either . . . until dinnertime. Then you might as well leave the French Quarter for a spell. Cross over the Greater New Orleans Bridge to the other side of the Mississippi to eat at one of the small, inexpensive and unpretentious restaurants there. The communities of Gretna and Algiers, both on the west bank, have many such places, among them one called Berdou's. The atmosphere here, outside and in, is more countrified somehow than that of the Quarter. As you pass moss-laden trees and catch a glimpse of the winter moon over the swirling brown river you think you are in some other city entirely, though you are only a 10-minute drive away. Sit down at one of the small tables and order crabmeat remoulade and pompano en papillote *(Recipe Index),* two of the best Creole dishes New Orleans has to offer.

The first will arrive on a small plate—fine large-lump crabmeat, picked by hand and covered with a cold sauce that contains among its ingredients parsley, shallots, celery, dill pickle, minced garlic, hot Creole mustard, horseradish, vinegar and oil, bay leaves, a few drops of lemon juice and a few of Tabasco sauce. Fresh lump crabmeat is itself a boon to mankind, but mixed with this sauce it becomes something so special that you cannot imagine how one could ever have been eaten without the other. Good remoulade sauce, a Creole cook will tell you, is supposed to make you think you look better and younger than you ever have—and if you *think* you look that way, she will add, then you *will* look that way. The taste of a well-made remoulade is so sharp that it feels astringent in the mouth; the blandness of fresh iced crabmeat is its best accompaniment, for the two tastes become indefinably different and better as one.

Then comes the pompano. This dish has a bit of crabmeat in it too, and most sane people will tell you not to follow crabmeat with crabmeat. I myself am insane on the subject; I can only tell you what I like—and what I like is just that. Simmered and then baked in parchment paper along with sautéed shrimp, crabmeat, green onions or shallots, cayenne, egg yolks, parsley and bay leaf, pompano makes one of the greatest foods imaginable. It is served in the paper, and when you tear the paper open a little cloud of steam billows out. Pompano is another proof of an old Creole rule: the fact that a food is good enough to eat plain is no excuse for not improving on it. Plain broiled pompano is excellent, and those who don't want crabmeat after crabmeat can have the fish that way. For me, there is something special in the rich flavor of pompano en papillote. The shellfish cooked with the pompano doubles the flavor of the fish, creating a dish that seems to represent the very soul of the sea.

Perhaps the best thing to do after eating such a dish is to have a cup of coffee and a slice of pecan pie. Corn syrup, sugar, vanilla and finely chopped pecans set in a flaky pastry . . . the quintessence of nuttiness in good pecan pie has to be savored to be believed. The proper complement to this dessert is a demitasse of strong black Creole coffee. To settle things, walk a while along the river, forgetting any warnings about damp night air. When the air is this soft, and the deep river flows silently around you, and the stars come out like silver needles, your meal will settle quietly and gently and your health will take care of itself.

Along about January or February or March comes the coldest part of the year in New Orleans, when ice forms like brittle fingers on the chinaberry trees. During one of those months you may find yourself leaving the restaurant circuit, at least for a time, to taste great food in a private kitchen. You may, for example, get a call, as I did, from a friend who is preparing *daube glacé,* glazed beef roast, for "just a few people," and who would welcome company during the cooking. In any other part of the country, the cooking of a *daube glacé* would be an ordeal; in New Orleans it is a good reason to collect a small gathering, otherwise known as a party. Phyllis Eagen, a friend of mine, does this every year. Phyllis is an attractive woman of Creole heritage, whose children are grown and married; she runs a hospital with one hand and with the other runs a home in which she supervises all of the cooking and often takes over the important parts of it herself. The Eagens live in a New Orleans suburb called Metairie, near the street where I grew up. It is a beautifully put together, green-looking area of spacious houses, and the Eagens' own house, on a street of flowering trees, is tastefully simple and comfortable.

Phyllis Eagen's grandmother spoke no English at all, and never put a recipe in writing—but recipes came down from generation to generation, from French to English, in much the way standards of manners or morals do in other places. Part of the pride that many women take in a Creole heritage is their knowledge of food, and Phyllis is no exception. Her kitchen is a large square roomy room with plenty of surfaces to work on and a table at the center to sit at. Join the friends who have dropped in for the occasion; have a glass of wine with them and watch the proceedings. On the table there will be a plate of hors d'oeuvre "just to keep things going": canapés made of shrimp combined with cream cheese, chili sauce, Worcestershire sauce and cayenne, spread on crackers; little balls of baked pork sausage meat, each pierced with a toothpick; stuffed eggs, spicy with Creole mustard and mayonnaise, and with bits of mysterious vegetables laced through them. A sip of wine with one of the hors d'oeuvre keeps your stomach warm and working, so that the sights and smells of cooking won't make you ravenous. Now watch:

No less than a dozen beef roasts, each weighing about two and a half pounds, are lined up on the sideboard—because Phyllis isn't going to make *daube glacé* for herself alone. Two or three of the people in the kitchen will walk off with one daube apiece, and there is the woman who lives a few blocks away—she's been promised one, and so have her children—and there is the relatively new invention of the freezer, which permits Phyllis to keep a few for the future. On the stove, about 20 pig's feet and pig's knuckles, about six pounds of veal and six of pork have been boiling for hours, along with onions, bay leaf, thyme, a few bunches of carrots and fresh parsley. The meat and bones will yield the natural gelatin needed to cover the *daube glacé.* If you ask Phyllis how long the boiling must go on to produce gelatin of the proper texture, she'll be vague—"Oh, well, three hours if you're in a hurry, six if you're not" —but most good Creole cooks tend to be vague in discussing their rec-

Opposite: "Tasting the delights of Heaven while beholding the terrors of Hell" was the way one visitor to New Orleans described his reaction to Antoine's version of *café brûlot diabolique,* a flaming mixture of coffee, brandy and spices. For dramatic effect, the lights are usually dimmed when *café brûlot* is served, leaving some unwary diners in puzzlement as well as darkness.

Prosaic but profoundly good, a *café au lait* with fresh *beignets* awaits a customer at the Morning Call Coffee Stand.

ipes, for cooking by tradition is not at all the same as cooking by a book.

Sooner or later, though, she will take the ingredients out of the boiling water and strain the liquid. Then—having put together a few more canapés and listened for a while to her friends' gossip—she will proceed to make the headcheese, explaining with a somewhat apologetic smile that her grandmother used to make it with real hogs' heads. Meticulously, yet quite effortlessly, she goes through the boiled ingredients in search of gristle. At this point, the friends pitch in and help, heeding her admonition that she wants only gristle removed, not fat. When this part of the job is done, she chops the gristle fine and also chops and adds the remaining pork and veal. What Phyllis calls headcheese is simply this combined chop-up, plus the remaining juices of the meats.

At her request, someone at one end of the kitchen table has been producing an even finer chop-up of garlic, dry bay leaf, a little thyme and much parsley, and a bit of cayenne pepper. Someone else has sliced a great many 1/16-inch-wide strips of unsalted pork fat, which appeared at the right moment from the icebox. Phyllis rolls the strips of pork fat in the garlic-and-herb chop-up, pierces the roasts here and there with a sharp knife, and lards them. The pork strips are pushed in with fingers rather than with a larding needle, possibly for the same reason that an icebox isn't called a refrigerator. Then she opens more wine for her friends and gets down to the heavy work—the cooking of the daubes.

One by one, the roasts are browned in a mixture of butter and a little oil. The particles that stick to the bottom of the browning pot are scraped up and splashed with brandy and champagne, then the mixture is poured over the roasts. She adds stock and lets the meat simmer slowly for a couple of hours. When they are ready, they are put in individual loaf pans; over them is poured all the stock and juices, the headcheese and some dried red pepper. They are refrigerated until good and cold, and by that time they will be surrounded by thick dark-brown jelly. The smells of cooking drift out the window, exchanging with the fragile, moist odor of sweet olive growing outside.

If you have stayed this long, and if you can manage to look like a hungry waif, Phyllis will give you a slice of the meat with some of the jelly over it. The cold *daube glacé* has a brilliant taste that is good now and will stay good, if the daube is frozen, through the summer. Thanks to the headcheese, the jelly has chewy bits in it, and it has been boiled so long that it seems to have more pure meat flavor per square inch than anything short of beef extract. The slice of cold roast is succulent and subtler in flavor. But the best quality of this fine dish is the taste of the two combined—together, the spice-hot, ice-cold jelly and the juicy roast make the sort of dish that will serve any purpose all the year round, from late-night snacks to elegant cold summer buffets.

Even now, the year is turning; the weather will soon begin to warm up. If you are a wise visitor to the city, you will go to a hotel in the French Quarter where you can rest and wait for spring. Some time off is necessary, even in a gourmet city, and you will need a long breather—a sort of *coup de milieu* of rest—to prepare you for the foods of the next and longest season in New Orleans.

CHICORY FOR COFFEE
The famous coffee that climaxes both Creole and Acadian cooking is usually made more pungent by the addition of chicory imported from Europe. Unlike the varieties of the plant grown for their leaves, for use in salads, the chicory used in coffee (above) is valued for its carrot-shaped roots, which grow as long as 14 inches and as thick as two inches at the top. White and fleshy when raw, the root is sliced, kiln-dried, and roasted with a little oil, then ground to the desired fineness. The final product tastes so much like coffee that it is sometimes used by itself to brew a substitute for the more expensive drink.

Custom dictates that Creole coffee be brewed in a drip pot such as the one at left. For Louisiana tastes, Latin American beans *(to*

ight) are roasted to a dark brown *(far right)*, ground, then flavored with imported chicory, shown fresh and roasted at center.

Chicken Rochambeau
CHICKEN AND HAM ON RUSKS WITH MUSHROOM AND BÉARNAISE SAUCES

This elegant chicken dish is said to be named for Count Jean Baptiste Donatien de Vimeur de Rochambeau, who commanded the French forces that supported Washington in the American Revolution.

To serve 4

MUSHROOM SAUCE
2 tablespoons butter
1 cup finely chopped scallions, including 3 inches of the green tops
1 teaspoon finely chopped garlic
2 tablespoons flour
2 cups chicken stock, fresh or canned
½ cup finely chopped fresh mushrooms (¼ pound)
½ cup dry red wine
1 tablespoon Worcestershire sauce
⅛ teaspoon ground hot red pepper (cayenne)
½ teaspoon salt

CHICKEN
2 one-pound chicken breasts, boned and halved but with the skin intact
1 teaspoon salt
½ teaspoon freshly ground black pepper
½ cup flour
12 tablespoons butter, cut into ½-inch bits

HAM
1 teaspoon butter
Four ¼-inch-thick slices Canadian bacon or lean cooked smoked ham

4 Holland rusks

First prepare the mushroom sauce in the following fashion: In a heavy 1- to 1½-quart saucepan, melt the 2 tablespoons of butter over moderate heat. When the foam begins to subside, add the cup of scallions and the garlic and stir for about 5 minutes, or until they are soft but not brown. Add 2 tablespoons of flour and mix well. Stirring constantly with a wire whisk, pour in the chicken stock in a slow, thin stream and cook over high heat until the sauce comes to a boil, thickens lightly and is smooth.

Stir in the mushrooms, reduce the heat to low and simmer partially covered for about 15 minutes, until the mushrooms are tender but still intact. Then add the wine, Worcestershire, ⅛ teaspoon of red pepper and ½ teaspoon of salt, and stir over low heat for 2 or 3 minutes. Taste for seasoning, remove from the heat and cover tightly to keep the sauce warm.

Pat the chicken breasts completely dry with paper towels and season them on all sides with the teaspoon of salt and the black pepper. Roll one piece of chicken breast at a time in the ½ cup of flour and, when evenly coated, shake vigorously to remove the excess flour.

Melt 12 tablespoons of butter bits in a heavy 10- to 12-inch skillet set over moderate heat. Do not let the butter brown. When the foam subsides, add the chicken breasts skin side down and, turning the pieces occasionally with tongs, cook over moderate heat until they are lightly brown on all sides. Reduce the heat to low, cover the skillet tightly and simmer the chicken for about 20 minutes, until it is tender and shows no resistance when pierced deeply with the point of a small sharp knife. As it simmers use a bulb baster or a large spoon to baste the chicken every 7 or 8 minutes with the pan juices.

Meanwhile preheat the oven to its lowest setting. In another large skillet, melt 1 teaspoon of butter over moderate heat and brown the ham. Turn the slices with tongs and regulate the heat so that they color richly and evenly on both sides without burning. When they brown, arrange the ham slices in one layer on a large baking sheet, drape loosely with foil and keep them warm in the oven. Place the Holland rusks side by side on another baking sheet and put them in the oven to warm.

About 10 minutes before the chicken is done, make the béarnaise sauce. Combine the vinegar, ¼ cup of scallions, tarragon, parsley and peppercorns in a small enameled or stainless-steel saucepan. Bring to a boil over high heat and cook briskly, uncovered, until reduced to about 2 tablespoons. Strain the liquid through a fine sieve into a small bowl, pressing down hard on the seasonings with the back of a spoon to extract all their juices before discarding the pulp. Set the strained liquid aside.

In a heavy 8- to 10-inch skillet, melt the 12 tablespoons of butter bits over low heat, stirring so that the butter melts evenly without browning.

Remove the pan from the heat and cover to keep the melted butter warm.

Working quickly, combine the egg yolks and water in a 1½- to 2-quart enameled or stainless-steel saucepan, and beat with a wire whisk until the mixture is foamy. Then place the pan over the lowest possible heat and continue whisking until the mixture thickens and almost doubles in volume. Do not let it come anywhere near a boil or the yolks will curdle; if necessary, lift the pan off the heat from time to time to cool it.

Still whisking constantly, pour in the reserved hot melted butter as slowly as possible and beat over low heat until the sauce thickens heavily. Beat in the reserved strained liquid, lemon juice, the ¼ teaspoon of red pepper and the salt, and taste for seasoning. Set it aside off the heat.

Before assembling the chicken Rochambeau, stir the mushroom sauce briefly and warm it over low heat if necessary. Arrange the rusks on a large heated platter or four individual serving plates. Place a slice of ham on each rusk and spoon the mushroom sauce over the slices, dividing it equally among them. Set a chicken breast on top of each ham slice and ladle 2 or 3 tablespoons of béarnaise over it. Pour the remaining béarnaise into a sauceboat and serve it at once with the chicken Rochambeau.

BÉARNAISE SAUCE
⅔ cup tarragon vinegar
¼ cup finely chopped scallions, including 3 inches of the green tops
1 teaspoon crumbled dried tarragon
4 sprigs fresh parsley
¼ teaspoon whole black peppercorns
12 tablespoons butter, cut into ½-inch bits
4 egg yolks
1 tablespoon water
2 tablespoons strained fresh lemon juice
¼ teaspoon ground hot red pepper (cayenne)
½ teaspoon salt

Petits Fours

Preheat the oven to 350°. With a pastry brush, spread 1 tablespoon of the softened butter over the bottom and sides of a 17-by-11-by-1-inch jelly-roll pan. Cut a piece of wax paper 19 to 20 inches long and fit it lengthwise into the pan, pressing it firmly into the bottom and against the ends. Brush the wax paper with the remaining tablespoon of softened butter, then sprinkle in the 2 tablespoons of unsifted flour and tip the pan to distribute it evenly. Invert the pan and rap the bottom sharply to remove the excess flour. Combine the ½ cup of sifted flour and the cornstarch, sift them together into a bowl and set aside.

In a small heavy saucepan, melt the 6 tablespoons of butter bits over low heat, stirring so that they melt completely without browning. Remove the pan from the heat, then skim off and discard the foam. Tipping the pan slightly, spoon the clear butter into a bowl and reserve it. Discard the milky solids that settle in the bottom of the pan.

Set a large heatproof mixing bowl over a pan of hot water off the heat. Place the eggs and the cup of granulated sugar in the bowl and, with a wire whisk or a rotary or electric beater, beat until they are thick, foamy and lukewarm. The sugar should be dissolved. Remove the bowl from the pan and continue to beat until the egg mixture has almost tripled in volume. It should be thick enough to stand in peaks when the beater is lifted from the bowl. (This will take about 15 minutes with an electric beater, and may require 30 minutes of continuous beating by hand.)

With a rubber spatula, gently fold in the flour-and-cornstarch mixture, a few tablespoonfuls at a time. Stir in the clarified butter, 1 teaspoon at a time, and add the vanilla extract.

Pour the batter into the paper-lined pan, spreading it evenly and smoothing the top with the spatula. Bake in the middle of the oven for 25 to 30 minutes, or until the cake begins to pull away from the sides of the pan and a toothpick or cake tester inserted in the center comes out

To make 5 dozen 1½-inch-square cakes

CAKE
2 tablespoons butter, softened, plus 6 tablespoons butter, cut into ½-inch bits
2 tablespoons unsifted flour plus ½ cup flour, sifted before measuring
½ cup cornstarch, sifted before measuring
6 eggs, at room temperature
1 cup granulated sugar
1 teaspoon vanilla extract

Petits fours *(opposite)* are perhaps the most elegant confection of the Creole cuisine. To make these dainty cakes, a 17-by-11-by-1-inch cake is trimmed and cut into quarters. Slice them horizontally and, for variety, fill each quarter differently. Then divide the quarters into 1½-inch-square petits fours and ice each group with a different color. Because the cakes are so small, the icing is kept fluid and poured over them, as at right.

RASPBERRY-KIRSCH FILLING
¾ cup raspberry preserves
3 tablespoons kirsch

COFFEE FILLING
¼ cup coffee liqueur
1 tablespoon granulated sugar
1 tablespoon water
2 teaspoons instant coffee,
  preferably instant *espresso*

CHOCOLATE AND MINT-CHOCOLATE
  FILLINGS
12 ounces semisweet chocolate,
  coarsely chopped
16 tablespoons butter (2 quarter-
  pound sticks), cut into ½-inch
  bits
2 cups confectioners' sugar
2 to 3 tablespoons crème de menthe

clean. Remove the cake from the oven and carefully turn it out of the pan onto a fresh piece of wax paper. Gently peel off the layer of paper on top of the cake, then set the cake aside to cool to room temperature.

Meanwhile, prepare the fillings. For the raspberry-kirsch filling, melt the preserves in a small pan set over low heat, and pour them through a sieve into a bowl to strain out the seeds. Cool, then stir in the kirsch.

For the coffee filling, combine the coffee liqueur, 1 tablespoon of granulated sugar, 1 tablespoon water and 2 teaspoons of instant coffee in a small bowl and stir until the ingredients are well mixed.

For the chocolate and mint-chocolate fillings, combine the 12 ounces of semisweet chocolate and 16 tablespoons of butter bits in a heavy 2- to 3-quart saucepan and, stirring constantly, melt them together over low heat. Remove the pan from the heat and stir in the 2 cups of confectioners' sugar, about ½ cup at a time. Spoon half of the mixture into a small bowl and add 2 to 3 tablespoons of crème de menthe, according to taste.

When the cake is cool enough to handle, use a long knife with a sharp serrated blade to trim off the rough edges and make a 15-by-9-inch rectangle. Cut the cake crosswise and lengthwise into four 7½-by-4½-inch quarters. Brush any loose crumbs off the top.

Place one of the quarters on a flat surface and, holding it firmly in place with one hand, cut it horizontally in half to make two thin layers.

Separate the layers, laying them cut side up, and brush one cut surface with the raspberry-kirsch filling. Reassemble the cake with the filling in the center and cover it tightly with foil or plastic wrap. Repeat the entire procedure with the three remaining cake quarters, spreading them successively with the coffee, chocolate and mint-chocolate fillings. To facilitate the final cutting of the cakes, freeze them for about 1 hour.

When you are ready to cut and ice the petits fours, prepare the icing in the following fashion: Combine the 5 cups of granulated sugar, the 2½ cups of water and the corn syrup in a heavy 6- to 8-quart casserole and stir over low heat until the sugar is dissolved. Using a hair-bristled (not nylon) pastry brush that has been dipped in cold water, wipe the sugar crystals that have formed on the sides of the pan back down into the syrup. Cover the pan tightly and cook the syrup over low heat for 5 minutes; its steam will dissolve any remaining crystals.

Increase the heat to high and boil the syrup uncovered and undisturbed for 5 minutes. Then remove the casserole from the heat and let the syrup cool to room temperature. (There will be about 4 cups of syrup.) Stirring the mixture constantly with a wire whisk, add the 12 cups of confectioners' sugar about 1 cupful at a time and beat until the ingredients are well combined. Place the casserole over low heat and, still stirring constantly, cook the icing until it is lukewarm and appears

ICING

5 cups granulated sugar
2½ cups water
1½ cups light corn syrup
12 cups (4 pounds) confectioners' sugar, sifted
Red and green liquid food coloring
2 teaspoons instant coffee, preferably instant *espresso*

smooth and shiny. Do not let the icing overheat or it will lose its gloss.

Ladle or pour the icing into four small heavy saucepans (preferably pans with pouring spouts), dividing it equally among them. For the raspberry-kirsch-filled cakes, stir a few drops of red food coloring into one pan of icing to tint it pink. For the coffee-filled cakes, add 2 teaspoons of instant coffee to another pan and stir until the coffee dissolves and the icing is light brown. For the mint-chocolate-filled cakes, mix a few drops of green food coloring into another pan of icing to tint it green. For the chocolate-filled cakes, leave the fourth pan of icing white.

Each quarter of the cake is cut into petits fours and iced separately. Remove one quarter from the freezer, check its filling, and select the appropriate icing. Let the other three pans of icing cool to room temperature, then cover them tightly with plastic wrap until you are ready to use them. Just before using each one, warm it over low heat.

With a large sharp knife, cut the quarter cake into 15 individual cakes, each 1½ inches square. Arrange the cakes an inch or so apart on wire racks set in a large shallow baking pan. Pour the icing generously over the tops of the cakes, letting it spread by itself and run down the sides.

With a metal spatula, scrape the excess icing from the bottom of the baking pan and return it to the saucepan. Stirring constantly, warm the icing over low heat until it is fluid again. Then pour it over any of the cakes that were not evenly coated before.

You can repeat the entire procedure—scraping, warming, and pouring the icing—as many times as necessary but be careful never to let the icing become too hot or it will lose its gloss.

Let the iced cakes dry on the racks for about 10 minutes, then transfer them to plates or wax paper. Following the same techniques identically, cut the three remaining cake quarters one at a time and cover the petits fours with the appropriate icing.

CAKE DECORATIONS (OPTIONAL)
15 crystallized violets
1½ ounces semisweet chocolate, coarsely chopped
8 tablespoons butter, softened
2 cups confectioners' sugar
Red and green liquid food coloring

If you like you can decorate the petits fours as shown on page 89. To ornament each white cake, center a crystallized violet in the top, pressing it gently into the icing. To trim the light brown cakes, melt 1½ ounces of coarsely chopped semisweet chocolate in a small heavy pan set over low heat and, using a fork, dribble lines of chocolate onto the tops of the cakes. For a more precise pattern, roll a piece of wax paper into a cone, cut off the bottom point to make a small hole and squeeze the chocolate through it onto the cakes.

To ornament the pink and green petits fours, cream the 8 tablespoons of softened butter by beating and mashing it against the sides of a bowl with the back of a large spoon until it is light and fluffy. Beat in the 2 cups of confectioners' sugar, about ½ cup at a time, and stir to a smooth, thick paste. Spoon half the mixture into another bowl and stir in two drops of red food coloring to shade it a dark pink. Add two drops of green food coloring to the paste remaining in the first bowl and stir until it is dark green. Using a pastry bag fitted with the decorative tips of your choice, pipe the pink paste onto the pink petits fours in whatever design you like, and pipe ribbons of the green paste onto the green petits fours.

Leave the petits fours uncovered for about 1 hour to let the icing dry completely. Then drape them loosely with wax paper. They can safely be kept at room temperature for about 24 hours.

Shrimp-stuffed Artichokes

With a small sharp knife, trim the bases of the artichokes flush and flat. Bend and snap off the small bottom leaves and any bruised outer leaves. Lay each artichoke on its side and slice about 1 inch off the top. With scissors, trim ¼ inch off the points of the rest of the leaves. To prevent discoloring, rub all the cut edges with lemon as you proceed.

In a 10- to 12-quart enameled pot, bring 5 quarts of water and 2 tablespoons of salt to a boil over high heat. Drop in the artichokes and one lemon half and return the water to a boil. Cook briskly, uncovered, for 15 to 20 minutes, or until the bases of the artichokes show no resistance when pierced with the point of a small sharp knife.

With tongs, invert the artichokes in a colander to drain. Discard the lemon and all but about 1 inch of the cooking liquid. Set the pot aside.

Meanwhile, shell the shrimp. Make a shallow incision down their backs with a small sharp knife and lift out the intestinal vein with the point of the knife. Wash the shrimp briefly in a colander set under cold running water. Then drop them into enough lightly salted boiling water to immerse the shrimp completely. Cook uncovered for 3 to 5 minutes, until they are pink and firm to the touch. Drain the shrimp and pat them dry with paper towels. Reserve four of the shrimp for garnish and chop the rest into fine bits. Set the shrimp aside.

Melt ½ pound of the butter bits in a heavy 12-inch skillet set over moderate heat, stirring so that the butter melts without browning. When the foam begins to subside, add the bread crumbs and stir over moderate heat until the crumbs are crisp and golden. With a rubber spatula, scrape the contents of the skillet into a bowl and set it aside.

In the same skillet, melt the remaining 4 tablespoons of butter bits over moderate heat. When the foam subsides, add the onions and garlic, and stir for about 5 minutes, until they are soft and translucent but not brown. Scrape the onion mixture over the bread crumbs, add the reserved shrimp, grated cheese, parsley and lemon peel, and toss the ingredients together gently but thoroughly with a spoon. Taste for seasoning.

Divide the shrimp mixture into four equal portions and stuff each artichoke in the following fashion: Starting near the base, gently ease the top of one leaf away from the artichoke and spoon about a teaspoonful of the shrimp mixture into the opening. Push the shrimp mixture down between the leaf and the artichoke, then press the leaf back into place.

Repeat until all of the large green outer leaves have been stuffed, then stand the artichoke upright on a large piece of heavy-duty aluminum foil. Fold the foil tightly up and around the artichoke, and twist the ends securely together at the top. To keep the stuffing in place, tie a short length of kitchen cord around the widest part of the foil package. Set aside. Stuff and wrap the remaining artichokes in the same way.

Stand the artichokes upright in the reserved pot and bring the liquid to a boil over high heat. Cover tightly and steam the artichokes for 20 minutes. With tongs, transfer the artichokes to a cutting board and remove the strings and foil. Arrange the artichokes attractively on a heated platter or four individual serving plates, and place one of the reserved whole shrimp on top of each one. Serve the Creole vinaigrette sauce separately as an accompaniment to the inner leaves and bottom of the artichokes.

To serve 4

4 large artichokes, each 4 to 5 inches
    in diameter at the base
1 lemon, cut in half crosswise
Salt
1 pound uncooked shrimp
½ pound plus 4 tablespoons
    butter, cut into ½-inch bits
6 cups soft fresh crumbs made from
    French- or Italian-type white
    bread, pulverized in a blender or
    finely shredded with a fork
1 cup finely chopped onions
4 teaspoons finely chopped garlic
2 cups freshly grated imported
    Romano or Parmesan cheese
½ cup finely chopped fresh
    parsley, preferably the flat-leaf
    Italian variety
2 teaspoons finely grated fresh
    lemon peel
½ cup Creole vinaigrette sauce
    (page 31)

To serve 4

1 pound fish trimmings: the heads, tails and bones of any firm white fish

3 cups water

2 medium-sized onions, peeled and coarsely chopped

1 medium-sized bay leaf, crumbled

6 whole black peppercorns

2 teaspoons salt

3 tablespoons butter, softened, plus 5 tablespoons butter, cut into small bits, plus 4 teaspoons butter, melted

4 eight-ounce pompano fillets, or substitute 4 eight-ounce sole or flounder fillets

½ cup dry white wine

½ pound uncooked small shrimp, preferably river shrimp (see Glossary, page 198)

¼ cup finely chopped scallions, including 3 inches of the green tops

2 tablespoons finely chopped fresh parsley, preferably the flat-leaf Italian variety

¼ cup flour

3 tablespoons heavy cream

¼ teaspoon ground hot red pepper (cayenne)

¼ pound freshly cooked, frozen or canned crabmeat, thoroughly drained and picked over to remove all bits of shell and cartilage

Pompano en Papillote
POMPANO FILLETS WITH SHRIMP AND CRAB BAKED IN PARCHMENT PAPER

Combine the fish trimmings and water in a 3- to 4-quart enameled saucepan and bring to a boil over high heat, skimming off the foam and scum as they rise to the surface. Add the onions, bay leaf, peppercorns and salt, reduce the heat to low, and simmer, partially covered, for 30 minutes. Then strain the fish stock through a fine sieve set over a bowl, pressing the trimmings and seasonings with the back of a spoon to extract all their juices before discarding the bones and pulp. Set the stock aside.

Preheat the oven to 350°. With a pastry brush, spread 1 tablespoon of the softened butter evenly over the bottom and sides of a 13-by-9-by-2-inch baking dish. Cut a piece of wax paper to fit over the dish and brush one side of the paper with 1 tablespoon of softened butter.

Place the fish fillets in the buttered dish and pour the reserved stock and the wine over them. Cover the dish loosely with the buttered paper and bake in the middle of the oven for 5 minutes, or until the fillets feel firm when prodded gently with a finger. With a large metal spatula, transfer the fish to a platter. Measure the stock remaining in the baking dish and reserve 1½ cups. Increase the oven temperature to 450°.

Meanwhile, shell the shrimp. Unless you are using the river variety, devein the shrimp by making a shallow incision down their backs with a small sharp knife and lifting out the intestinal vein with the point of the knife. If the shrimp are over 1 inch long, cut them into pieces. Wash the shrimp briefly in a colander and pat them dry with paper towels.

Melt 2 tablespoons of the butter bits in a small skillet set over moderate heat. When the foam begins to subside, add the shrimp and stir for 2 to 3 minutes, until they are pink and firm to the touch. Set the shrimp aside off the heat. Cut four parchment-paper hearts about 11 inches long and 15 inches wide (as shown opposite) and brush one side with the melted butter. Set the hearts aside.

In a heavy 1- to 1½-quart saucepan, melt the remaining 3 tablespoons of butter bits over moderate heat. Add the scallions and parsley and, stirring frequently, cook for about 5 minutes, until they are soft but not brown. Add the flour and mix well. Then, stirring constantly with a wire whisk, pour in the reserved 1½ cups of stock in a slow, thin stream and cook over high heat until the sauce comes to a boil, thickens and is smooth. Reduce the heat to low and simmer the sauce uncovered for 3 minutes. Stir in the cream and red pepper, and taste for seasoning.

To assemble each pompano en papillote, place a fish fillet on one side of a paper heart and cover the fillet with about ¼ cup of shrimp and ¼ cup of crabmeat. Spoon the sauce over the top, dividing it equally among the four portions. Fold over the exposed side of the paper so that the edges of paper meet. Starting at the upper end of the fold, seal the edges by crimping them at about ½-inch intervals. Before crimping the bottom point of the heart, open the seam slightly and blow through the hole to inflate the papillote. Then quickly crimp the bottom point closed.

Brush a large baking sheet with the remaining tablespoon of softened butter and place the papillotes on it. Bake in the middle of the preheated 450° oven for 8 to 10 minutes. The paper should turn a golden brown. Serve the papillotes at once, opening the paper at the table.

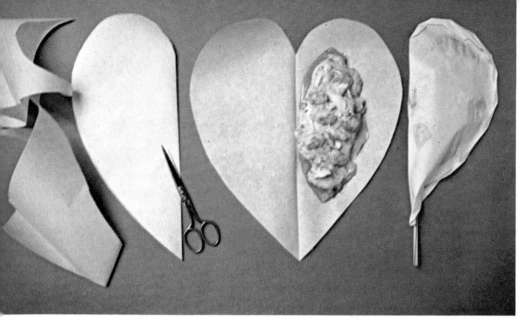

Pompano en papillote
(below) was added to
Antoine's menu to honor a
visiting balloonist, and the
papillote does in fact swell
up like a balloon. To
prepare the dish *(left)*,
cut an 11-by-15-inch
parchment-paper heart.
Place the fish and sauce on
one side, fold the heart,
and crimp the edges shut.
Before sealing the tip,
blow air into the papillote
with a paper straw.

IV

Voodoo Soup and Birds in Birds

In 1948, novelist Frances Parkinson Keyes wrote the bestseller *Dinner at Antoine's,* which called national attention to a restaurant that New Orleans natives had known and treasured for generations. Simplicity of service combined with excellence of cuisine—illustrated here by a plate of shrimp remoulade displayed on gleaming linen—aptly sums up Antoine's. But while this image suggests the quality of New Orleans' restaurants, it gives no hint of their splendid variety. For that, one must go there, explore and eat.

A love for Creole food is easily come by but not so easily left behind, and so one great hazard of visiting New Orleans is the difficulty of getting away. There are many ways of leaving the city quickly and painlessly by land, water or air, but I have never found a really satisfactory one (the Creole way, of course, is simply not to leave at all). As the chill weather warms into balmy spring, a strange inertia sets in. The Hotel Richelieu in the French Quarter, where I stayed on my last visit to the city, is an attractive place. It has many large suites and an old-style patio with a swimming pool surrounded by terra-cotta-colored walls and lush green plants; the bar, just inside, offers a Creole Bloody Mary with a richness and a wasplike sting that make all other versions of the drink seem tame and tasteless. On Sundays, people gather at the Richelieu to sip their drinks in the open, under the lazy drifting April skies—and Sunday follows Sunday with frightening rapidity.

Don't think of leaving New Orleans yet, friends say to you; stay on and enjoy the good weather. Stay a day; stay a year; stay a lifetime. Well, stay a few weeks, anyway. . . .

There is good reason to stay, for with the coming of spring you will want to visit a few more of the restaurants in and out of the French Quarter. Crawfish are beginning to be in season, and crawfish bisque is one of the city's most notable culinary achievements. The young, tender-shelled spring crawfish make the best bisque, and one of the best places to eat it is Galatoire's, a "family" place that many New Orleans residents consider to be the finest restaurant in the city. Galatoire's also has the distinction of being one of the few truly great restaurants in this country that won't take a reservation for anybody—anybody at all, ever. If you want to eat at Galatoire's, you had better get used to waiting in line; there is no other way to get in. Famous politicians and movie stars have complained about that, and the complaints have gone unheard.

So relax and wait; and while standing on line look and listen around you. Galatoire's is on Bourbon Street, once the home of New Orleans' French opera house. Through the years, especially after the birth of jazz, the street declined in elegance; at the moment, it is a garish promenade lined by strip joints and full of clashing neon lights, the loud calls of barkers and the sounds of music fighting music, block after block. Authentic Dixieland jazz is hard to find today, though there are still a couple of places where jazz aficionados still go—most notably Preservation Hall, a few blocks up Bourbon and half a block to the right. If you have grown up with them, real jazz and good blues make today's popular music sound like the pantings of a puppy. But you can still hear the old sounds on Bourbon Street now and then, and Galatoire's still stands as a reminder of the old ways of life.

Once inside Galatoire's, you may wonder if you had been waiting in the wrong line, for the place probably looks less like a great restaurant than any other you have ever entered. There is only one room, a big one, with mirror-lined walls, an immaculate tile floor and wall hooks for coats. The effect is to make Galatoire's look like an outsized barbershop. Pay no attention to the décor—or rather, note it well, for it perfectly exemplifies the New Orleans tradition that a restaurant builds its reputation in its kitchen and its kitchen alone.

Order a bowl of crawfish bisque *(Recipe Index)* and watch it arrive, trailing white steam like a toy ocean liner. The bisque is a curious combination of aristocratic cuisine and the kind of cooking that is today called "soul food." Thyme, bay leaf, garlic, onion, celery, parsley, cloves and other ingredients all figure in a good crawfish bisque, and the thick brown soup has a bright taste that seems to marry quiet elegance with loud jazz, as if the past of Bourbon Street itself had condensed into the dish. Floating in the bisque are red heads of crawfish, stuffed with a chop-up of their tails mixed with bread crumbs and herbs, vegetables and spices. You can scoop out most of the stuffing with your spoon, but when you get down to the bits that cling to the inside of the heads you will want to suck them out. In the old days, the most exquisite Creole ladies saw nothing wrong in sucking loudly on a crawfish head at the table; having done so, they would hang the empty shells delicately around the rim of the bowl, so that the dish looked more decorative empty than full. After your bisque, if you are anything like me, you will simply want more bisque. The soup can be made just as well with shrimp as with crawfish, and I don't know why anybody would want anything more for a meal than a couple of bowlfuls of either one, accompanied by a tart tossed salad, French bread, cheese and a good bottle of wine.

If you want to stretch your menu out, though, Galatoire's is the place to do it. All the fish and shellfish dishes are good, and the trout Marguery *(Recipe Index),* a combination of trout with shrimp, mushrooms

Two generous handfuls of home-grown mirlitons are proudly displayed by their grower, Weston Champagne of St. Martinville, Louisiana. Technically a tropical squash, the mirliton is popular not only in Louisiana, but also in the Caribbean area and Latin America where it is variously called *chayote*, *christophene* or *chocho*. Fully ripe mirlitons range from three to eight inches long, and a single trellised vine like the one in the background can produce over a hundred of them. The flesh is firm, crisp and white, with a flavor even more delicate than that of summer squash.

and truffles in a hollandaise sauce, stands out as something special. It has richness, yet a light taste; something about the way Creole chefs prepare it makes it a new version of the dish, for in Creole hands classic French foods quickly become Creole foods. Galatoire's hollandaise sauce has a superb deep tang; served on fresh broccoli or asparagus it leaves a lingering, lovely aftertaste. On another visit, you may want to try the Galatoire version of oysters Rockefeller, for though it looks much the same as Antoine's it is as different as another food would be—and some people claim that Galatoire's is the better of the two. This difference of opinion is perfectly proper; no two Creole chefs ever cook alike, or want to. If you have the same dish in five different places you will probably have five quite different eating experiences, all on a par with the best food in other cities. When the old Creoles passed recipes on to their children they didn't say them aloud, let alone write them down, but merely whispered them, and this very secretiveness is what has produced the marvelous individuality of Creole dishes.

One of the ways to savor this quality, between visits to the fine restaurants of New Orleans, is to sample the cooking in almost any private

kitchen in the city. Some of the best Creole foods are still prepared in privacy by women, white and black, who think of these dishes as everyday routine. Last year I went to see an old friend, Louise George, now a grandmother, who happened to be visiting one of her children in New Orleans. One of the most remarkable things about Louise is that she can cook with her left hand alone (and she is not left-handed) while she uses the right hand mainly to accentuate her conversation. Most of the time you wouldn't know she was cooking at all unless you stepped around behind her and watched the pot.

As we visited, she was telling me a story about something that had happened to a mutual friend, accompanied by appropriate gestures of her right hand; with her left hand she was smoking a cigarette and also parboiling four large eggplants, which she then stuffed in a rather complicated way. Yet all I saw was the dark-skinned hand with the cigarette that reached out occasionally, accomplished a little something, and returned to its owner as if it had gone off briefly on an errand of its own. The left hand sliced the eggplants in two, lengthwise, and scooped out the parboiled centers. In a black iron skillet the hand fried some cubes of ham, chopped onion, green pepper and celery; the hand then added the eggplant centers, some bread crumbs and a few herbs and spices; it mixed them all together and put the mixture back into the empty eggplant shells; then it sprinkled a few more bread crumbs over the top, dotted them with butter and slipped the dish into the oven to bake—all, apparently, without needing or getting any advice from the hand's owner, who was too busy telling her story to give the hand more than a glance now and then, just to be sure that it was doing its duty. Watching it, you got the feeling that the hand didn't dare interrupt Louise's story for the preparation of a Creole dish that it had been making for decades.

When the sizzling ham-stuffed eggplant *(Recipe Index)* was ready, I was given a big scoop of it as a snack. Its taste was wonderfully whole, yet mingled, and completely free of the acid flavor that eggplant often imparts. It was an excellent example of the local way in which a vegetable is unceremoniously removed from itself, and returned to its shell only when the cook has shown it what it should have tasted like in the first place. Shrimp is often used in the stuffing instead of ham, and a squash is often given the same treatment as an eggplant. The same goes for a mirliton —the maverick vegetable of South Louisiana that looks like the illegitimate offspring of an eggplant and a squash with a melon somewhere in its ancestry. There are, in fact, few large vegetables that cannot be treated this way, and watching a good New Orleans cook prepare them can make you suspect that what really goes on in the kitchen of a great restaurant is endless conversation, or perhaps a poker game, with some cooking done on the side as the need arises. The suspicion is not completely unfounded, for there isn't a Creole cook alive who cannot produce fine food while giving three quarters of his or her attention to something else. The Creole kitchen is, in truth, the kitchen of the subconscious.

But you will not think so if you are sitting in, say, the Caribbean Room of the Pontchartrain Hotel; you will think that four chefs must be lying exhausted on the kitchen floor. You may also wonder how it is that they

Opposite: Creole cooks transform the lowliest vegetables into fancy fare by hollowing them out and stuffing their shells with savory mixes of puréed or minced pulp, bread crumbs and meat or seafood. The three combinations shown here are chicken-stuffed tomatoes *(top left),* shrimp-stuffed mirliton *(top right)* and ham-stuffed eggplant *(foreground).* Recipes for all three are listed in the Recipe Index.

happen to be working in a hotel, and conclude that another of the many clichés of American life should be discarded: the Pontchartrain is living proof that hotel cooking can be fully as good as that of the finest restaurant or the best-run home. Lysle Aschaffenburg, who owns and operates the hotel, has been given award after award for the products of his kitchen. He is a man with a flair for the theater and for food, and he does honor to them both. His hotel is on St. Charles Avenue, a wide street with a central lane on which streetcars run. At one time St. Charles was one of the city's most splendid residential avenues; even today, though its grandeur is much diminished, it has the look of a street on which marble mansions grow as naturally as crape myrtle or wax-white magnolias, and the rattling of the streetcars makes a pleasant sound. The hotel itself is relatively small, and so is its Caribbean Room, which is decorated in cool, glowing colors with comfortable tables and soft lighting.

Here you *do* make a reservation (it is hard in New Orleans to keep track of where you do and where you don't). Once seated, you have a delightful problem: should you order iced lump crabmeat with two sauces, or oysters en brochette, or shrimp Saki? I would, I confess, order all three. But choose two of them, anyway, and let your choice be based on what you have already eaten in New Orleans and what you have missed. Spooned over the crabmeat, the Creole mustard-mayonnaise and the Pontchartrain version of French dressing, with a taste like creamy tart brandy, are very good, either separately or mixed together as you wish. Served on a bed of crushed ice and eaten with a little chilled Chablis, this is one of the simple dishes that make you wonder why the Creole cooks ever bother with more than simple boiling. You need not wonder very long; order the oysters en brochette, skewered with bits of bacon and broiled with butter. There is a taste to this that reminds the tongue of what oysters are all about—sweet-salt, moist-dry—but in this case the taste is as different from that of raw oysters as the taste of pork would be. The Caribbean Room's shrimp Saki, too, is evidence of the Creole ability to teach new tricks to an old shellfish. The shrimp are first baked, then broiled, and they are served with lemon butter. Both the delicacy and the sweetness of shrimp are brought out in this dish, because Creoles know how to emphasize and concentrate natural flavor with the addition of one or two contrasting ingredients.

As the air turns warmer, New Orleans burgeons with flowers and freshness, with breezes from the river, and with a sudden sense of newness. The heat will come soon enough, so take advantage of the weather and go outdoors. Buy a fried-oyster sandwich on French bread at one of the little inexpensive French Quarter restaurants. There is no better place in the world to eat fried oysters than in this city, and no better way to have them than in a crisp, hot loaf with a few shreds of lettuce and perhaps some thinly sliced tomatoes making a vegetable oyster bed inside the bread. The oysters have been dipped in a batter of beaten egg yolks and milk, then in a mixture of cracker crumbs and either cornmeal or bread crumbs, and fried quickly in deep fat. Like the bread, they are crisp, hot and incredibly good, and the fresh cold garden vegetables join the bread to make a jaunty combination of tastes. Eat the sandwich as you walk

Opposite: Hot bread pudding Creole style *(Recipe Index)* is a far cry from the bland nursery dessert of tradition. Though it is composed of familiar ingredients—it contains French bread, eggs, milk, sugar, vanilla and raisins—the pudding is liberally laced just before serving with a rich, buttery whiskey sauce.

In the parlor of Corinne Dunbar's, a waiter serves predinner cocktails to two patrons. Mrs. Dunbar, a Creole aristocrat, launched her restaurant in 1935 by simply opening her own home to paying dinner guests. Recently the establishment moved to new quarters, but it retains the aura of a private mansion—no menus and no clatter or bustle. Only an unobtrusive brass plaque on the outside announces its existence.

through the residential parts of the Quarter under the fresh sun, past the pastel-colored houses and the grillwork adorned with pots and window boxes of flowers that send out a smell of new blooms in the soft breeze.

Leave the Quarter now, and cross the wide avenue on the side farthest from the river *(map, page 6),* for a visit to the last place you would expect to go in this season of birth—the St. Louis Number One Cemetery. In this city of exceptions there are many old cemeteries worth seeing; this one is the oldest and the most unusual. On All Saints' Day, many people come here on a sort of excursion, bringing all sorts of refreshments prepared for the occasion. St. Louis Number One was built when it was considered a desecration to dig graves in the swamp earth, where the water might destroy them. Instead, the oldest cemeteries consist entirely of mausoleums. By now the mausoleums have sunk partly into the earth; you stroll along white clamshell paths past little white, pink, gray and mottled stone houses that stick up into the sky at odd angles. Some are no more than half visible, as if someone had spread wheelbarrows full of earth around among the tombs. There are black iron grillwork doors on many of the mausoleums, and marble benches in front of them to sit on and read the inscriptions, nearly all of them in French.

There is one tomb that stands, shining and pristine, strangely out of place among its tilted neighbors. This tomb has a story: it is said to be the burial place of Marie Laveau, the reigning voodoo queen of New Orleans in the latter half of the 19th Century. Many powerful people, from restaurateurs to politicians, went to her for advice and help. Sometimes, even today, you will see stars and half-moons and other signs drawn on her tomb with pieces of crumbled red brick. Ask about Marie Laveau or the markings of her tomb and you will get either a blank stare or a certain evasive look, for the practice of voodoo is now outlawed. But there are still ways of finding out about it. One of my own is worth telling.

On an earlier visit to New Orleans I had wanted to learn about voodoo for an article I was writing; I did some checking and found myself finally in a remote part of town, at the home of an old black woman, who shall for her own sake be nameless. The room I walked into that night smelled sharply of a soup slowly simmering in a pot in the kitchen. I had arrived recommended by a friend (who knew a friend, who had a friend) but the old woman looked at me with some suspicion; she didn't seem to know what I was talking about when I told her that I was trying to buy a "gris-gris," a voodoo charm, to take away with me. I had lost my New Orleans accent and I had been away a long time—too long, she seemed to feel. I knew enough not to press the point, and instead sat down and talked about other things.

After a while I was given a bowl of the soup. I tasted it with a shaky feeling at the pit of my stomach, for if this truly was a voodoo woman, there was no telling what might be in the soup besides food. Whatever there was, the soup was good to eat, made from black beans and ham hocks, with the gentlest flavor of onion—and something else that I could not quite identify. But it was all thick, with a taste like the night: dark and heavy and warm. I asked for a second bowl, and something at the back of the woman's eyes flickered at me for a moment. There is no better way to gain a woman's confidence in New Orleans than by enjoying her cooking; and you cannot fake enjoyment, because she will know. This old woman refilled my bowl, and while I was eating, she began to toy with a tiny ivory snuffbox, yellow with age. When I had finished the second bowl, she flipped the box toward me on the table and suggested offhandedly that I might want to take it to the St. Louis Number One Cemetery next day. There I should pick up a bit of the crumbled brick from the bottom of Marie Laveau's tomb, and put it in the box. Bring the box back tomorrow, she said; something might be arranged. I did as I was told, and came back the next day with a sliver of red brick in the tiny box, which I had been flicking open and shut in my coat pocket all afternoon. The woman asked me to open the box and hold it out to her in my hand. I did. Without touching it, she made several motions in the air over it, and asked me to close it. Then she explained that the box could not open again until I wanted it to open badly enough—which would be when I craved something, some wish, that seemed unobtainable. I asked her what kind of wish—for good or for evil—it was to be; and the old woman replied that it was up to me. Then she shrugged and turned away, pocketing the small amount of money she had asked in return for the favor and the ivory box. That night I took the box out again and decided to make a wish. But something odd had happened; the box wouldn't

Continued on page 112

Some Reasons Why New Orleans Is a Great Restaurant City

To visiting English novelist William Makepeace Thackeray, New Orleans was "the city in the world where you could eat and drink the most and suffer the least"—but one need not have the appetite of a Victorian gourmand to enjoy the range and refinement of New Orleans' eating places. Traditionally, the city's restaurants complement rather than compete with one another, in the happy belief that each has its particular virtues of setting, cuisine, scope of menu and secret specialties. Most of them are self-contained family businesses, engaging the talents and attention of everyone from *grand'mère* down. On these pages are shown a few—but by no means all—of the most notable reasons for dining out in New Orleans.

BRENNAN'S
By local restaurant standards Brennan's is a youngster. Founded by Owen Brennan in 1946, it is now managed by his sister Ella and his son Owen Jr., better known as "Pip" *(above)*, who have continued his custom of serving gargantuan breakfasts. Typical breakfast items include *(clockwise from bottom left)* Creole cream cheese and strawberries, eggs *hussarde*, eggs Nouvelle Orléans and eggs Sardou, with a bottle of chilled rosé.

GALATOIRE'S
Dating back to 1905, Galatoire's retains a direct link to its past through the founder's nephew, Justin Galatoire *(right)*, his daughter Yvonne Wynne and his grandson Chris Ansel Jr. A proud sample of its cuisine is redfish courtbouillon *(foreground)*, displayed with its ingredients.

ANTOINE'S

Partly because of its great age (Antoine Alciatore, a native of Marseilles, founded it in 1840), partly because of its location in a fine old building in the heart of the French Quarter, but mostly because of its superb food, Antoine's is New Orleans' most famous restaurant. It also boasts oysters Rockefeller, a sumptuous dish invented by Antoine's son Jules in adaptation of a French recipe for snails and named in honor of the richest man Jules could imagine, John D. Rockefeller Sr.—who actually never set foot in Antoine's. At left, seated behind a platter of oysters Rockefeller *(foreground)* and another of raw oysters, is Antoine's present owner, a third-generation Alciatore, Roy. His cousin Angelo Alciatore, the manager, stands behind him, and at right is the oldest waiter on the staff—Willie Gaudin, veteran of more than 30 years of dinners at Antoine's.

THE CARIBBEAN ROOM OF THE PONTCHARTRAIN HOTEL

Hotel owner E. Lysle Aschaffenburg opened his Caribbean Room in 1948, with the idea of creating a restaurant on the order of New York's elegant Pavillon. It was a flop, but when he turned instead to Creole and French food produced by local chefs and served by a local staff, the Caribbean Room quickly caught on. Aschaffenburg is still in charge, assisted by his son Albert. They are shown at right with a few of their seafood specialties: broiled oysters and bacon en brochette *(left, rear);* shrimp Saki; and backfin lump crabmeat with two house dressings, mustard and French.

CHEZ HELENE
A fine New Orleans restaurant is not necessarily a fancy one. Chez Helene, owned by Mrs. Helen DeJean Pollock, is simple and fragrant with the aromas of soul food—fried chicken, mustard greens, grits—and Creole dishes. The staff includes two chefs in their chef's hats: Sidney DeJean *(left)*, Helen's brother; and Austin Leslie, her nephew. Mrs. Pollock is third from right.

BON TON CAFÉ
Al Pierce, who owns the Bon Ton
Café *(left)*, has an odd but
manifestly effective idea about
hiring cooks. He doesn't want them
to be experienced; instead, he
believes in training them from the
start "before they acquire bad habits
or try to make you cook *their* way."
Whatever the logic of Pierce's
personnel policy, it has paid off in
loyalty: cooks Louise Joshua
(center) and Loretta Barcony have
been with him 22 and eight years,
respectively, and the Bon Ton's
food is its own justification. Its style
is Acadian, which (like Pierce
himself) comes from the bayou
country, and its specialty is seafood,
notably crawfish. Shown at left are
a crawfish bisque *(foreground)*,
shelled crawfish *(left)* and stuffed
crawfish heads. Crawfish dishes are
served all during the crawfish
season, from November to July.

GUMBO SHOP
"Authentic and unpretentious" is
the way one guidebook, *The New
Orleans Underground Gourmet*,
describes the Gumbo Shop. Run by
an adopted New Orleans lady, Mrs.
Margaret Porpora, who bought it
soon after World War II, the
restaurant specializes in a lusty
Louisiana gumbo made with crab,
shrimp and okra. Prices are modest,
even for more elaborate dishes.
Every year, Mrs. Porpora and her
husband travel to Europe, where she
picks up new recipes for adaptation
back home, but the gumbo *(right)*
is perennial and basic.

open. I pried at it with a knife and even took a pair of pliers to it, without success. The box wouldn't open again and that was that.

Five years later I was in New York, visiting an actress friend who had come down with pneumonia and was too ill to perform in a play that was due to open in a couple of days. No medicine had worked, and she was in despair. On the afternoon I went to see her, I remembered the little ivory gris-gris from New Orleans, which had been lying forgotten on a bookshelf. I brought it to my friend as a present, more to distract her than for any other purpose, and as I began to tell her how I had acquired it, she picked it up and looked at it. Suddenly, midway in the story, I stopped, and I never finished telling it. The box had fallen open in her hand! I realized that I had been caught up in one of those incidents that no one will ever believe, even if you swear to it. I left the box with its new owner and went about my business. She was up and about the next day and opened in the show, which was—of course—a hit.

The following month I was in New Orleans again. I went to see the old voodoo woman—but her house had been demolished to make way for a store, and she was not to be found. I might have thought that I had dreamed the whole thing, were it not for my memories of the smell and the taste of that dark soup, and the look in the old woman's eyes. But Marie Laveau's tomb is not gone—it rises as always, clean and shining, in the strange old cemetery.

On a late spring night in New Orleans, if you are well dressed and have an appetite, you may want to take a very different sort of walk, back under the trees of St. Charles Avenue, to dine at Corinne Dunbar's, another unique eating place. At this restaurant you not only must make a reservation but had better make it at least three days in advance—the place is that heavily booked. Mrs. Corinne Dunbar was a Creole aristocrat who long ago opened her home in the then-fashionable Garden District to paying guests. The house eventually became a restaurant, with the food served on Mrs. Dunbar's old silver and china, in a setting of her own family antiques. The restaurant is now owned and operated by James Plauché, a distant cousin of Mrs. Dunbar's, and has moved to another old house across the street from the original location.

As you arrive at Corinne Dunbar's, you feel that you are about to enter a private home, for the door is locked and you must ring the bell. A butler ushers you into the parlor, where you are seated and given a cocktail to sip until a waitress shows you into the dining room. This has the cool look of an aquarium; it is decorated in gold, blue and white, and slivers of light glint from a crystal chandelier. The only reminder that you are in a restaurant comes from seeing diners at other tables; otherwise, there is a sense of being here by invitation.

The restaurant provides no menu. Your first course is always a fresh fruit dish, an old Creole custom; at Dunbar's it is usually melon balls, with a sweet sauce passed separately, to brighten the taste buds for what is to follow. And the rest of the meal takes some getting through, simply in terms of quantity. There is a soup—a gumbo or a bisque—served with toast. Then you may have oysters and artichokes, a specialty that has kept Dunbar's kitchen famous. It comes in a small round dish rimmed by artichoke leaves, with French bread to dip in the chopped-oyster sauce.

Your main course may turn out to be a Creole bouillabaisse, containing among other ingredients redfish, soft-shell crabs, shrimp and scallops, with a sharpness derived from cayenne pepper and saffron. Or you may be served a hot daube or beef with Burgundy sauce, accompanied by a seemingly endless array of vegetables, served separately, and by such surprise side dishes as banana puffs. Hot biscuits are served with the main course, and there is a "simple" dessert—what the Creoles called a *goûté*, or taste of sweet—perhaps pecan ice cream and a platter of multicolored petits fours. Finally, a demitasse.

Now and then the owner of Corinne Dunbar's will work up a special dinner for a few friends, served not at the restaurant but in a private room at a hotel in the French Quarter where he can collar some chef to do his bidding for the two or three days it takes to prepare the meal. On one such memorable occasion, Jimmy Plauché's idea of a "simple" first course was raw oysters on the half shell, with a heaping spoonful of fresh beluga malossol caviar on each of them—an idea he got one day when he was "stuck for a new way to begin a meal." Next came a cold soup, a trout dish and an artichoke. Then came the stunning main course. It seems that Jimmy had heard somewhere that you can stuff a bird into a bird into a bird just as long as you can find a bird big enough to contain the last one. He found nine birds around town, and tried it. The dish he served consisted of a snipe that was stuffed into a dove that was inserted into a quail that was placed in a squab that was put into a Cornish game hen that was tucked into a pheasant that was squeezed into a chicken that was pushed into a duck that was stuffed into a turkey. All the birds had been boned, and each had been boiled separately with seasoning to make a stock. A stuffing of wild cherries and almonds was placed around each bird to make it fit snugly into the next. The final nine-bird result was poached in all the combined stocks. When the chef carved it, the partakers felt as if they were eating a single legendary bird, a sort of poached phoenix. Little onions boiled in champagne were served with it, along with a lettuce-and-vinaigrette salad, and there was fresh fruit for dessert. Let a man from an old Creole family arrange a dinner for you and, of course, black, black coffee could be the only proper ending to the meal. That and deep, slow breathing.

By now, you will have fallen total victim to the New Orleans Creole fever that keeps you going to "just one more" restaurant for "just one other dish" you have heard about. If you listen to any local citizens on the subject you are lost, for they talk in a special way when it comes to food.

Let's see now, they will say. Yes, you've probably had the best dishes in the best eating places of the city . . . but wait, have you been uptown to Pascal Manale's, a simple place with fabulous Creole fare? If you want to know what a butter-pepper sauce ought to taste like, you must try their barbecued shrimp—and at the same time you can sample the Spanish tradition in eating shrimp, in which bits of their shells are chomped up along with them. And oh, while we're on the subject, Manale's does a dish of spaghetti with oysters that puts Italian clam sauces to shame. And before you finish your eating tour, you should try one of the newer lake-

New Orleans' mixed drinks are as complex as its foods. The three at left incorporate the licorice flavor of anise: Ojen cockta

zerac and absinthe frappé. At right are a milk punch, an absinthe *suissesse* and a gin fizz. All are included in the Recipe Index.

front restaurants. They're just as good as the old ones were, if you happen to like spicy shellfish—and if you don't, you ought to go out there and learn to like them. And for heaven's sake, don't tell me you haven't been to Tujague's on Decatur Street in the Quarter! It's one of the oldest places in the city, plain as an old kitchen, another of the restaurants that don't have menus—but if you like boiled beef brisket with a thick sharp horseradish sauce that only a Creole could make, you mustn't miss it. And there's Le Ruth's, across the river in Gretna—it's a new restaurant, really more French than Creole, but one of the best in the country. And then there's. . . .

You're leaving? You say you're going off for a trip through the bayou country to try out the food down there? Well, *che* [a charming diminutive of the French *cher,* or "dear"], that's up to you. But you can't just walk out of New Orleans in the middle of the day without something good to eat. You can't leave a gourmet city that way.

You're leaving at noon? Well, that's easy—just go and have breakfast at Brennan's before you leave. You what? You haven't been to Brennan's yet? Good Lord, what have you been doing all this time? Well, no harm done, I'm just glad I caught you before you left. I mean, if you haven't had breakfast at Brennan's, you haven't really been to New Orleans at all, you know, *che?* Well, go there, you hear? Go there.

Brennan's, perhaps the best-looking restaurant in the city, is on Royal Street in the heart of the French Quarter. It has everything a restaurant needs in the way of décor: candlelight, a winding staircase, very separate tables and small separate rooms. Each of the 13 rooms is decorated differently, and an easy sense of quiet comfort is everywhere. There is even a large patio shaded by banana trees, a fine place to sit in good weather and —since you forgot to make a reservation for breakfast—a fine place to relax while waiting for a table. You will want to sit there anyway, for you can't have a traditional breakfast in New Orleans without having a drink first. Sit in the morning shade and take a look at the breakfast menu. It won't help you in ordering your breakfast, but you might as well know what it says. If you want to know what to order, you had best check first with one of our New Orleans food writers—say, Richard H. Collin, who knows everything there is to know about the city's restaurants. Read what he says in his book *The New Orleans Underground Gourmet.* Or get some author to go with you—an author who lives in the city.

If you can, get Harnett Kane. Traditionally, the French Quarter has always been full of novelists and playwrights—William Faulkner for a time, and Roark Bradford, and Sherwood Anderson, and Tennessee Williams, among others—but Harnett Kane has written more factual books about the city than anybody else, and probably knows more about it than anybody alive. He will tell you what to have at Brennan's.

The first group on the menu is a list called "Eye Openers." Harnett will suggest an absinthe *suissesse,* or a milk punch made with bourbon and nutmeg, or perhaps a Ramos gin fizz, or how about a Sazerac? It depends on whether you want to start your day with the licorice, oddly blue taste of Pernod or Herbsaint (the "absinthe" drinks), or with whiskey (the punch), or with the bouquet flavor of gin mixed with cream and

Opposite: Eggs *hussarde,* a subtle composition of eggs, tomato and two separate sauces, may represent the pinnacle of the lavish breakfast dishes of New Orleans. Toasted Holland rusks are covered by slices of fresh tomato, blanketed by *marchand de vin* sauce and topped with freshly poached eggs smothered in hollandaise sauce *(Recipe Index).* The exotic name of the dish may have been borrowed from the European mercenary soldiers called hussars, who wore bright tomato-red uniforms.

egg white and orange-flower water (the gin fizz), or with whiskey sweetened by sugar and Herbsaint and sharpened by both Peychaud and Angostura bitters (the Sazerac). The decision is simple. Harnett likes the absinthe *suissesse* best; Richard Collin seems to like the gin fizz; I like the Sazerac. Make up your own mind.

Now that we have helped you with that decision, let us go on to more serious matters. Take the huge menu with you, leave the patio for your table inside and consider what you would like to eat. There is a New Orleans food called Creole cream cheese, made from milk curd mixed with cream. At Brennan's, ripe fresh fruit is added to it to make a wonderful, wakening taste that does for your stomach what the drink just did for your head. It will put you in the right mood for an egg dish—say eggs Sardou *(Recipe Index),* which are artichoke bottoms set on a bed of creamed spinach and topped with poached eggs and hollandaise sauce. It is my personal favorite. Harnett doesn't like it as much as I do—he prefers the eggs Nouvelle Orléans *(Recipe Index),* which are poached eggs with lump crabmeat and a cream sauce made with brandy. Richard Collin's favorite is eggs *hussarde (Recipe Index),* grilled ham on Holland rusks with *marchand de vin* sauce, topped by poached eggs with hollandaise. If you want to know which of them is best, I repeat, just ask a writer; it's a New Orleans tradition, and writers know these things.

Now for some dessert; who ever heard of having breakfast without dessert? You might as well try the bananas Foster *(Recipe Index).* This is bananas flamed with rum at your table and served over ice cream, and it makes bananas taste hot and cold at the same time, sweet but not too sweet, a smooth finish to the meal. And coffee, of course, because Brennan's makes a coffee that is dark even for a New Orleans brew, and it burns you awake all over again. Now you are ready to jump in your car and leave on your trip.

Oh, really? say your New Orleans friends. You're too full?

Well, leave tomorrow, not today. That's a tradition too. You can go for a long walk now and come back to Brennan's tonight for dinner. I wasn't going to mention it, but you missed their best dish. It's the baked oysters—two Bienville, two Roffignac, two Rockefeller. I know you've already had the Rockefeller, but the other two are completely different—almost like other foods—and you will never taste anything like all three together. Come and sit in the evening candlelit shadows and try them. The Bienville have golden toppings with shallots and chopped shrimp and other things; they have a piquant soft taste and they melt like butter on the tongue. The Roffignac are reddish, made with mushrooms and red wine and shrimp and scallions; their flavor is quick, more glowing somehow, and fuller. The platter looks gay and symmetrical too, with the alternating colors of topping—red, yellow, green. The Creoles always knew how to make food as good to look at as it is to taste.

That reminds me. Before you go tomorrow, you should try the breakfast at a place called. . . . No? You've heard about the beauty of the bayou country and you want to get an early start?

You mean you're going to leave New Orleans on an empty stomach? Are you from up North somewhere?

Opposite: Bananas Foster, a specialty of Brennan's Restaurant, is a spectacular but easily assembled dessert. The bananas are peeled and halved, then cooked at the table in a brown-sugar syrup. In a final blaze of glory they are flamed with banana liqueur and rum and served at once, over vanilla ice cream.

To serve 4 as a main dish or 8 as a
   first course

CRÊPES
½ cup unsifted flour
⅛ teaspoon salt
2 eggs
½ cup milk
2 to 4 tablespoons melted butter

1 tablespoon butter, softened

SAUCE AND FILLING
4 tablespoons butter, cut into small
   bits
½ cup finely chopped scallions
¼ cup flour
1½ cups chicken stock, fresh or
   canned
½ cup dry white wine
¼ teaspoon ground hot red pepper
   (cayenne)
½ teaspoon salt
2 egg yolks, lightly beaten
1½ cups fresh, frozen or canned
   crabmeat, thoroughly drained and
   picked over to remove all bits of
   shell and cartilage
2 tablespoons finely chopped fresh
   parsley, preferably the flat-leaf
   Italian variety

Crabmeat Crêpes

To prepare the crêpes, combine the ½ cup of flour and ⅛ teaspoon of salt and sift them into a deep bowl. Add the eggs and stir with a wire whisk until the batter is smooth. Whisking constantly, pour in the milk in a slow, thin stream. Cover the bowl tightly with plastic wrap and let the batter rest at room temperature for about 1 hour before using it.

Heat an 8-inch crêpe pan or skillet over high heat until a drop of water flicked into it evaporates instantly. With a pastry brush, lightly grease the bottom and sides of the pan with a little of the melted butter. Pour about ¼ cup of the batter into the pan and tip the pan so that the batter quickly covers the bottom; the batter should cling to the pan and begin to firm up almost immediately.

At once tilt the pan over the bowl and pour off any excess batter; the finished crêpe should be paper thin. Cook the crêpe for a minute or so, until a rim of brown shows around the edge. Turn it over with a spatula and cook the other side for a minute longer. Slide the crêpe onto a plate. Then brush melted butter on the skillet again and proceed with the rest of the crêpes; you should have enough ingredients to make eight or nine in all. The crêpes may be made hours or even days ahead of time and kept, tightly covered, in the refrigerator or freezer. If you do this, let them return to room temperature before attempting to separate them.

Preheat the oven to 400°. With a pastry brush, spread the tablespoon of softened butter evenly over the bottom and sides of a 13-by-9-by-2-inch baking-serving dish, and set it aside.

To prepare the sauce and filling, melt the 4 tablespoons of butter bits over moderate heat in a heavy 1- to 1½-quart saucepan. When the foam begins to subside, add the scallions and, stirring frequently, cook for about 5 minutes, or until they are soft but not brown. Add the ¼ cup of flour and mix well. Stirring constantly with a wire whisk, pour in the chicken stock and wine in a slow, thin stream and cook over high heat until the sauce mixture comes to a boil, thickens lightly and is smooth.

Stir in the red pepper and the ½ teaspoon of salt, reduce the heat to low and simmer for about 3 minutes to remove any taste of raw flour. Ladle about 3 tablespoons of the sauce into the beaten egg yolks and whisk together thoroughly. Then, whisking the mixture constantly, pour the egg yolks slowly into the sauce and simmer for 2 or 3 minutes longer to cook the egg yolks. Do not let the sauce come anywhere near a boil or the yolks will curdle. Taste for seasoning.

Ladle 1 cup of the sauce into a bowl and stir in the crabmeat. Set the remaining sauce aside off the heat.

Place 3 tablespoons of the crabmeat mixture on the lower third of each crêpe and roll it up into a cylinder; do not tuck in the ends. Arrange the filled crêpes side by side in the buttered baking dish and pour the reserved sauce over the center of the row of crêpes, leaving the ends unsauced. Bake in the upper third of the oven for 10 minutes, or until the sauce bubbles. Sprinkle the crêpes with the parsley and serve at once, directly from the baking dish.

Choices for a lively start to a Creole dinner include shrimp remoulade *(left)*, two crabmeat crêpes, and oysters and artichokes.

Shrimp Remoulade

To prepare the remoulade sauce, combine the mustard, paprika, red pepper and 4 teaspoons of the salt in a deep bowl and stir with a wire whisk until all the ingredients are thoroughly combined. Beat in the vinegar. Then, whisking constantly, pour in the oil in a slow, thin stream and continue to beat until the sauce is smooth and thick. Add the scallions, celery and parsley, and mix well. Cover the bowl tightly with plastic wrap and let the sauce rest at room temperature for at least 4 hours before serving.

Meanwhile, shell the shrimp. Devein them by making a shallow incision down their backs with a small sharp knife and lifting out the black or white intestinal vein with the point of the knife. Wash the shrimp briefly in a sieve or colander set under cold running water.

Drop the shrimp into a heavy 5- to 6-quart saucepan and add 2 quarts of water and the remaining teaspoon of salt. The water should cover the shrimp completely; if necessary, add more. Bring to a boil over high heat, reduce the heat to low and simmer uncovered for 3 to 5 minutes, until the shrimp are pink and firm to the touch. With a slotted spoon, transfer the shrimp to a plate to cool. Then chill them until ready to serve.

Just before serving, mound the shredded lettuce attractively on six to eight chilled individual serving plates and arrange the shrimp on top. Spoon the remoulade sauce over the shrimp and serve at once.

To serve 6 to 8 as a first course

¼ cup Creole mustard *(see Glossary, page 198)*
2 tablespoons paprika
1 teaspoon ground hot red pepper (cayenne)
5 teaspoons salt
½ cup tarragon vinegar
1⅓ cups olive oil
1½ cups coarsely chopped scallions, including 3 inches of the green tops
½ cup very finely chopped celery
½ cup coarsely chopped fresh parsley, preferably the flat-leaf Italian variety
3 pounds medium-sized uncooked shrimp (about 20 to 24 to a pound)
1 large iceberg lettuce, trimmed, quartered lengthwise and cut into ¼-inch-wide shreds

121

To serve 6 as a first course

6 large artichokes, each 4 to 5 inches
    in diameter at the base
1 quart cold water combined with
    2 tablespoons fresh lemon juice
1 dozen medium-sized oysters,
    shucked, with all their liquor
    reserved
3 tablespoons butter
¼ cup soft fresh crumbs made
    from French- or Italian-type
    bread with all the crusts removed
    and pulverized in a blender or
    finely shredded with a fork
1½ teaspoons finely chopped
    garlic
2 tablespoons paprika
1 cup chicken stock, fresh or canned
¼ cup cornstarch mixed with
    3 tablespoons cold water
1 tablespoon strained fresh lemon
    juice
¼ teaspoon ground red pepper
    (cayenne)

Oysters and Artichokes

Wash the artichokes under cold running water and bend and snap off the small bottom leaves and any bruised outer leaves. Then drop the artichokes into enough lightly salted boiling water to cover them completely and cook briskly, uncovered, for 15 to 20 minutes, or until the bases show no resistance when pierced with the point of a small sharp knife.

With tongs, transfer the artichokes to a colander and invert them to drain. Cut off the stems flush with the bases of the artichokes, and drop the stems into a small bowl. Cut or pull off about two dozen of the large outside leaves of the artichokes and, with a spoon, scrape the soft pulp from each leaf into the bowl with the stems. (Discard the scraped leaves.) Using the back of a fork, mash the pulp and stems to a purée. There should be about ½ cup of purée; if necessary, pull off and scrape more leaves.

Cut or pull off the remaining green leaves of the artichokes, cover with foil or plastic wrap, and refrigerate until ready to serve. Following the diagrams in the Recipe Booklet, pull the thistlelike yellow leaves and hairy inner chokes away from the artichoke bottoms. Trim the surface of the artichoke bottoms, drop them into a bowl and pour the water-and-lemon-juice mixture over them. The liquid should cover the artichoke bottoms completely; if necessary, add more water. Set the bottoms aside.

About 15 minutes before you plan to serve the oysters and artichokes, drain the oysters and their liquor through a fine sieve lined with a double thickness of dampened cheesecloth and set over a bowl. Measure and reserve 1 cup of the oyster liquor. (If there is less than 1 cup, add fresh or bottled clam broth to make that amount.)

Pat the oysters dry with paper towels and cut them into quarters. Rinse the artichoke bottoms briefly under cold water, pat them dry with paper towels and cut them into ¼-inch dice. Reserve the oysters and artichoke-bottom dice in a bowl. In a heavy 6- to 8-inch skillet, melt 2 tablespoons of the butter over moderate heat, add the bread crumbs and stir until they are crisp and golden. Remove the pan from the heat and set aside.

Prepare the oyster-and-artichoke sauce in the following manner: In a 1- to 1½-quart enameled or stainless-steel saucepan, melt the remaining tablespoon of butter over moderate heat. When the foam begins to subside, add the garlic and stir for 1 minute. Add the paprika, then stir in the reserved artichoke purée, the oyster liquor and chicken stock. Stirring constantly with a wire whisk, bring to a boil over high heat. Reduce the heat to low, cover the pan partially and simmer for 10 minutes.

Transfer the entire contents of the saucepan to the jar of an electric blender and blend at high speed for about 30 seconds to reduce the mixture to a smooth purée. Return the purée to the saucepan and set over high heat. Give the cornstarch-and-water combination a quick stir to recombine it, then pour it slowly into the purée and whisk constantly until the mixture comes to a boil. Stir in the oysters and diced artichoke bottoms, reduce the heat to low and simmer for 2 or 3 minutes. When the oysters plump and their edges begin to curl, add the reserved bread crumbs, the lemon juice and the red pepper, and taste the sauce for seasoning.

To serve, ladle the sauce into six small bowls, dividing it evenly among them. Place each bowl in the center of a serving plate and arrange the chilled artichoke leaves attractively around it.

Bananas Foster

This elegant dessert of flamed bananas and ice cream, created at Brennan's over 20 years ago for a regular patron named Richard Foster, has become one of the restaurant's most popular dishes.

Prepare and assemble the bananas Foster at the dinner table when you are ready to serve them. Light an alcohol burner or table-top stove and set a 12-inch copper *flambé* or crêpe-suzette pan over the flame. Arrange all the ingredients conveniently beside the pan. Place a scoop of ice cream on each of four chilled individual dessert plates and set them to one side.

Combine the butter and brown sugar in the *flambé* pan and stir until the mixture becomes a smooth syrup. Add the bananas and baste them with the syrup for 3 or 4 minutes, then sprinkle in the cinnamon.

Carefully pour in the banana liqueur and rum, and let the liquors warm for a few seconds. They may burst into flame spontaneously. If not, ignite them with a match. Slide the pan back and forth until the flames die, basting the bananas all the while. Place two banana halves around each scoop of ice cream, spoon the sauce over the top and serve at once.

To serve 4

1 pint vanilla ice cream
8 tablespoons butter, cut into ½-inch bits
½ cup brown sugar
4 firm ripe bananas, peeled and cut lengthwise into halves
½ teaspoon ground cinnamon
½ cup banana liqueur
1 cup rum

Shrimp-stuffed Mirliton

Drop the mirlitons into enough boiling water to immerse them completely. Cook briskly, uncovered, for about 45 minutes, or until they show no resistance when pierced with the point of a small sharp knife.

Meanwhile, shell the shrimp. Devein them by making a shallow incision down their backs with a small sharp knife and lifting out the intestinal vein with the point of the knife. Wash the shrimp briefly in a colander set under cold running water, then drop them into enough boiling salted water to cover them completely. Cook briskly, uncovered, for 3 to 5 minutes, or until the shrimp are pink and firm to the touch. Drain the shrimp and pat them completely dry with fresh towels. Put the shrimp, ham, onion and garlic through the medium blade of a food grinder, stir in the parsley, thyme, red pepper and salt, and set aside.

Preheat the oven to 375°. With a pastry brush, spread the tablespoon of softened butter over the bottom and sides of a shallow baking dish large enough to hold the squash snugly in one layer.

Drain the mirlitons and, when they are cool enough to handle, cut them lengthwise into halves. Remove the seeds, and hollow out each half with a spoon to make boatlike shells about ¼ inch thick. Invert the shells on paper towels to drain. Purée the pulp through a food mill set over a bowl or drop the pulp into a bowl and, with the back of a fork, mash it to a purée. Transfer the pulp to a heavy ungreased 12-inch skillet and, stirring constantly, cook over moderate heat until all of the liquid in the pan evaporates. Add 8 tablespoons of the butter bits to the purée and, when it melts, stir in the ground shrimp mixture. Taste for seasoning.

Spoon the shrimp-and-squash stuffing into the reserved mirliton shells, dividing it equally among them and mounding the tops slightly. Sprinkle the bread crumbs and the remaining 3 tablespoons of butter bits over the mirlitons. Arrange the shells in the buttered dish and bake in the middle of the oven for 30 minutes, or until the tops are brown. Serve at once.

To serve 8

4 eight-ounce mirliton squash *(see Glossary, page 198)*
½ pound uncooked shrimp
½ pound lean cooked smoked ham, coarsely chopped
1 medium-sized onion, peeled and coarsely chopped
2 medium-sized garlic cloves, peeled and coarsely chopped
¼ cup finely chopped fresh parsley, preferably the flat-leaf Italian variety
¼ teaspoon ground thyme
½ teaspoon ground hot red pepper (cayenne)
½ teaspoon salt
1 tablespoon butter, softened, plus 11 tablespoons butter, cut into ½-inch bits
1 cup soft fresh crumbs made from French- or Italian-type white bread, pulverized in a blender or finely shredded with a fork

To serve 4 as a first course

Rock salt
2 dozen large oysters, shucked, with all their liquor and the deeper halves of their shells reserved
Fresh or bottled clam broth
3 cups coarsely chopped scallions, including the green tops
3 cups coarsely chopped fresh parsley, preferably the flat-leaf Italian variety
1½ pounds fresh spinach, washed, trimmed, patted dry with paper towels and torn into 1-inch pieces
¾ pound unsalted butter, cut into ½-inch bits
4 teaspoons finely chopped garlic
¾ cup flour
3 tablespoons anchovy paste
¾ teaspoon ground hot red pepper (cayenne)
1½ teaspoons salt
¾ cup Herbsaint or Pernod

To serve 4

SAUCE
3 tablespoons butter
2 tablespoons finely chopped onions
3 tablespoons flour
1½ cups milk
2 tablespoons brandy
1 teaspoon strained fresh lemon juice
⅛ teaspoon ground hot red pepper (cayenne)
1 teaspoon salt

Oysters Rockefeller
BAKED OYSTERS TOPPED WITH ANISE-FLAVORED GREEN SAUCE

Oysters Rockefeller was created in 1899 by Jules Alciatore, the son and successor of M. Antoine Alciatore, who founded Antoine's Restaurant in 1840. It is told that he called the dish Rockefeller because the sauce was so rich. While Antoine's keeps its own recipe secret, there are many other versions. This one includes spinach in the green sauce.

Preheat the oven to 400°. Spread the rock salt to a depth of about ½ inch in four 8- or 9-inch pie pans. Arrange the pans on baking sheets and set them in the oven to heat the salt while you prepare the oysters.

Drain the oysters and their liquor through a fine sieve lined with a double thickness of dampened cheesecloth and set over a bowl. Measure and reserve 3 cups of the oyster liquor. (If there is less than 3 cups, add fresh or bottled clam broth to make up that amount.) Transfer the oysters to a bowl. Scrub the oyster shells, then pat them dry with paper towels.

Put the scallions, parsley and spinach through the finest blade of a meat grinder, and set aside. In a 2- to 3-quart enameled or stainless-steel saucepan, melt the butter over moderate heat, stirring so that it melts evenly without browning. Add the garlic and stir for a minute or so, then add the flour and mix well. Stirring constantly with a wire whisk, pour in the 3 cups of oyster liquor in a slow, thin stream and cook over high heat until the sauce comes to a boil, thickens heavily and is smooth.

Stir in the anchovy paste, red pepper and salt. Then add the ground scallions, parsley and spinach, and reduce the heat to low. Stirring occasionally, simmer uncovered for 10 minutes, or until the sauce is thick enough to hold its shape almost solidly in the spoon. Remove the pan from the heat, stir in the Herbsaint or Pernod and taste for seasoning.

Arrange six oyster shells in each of the salt-lined pans and place an oyster in each shell. Spoon the sauce over the oysters, dividing it equally among them. Bake in the middle of the oven for 15 minutes, or until the sauce is delicately browned and the oysters begin to curl at the edges. Serve the oysters Rockefeller at once, directly from the baking pans.

NOTE: While the bed of salt helps to keep the shells from tipping and, if heated beforehand, will keep the oysters hot, it is not indispensable. You may, if you like, bake the oysters in any shallow pan large enough to hold the shells in one layer, and serve them from a heated platter.

Eggs Nouvelle Orléans
POACHED EGGS AND CRABMEAT WITH BRANDIED CREAM SAUCE

First prepare the sauce in the following manner: In a heavy 2- to 3-quart saucepan, melt the 3 tablespoons of butter over moderate heat. When the foam begins to subside, add the onions and, stirring frequently, cook for about 5 minutes or until they are soft and translucent but not brown. Add the flour and mix well. Stirring constantly with a wire whisk, pour in the milk in a slow, thin stream and cook over high heat until the sauce comes to a boil, thickens and is smooth. Reduce the heat to low and simmer uncovered for 2 or 3 minutes to remove any taste of raw flour.

In a small pan, warm the brandy over low heat and ignite it with a

Colorful sauces distinguish oysters Rockefeller, in green; oysters Roffignac, in red; oysters Bienville, in gold *(Recipe Index)*.

match, then slide the pan back and forth gently until the flames die. Stir the brandy, the lemon juice, ⅛ teaspoon of ground red pepper and 1 teaspoon of salt into the sauce and taste for seasoning. Remove the pan from the heat and cover to keep the sauce warm until you are ready to use it.

Preheat the oven to 450°. In a heavy 12-inch skillet, melt 6 tablespoons of the butter bits over moderate heat. Add the crabmeat and toss gently about with a spoon until the meat is hot and evenly moistened. Stir in ⅛ teaspoon of red pepper and ½ teaspoon of salt and, with a rubber spatula, scrape the contents of the skillet into an 8- to 10-inch round shallow baking-serving dish. Drape with foil to keep the crabmeat warm.

To poach the eggs, pour cold water into a 12-inch skillet to a depth of about 2 inches. Bring to a simmer, then reduce the heat so that the surface of the liquid barely shimmers. Break the eggs into individual saucers. Gently slide one egg into the water and, with a large spoon, lift the white over the yolk. Repeat once or twice more to enclose the yolk in the white.

One at a time, slide the seven other eggs into the pan, enclosing them in their whites and spacing them an inch apart. Poach the eggs for 3 or 4 minutes, until the whites are set and the yolks feel soft to the touch.

With a slotted spatula, arrange the poached eggs on the crabmeat. Spoon the brandied cream sauce over the eggs and sprinkle the top with the remaining 2 tablespoons of butter bits and the paprika. Bake in the middle of the oven for 10 minutes, or until the top is golden brown. Serve the eggs Nouvelle Orléans at once, directly from the baking dish.

CRABMEAT AND EGGS

8 tablespoons butter, cut into ½-inch bits

1 pound fresh, frozen or canned crabmeat, thoroughly drained and picked over to remove all bits of shell and cartilage

⅛ teaspoon ground hot red pepper (cayenne)

½ teaspoon salt

8 very fresh eggs

½ teaspoon paprika

To serve 4

3 tablespoons butter
4 slices Canadian bacon
4 Holland rusks
½ cup *marchand de vin* sauce
   (Recipe Booklet)
1 large firm ripe tomato, washed,
   stemmed and cut crosswise into
   four ¼-inch-thick rounds
4 large very fresh eggs
½ cup freshly made hollandaise
   sauce *(Recipe Booklet)*
Paprika

To serve 4 or 8

6 tablespoons butter
2 tablespoons flour
1 cup milk
1½ pounds fresh spinach, cooked,
   drained, squeezed dry and finely
   chopped (about 2 cups)
1 teaspoon salt
¼ teaspoon ground white pepper
8 canned artichoke bottoms, drained
8 very fresh eggs
1 cup freshly made hollandaise
   sauce *(Recipe Booklet)*

Eggs Hussarde
POACHED EGGS, CANADIAN BACON AND TOMATO
ON RUSKS WITH MARCHAND DE VIN AND HOLLANDAISE SAUCES

Preheat the oven to 250°. In a heavy 12-inch skillet, melt the butter over moderate heat. When the foam begins to subside, add the bacon. Turn the slices frequently with tongs and regulate the heat so that they color richly and evenly on both sides without burning.

As they brown, place the bacon slices on top of the Holland rusks. Remove the skillet from the heat and reserve it. Place the rusks on four individual heatproof serving plates and ladle the *marchand de vin* sauce over the bacon, dividing it equally among the slices. Set the plates in the oven to keep the bacon and sauce warm.

Add the tomato slices to the fat remaining in the skillet and, turning them frequently with a wide metal spatula, cook over moderate heat until the slices are golden brown on both sides. Place the tomato slices in one layer in a separate shallow baking dish and set them in the oven.

To poach the eggs, pour cold water into a 10- to 12-inch skillet to a depth of about 2 inches. Bring to a simmer, then reduce the heat so that the surface of the liquid barely shimmers. Break the eggs into individual saucers. Gently slide one egg from its saucer into the water and, with a large spoon, lift the white over the yolk. Repeat once or twice more to enclose the yolk completely in the white.

One at a time, slide the three other eggs from the saucers into the pan, enclosing them in their whites and spacing them at least 1 inch apart. Poach the eggs for 3 or 4 minutes, until the whites are set and the yolks feel soft when prodded gently.

With a slotted spatula transfer the poached eggs to a large bowl half-filled with lukewarm water and set them aside while you prepare the hollandaise sauce.

Before assembling the eggs *hussarde,* transfer the poached eggs to a linen towel with a slotted spatula and let them drain briefly.

Place a tomato slice on each of the sauced, ham-topped rusks and carefully place the poached eggs on the tomatoes. Ladle about 2 tablespoons of the hollandaise sauce over each egg and sprinkle the tops lightly with the paprika. Serve at once.

Eggs Sardou
POACHED EGGS WITH ARTICHOKE BOTTOMS AND CREAMED SPINACH

In a heavy 1- to 2-quart saucepan, melt 2 tablespoons of the butter over moderate heat. When the foam begins to subside, add the flour and mix well. Stirring constantly with a wire whisk, pour in the milk in a slow, thin stream and cook over high heat until the sauce comes to a boil, thickens lightly and is smooth. Reduce the heat to low and simmer for about 3 minutes to remove any raw taste of the flour. Then stir in the spinach, ½ teaspoon of the salt and the white pepper. Taste for seasoning, remove the pan from the heat and cover tightly.

Melt the remaining 4 tablespoons of butter in a heavy 10- to 12-inch skillet. Add the artichoke bottoms, concave side down, and baste them with the hot butter. Sprinkle them with the remaining ½ teaspoon of salt, reduce the heat to the lowest possible point, cover tightly and cook for several minutes until the artichoke bottoms are heated through. Do not let them brown. Remove the skillet from the heat and cover tightly to keep the artichoke bottoms warm.

To poach the eggs, pour cold water into a 12-inch skillet to a depth of about 2 inches. Bring to a simmer, then reduce the heat so that the surface of the liquid barely shimmers. Break the eggs into individual saucers. Gently slide one of the eggs from its saucer into the water, and with a large spoon, lift the white over the yolk. Repeat once or twice more to enclose the yolk completely in the white.

One at a time, slide the seven other eggs into the pan, enclosing them in their whites and spacing them about an inch apart. Poach the eggs for 3 or 4 minutes, until the whites are set and the yolks feel soft when prodded gently. With a slotted spatula, transfer the poached eggs to a large bowl half-filled with lukewarm water and set them aside while you prepare the hollandaise sauce.

Before assembling the eggs Sardou, transfer the poached eggs to a linen towel with a slotted spatula to drain briefly. If the creamed spinach and artichoke bottoms have cooled, warm them over low heat.

Spread the creamed spinach smoothly on a heated serving platter to make a bed about ¼ inch deep. Arrange the artichoke bottoms, concave sides up, on the spinach and place an egg in each one. Spoon the hollandaise sauce over the eggs and serve at once.

Bread Pudding with Whiskey Sauce

To serve 8 to 10

Preheat the oven to 350°. With a pastry brush, spread the softened butter evenly over the bottom and sides of a 13-by-9-by-2-inch baking-serving dish. Set the dish aside.

Break the bread into chunks, dropping them into a bowl as you proceed, and pour milk over them. When the bread is softened, crumble it into small bits and let it continue to soak until all the milk is absorbed.

In a small bowl, beat 3 eggs and 2 cups of sugar together with a wire whisk or a rotary or electric beater until the mixture is smooth and thick. Stir in the raisins and vanilla extract, then pour the egg mixture over the bread crumbs and stir until all the ingredients are well combined.

Pour the bread pudding into the buttered dish, spreading it evenly and smoothing the top with a rubber spatula. Place the dish in a large shallow roasting pan set on the middle shelf of the oven and pour boiling water into the pan to a depth of about 1 inch. Bake for 1 hour, or until a knife inserted in the center of the pudding comes out clean.

Meanwhile, prepare the sauce in the following fashion: Melt the butter bits in the top of a double boiler set over hot, not boiling, water. Stir 1 cup of sugar and 1 egg together in a small bowl and add the mixture to the butter. Stir for 2 or 3 minutes, until the sugar dissolves completely and the egg is cooked, but do not let the sauce come anywhere near a boil or the egg will curdle. Remove the pan from the heat and let the sauce cool to room temperature before stirring in the bourbon.

Serve the bread pudding at once, directly from the baking dish, and present the whiskey sauce separately in a sauceboat or small bowl.

PUDDING
2 tablespoons butter, softened
A 12-ounce loaf day-old French- or Italian-type white bread
1 quart milk
3 eggs
2 cups sugar
½ cup seedless raisins
2 tablespoons vanilla extract

SAUCE
8 tablespoons butter (1 quarter-pound stick), cut into ½-inch bits
1 cup sugar
1 egg
½ cup bourbon

V

The Finest Food of the Bayous

Two youthful bayou fishermen, Patrick Willis and his brother John, demonstrate the use of the most basic of all implements for catching crawfish—a stick and a string baited with a chunk of meat. Their fishing ground is a flooded rice field located near their home in St. Martinville; their modest objective is a catch of enough "crawdaddies" to suffice for a single but succulent dinner.

West and southwest of New Orleans, bordering the Gulf of Mexico, is an area that from the air looks as though a tipsy spider had been weaving webs too close to each other. This is the country of the bayous, those sluggish streams that meander amid swamps and marshlands, past low-lying farms and plantations, going everywhere and anywhere in an endless, slow processional. Traveling through bayou country is like taking a trip into a different world, for there is a silence and strangeness and almost eerie beauty here. The moody skies, the tree shadows, the very texture of the damp earth seem to contain an unspoken threat, and indeed the history of this watery land is filled with violence. Wild winds have slashed through it, bringing flood and destruction and plague in their wake. Wars have raged across its uncertain terrain. Pirate ships have used the bayous as hiding places; hunted men have come here and become hunters. And lurking in the swamps and the marshlands there have been other kinds of danger, from poisonous snakes to gently waving grass over deceptively solid-looking soil that is not soil at all but quicksand.

It is in this place where doom seems ever present yet the earth appears at its most beautiful—where lushness and horror live side by side—that the Acadians have made their homes. Theirs, too, is a history of violence: it is as though the people and the land shared a common past, and have come together not as opponents but as old friends. For both, survival alone is a cherished prize. And once an Acadian has survived, he expects to enjoy all he can in the small space of dry earth he owns and the short time he has before the next danger arrives.

Stately in a somber sunset, Bayou Teche reflects the shadows of huge old live oaks along its banks. By far the richest and most patrician of all the bayous, the Teche rises in central Louisiana and flows south about 170 miles to the Atachafalaya River. The stretch shown here is near the town of St. Martinville.

Eating is a fundamental part of that enjoyment. Acadian cooking is simple—often the ingredients of a meal are all together in one black iron pot —and extraordinarily good. It is marked by unexpected combinations of flavors, and often by a sudden lash of hot spices; just as things happen often without warning in the simplest day-to-day Acadian existence, so a new taste appears, unheralded, in the simplest dish. The food reflects not only the kind of life that is led in this land but also the land itself. There is a genuine feel of the marsh in Acadian dishes; in an odd way, what you are eating becomes inexorably bound up with the glint of sunlight on a swamp flower, with the touch of sweet yet bitter marsh air on your body, with the presence of water stretching under and around and beyond you in every direction.

A liking for Acadian foods, like a love of the bayou country, is a special taste that can never be lost once found. Finding it, however, is not easy. At first the newcomer may feel hopelessly confused, for a detailed, complete gastronomic tour of all the Acadian towns and bayous of South Louisiana is as impossible an undertaking as a listing of all the Creole dishes served in New Orleans. Perhaps the best way to begin to understand the Acadians and their cooking is to steep oneself in the beauty and quiet majesty of a bayou. And of all of them none can compare in grandeur, or in serenity, to Bayou Teche.

Stretching from above the town of Breaux Bridge in a wavering vertical line south to Berwick Bay and thence to the Gulf, the Teche is in every sense the richest and loveliest of South Louisiana's bayou waterways. It is, and always has been, the elegant bayou. Much of its past was

opulent, for there was great Creole luxury here along with Acadian simplicity. Indeed the Teche offers the ideal transition from Creole to Acadian cuisine. But approach it slowly, for life here is a slow business, to be savored with the whole body. Well before you see the Teche, give yourself time to get into the proper mood; you must prepare your taste buds and your other senses for the noblest of the bayous as you would for a great wine. Begin by going first to the city of Lafayette, the capital of the Acadian country, a few miles west of the Teche.

A morning's drive, or a 20-minute plane ride from New Orleans over miles of gray-green, mysteriously glistening land, will bring you to Lafayette in time for lunch or dinner. Go to Don's, a small, warm restaurant that serves many of the best Acadian dishes cooked in the best way. It consists of only one room, gaily and artlessly decorated, as if a child had done it overnight to please his parents. On the menu you will note the predominance of foods taken from the water—except that water here means both fresh and salt water as well as watery land and even watery air. Crabmeat, shrimp, oysters, redfish, red snapper, flounder, trout, catfish, frogs' legs and, most important, crawfish may be eaten in almost any combination—singly, one stuffed inside the other or two cooked together, as if in swimming, crawling or flying they had just joined forces and become one. There is a rich smell in the room that is like one edible concentrate.

Under the single heading of crawfish on the menu, you will find crawfish bisque, crawfish *étouffée,* fried crawfish tails, crawfish patty, stuffed crawfish heads, crawfish jambalaya and crawfish salad. The mind stum-

Crawfish: The Lobsterlike Morsel from Louisiana's Waters

Except for the fact that they live in lakes and rivers rather than the sea, Louisiana crawfish rather resemble tiny lobsters. Like lobsters, most crawfish are mahogany-colored when alive, bright red when boiled. Their meat, like lobster meat, is white and sweet, but a typical crawfish is so small—usually only three to five inches long—that only its tail yields much meat.

Crawfish (or crayfish, as they are also known) are usually caught in the wild during a short season that runs from May to July. In recent years, however, Louisianians have begun raising them in flooded fields, and an average harvest of the crustaceans now comes close to 18 million pounds a year. Since an average crawfish weighs only an ounce or so, it takes over a quarter of a billion of them to satisfy the appetites of America's crawfish aficionados.

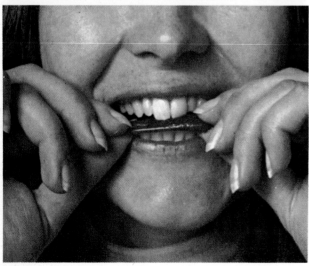

Eating boiled crawfish is a basic skill in Louisiana —but one that outsiders can easily master. (1) Holding the crawfish in both hands, snap off the ridged tail. In most cases, the yellow fat can then be pulled out of the head shell, as shown here. (2) With your thumbs, break the tail shell in half lengthwise. (3) Then pull the meat out of the tail. This is the most edible part of the crawfish, though any yellow fat left in the head shell, scooped out with the tip of a finger, is also delicious. (4) Before discarding the shells, you may want to crack the larger claws with your teeth and suck out the delicate claw meat.

Crawfish come to the table in plain and fancy guises. At their simplest, they are boiled and served in the shell, like the ones on the platter in the foreground. More elegantly, crawfish meat and fat are incorporated into such classic dishes as a crawfish bisque *(center left)*, containing shells stuffed with ground spiced crawfish meat. Crawfish jambalaya *(top left)* combines the meat with rice and vegetables, while deep-fried crawfish balls *(top right)* blend the meat with bread crumbs and seasonings. Crawfish *étouffée (center right)* is a peppery stew accompanied by rice. *(For details, see the Recipe Index.)*

bles through the list, and for a while you won't even begin to know what to order. Listen to the voices around you and you will be no less confused; many are speaking a language that sounds as if 17th Century French had come to Canada, been bounced out of Nova Scotia, wandered aimlessly for a time and then been squeezed through a Louisiana bayou and tinged with Indian, Spanish and English. Modern Acadian French sounds that way because that is exactly how it came into existence; it has a lilt almost like singing. The waitress will echo it when, at last, you turn to her for help in ordering. *"Ça depend,"* she will say, "I like the pie, me . . . *pourquoi pas le* crawfish pie?"

Take her advice and you will have learned the first rule: always eat what is suggested in "Acadiana." The pie will arrive steaming, and if you are a "foreigner" (a non-Acadian American) it will come with a small side dish of salad to make you feel at home—only the salad will be crawfish salad. The pie has a flaky crust and looks like any other pie—except that it contains crawfish tails, crawfish fat, onions, green onions, parsley and celery, all cooked together with just enough cayenne to give it a peppery lift. There is a stunning richness to the flavor that is not exactly of the land or of the sea, but from somewhere in between. You won't know where to fit it into your eating experience if all your life you have been used to separating earthy flavor from watery tang, but it is the basic taste of the best Acadian food, and a good way to begin to understand that food. Take a forkful of the crawfish salad; the fresh, crisply tart garden taste will balance the full deep flavor of the pie. Finish with a flaming *café brûlot;* it will sear all the tastes together and make you think that they are cooking all over again inside you.

Then go out and walk awhile at the edge of the city under great moss-draped oaks that stretch and arch like friendly demons overhead, past azalea bushes that bloom lazily, their purple and red and white blossoms resplendent. The air here is so heavy with moisture that you move slowly without realizing it. Your body seems to be suspended, as if you were walking underwater. Floating about you is an odor that is fresh, yet with the hint of something faintly rotten in it—a strange scent both dark with stagnant gloom and bright with the promise of green growth. All around you are the houses of Lafayette, white porticoes adjoining gray clapboards, neatly vertical on the flat earth. But the bayous and the swamps are not far away, and you can sense them in the air.

Get into your car and drive just a few miles to the town of Breaux Bridge, situated right on Bayou Teche. En route the car radio will blare the local news sometimes in English, sometimes in French. Road signs are bilingual, the gas-station attendants speak French, and as you approach Breaux Bridge you will think you have left the United States. Founded in 1859, the town has a population of a little over 5,000. It was once an advance post for trading with the Attakapa Indians, who were said to be cannibalistic. It has since become famous for another and very different reason: in honor of its centennial year, the Louisiana legislature in 1958 officially designated Breaux Bridge "La Capitale Mondiale de l'Écrevisse"—the Crawfish Capital of the World. Before you go to see the bayou, pause and watch the harvesting—and eating—of the crustaceans that have been estimated to bring the Breaux Bridge area more than a million and a half dollars in a year.

The crawfish (alias the crayfish or crawdad or creekcrab or yabbie) is a funny-looking thing to anyone unfamiliar with it, resembling a small lobster but ranging in color from cream, yellow, blue, red or green to black. Its size varies widely too; the smallest of the Louisiana species grows to only about an inch long, while a giant type in Australia reportedly reaches 16 inches. Though it is found in fresh waters on all continents except Africa, this amphibious-looking morsel—a visual emblem of the joining of land and water—is relatively unknown in North America outside of Louisiana and Texas. The state harvests more crawfish than any other area its size in the world, yet four fifths of what it harvests it eats—a sure measure of the local affection for crawfish as a food.

Unlike the famous Louisiana shrimp, which are caught in trawling nets, the crawfish are trapped in vast numbers—an estimated 20 million pounds a year—in ponds, flooded fields, lakes and practically all the marshy areas of the Atchafalaya River Basin. During the crawfish season, late winter to the end of June, thousands of trappers drop chicken-wire cages shaped like puffed hollow pillows to the bottoms of ponds, lakes and swamps. The traps, designed with a hole in one end that allows the crawfish to enter but not to leave, are baited with small pieces of meat, and a wooden stake tied with a bit of colored cloth is set up to mark the place where each trap has been sunk.

Such is the growing awareness of the delights of crawfish that rice farmers around Breaux Bridge have taken to harvesting their rice crops in the fall and then flooding their fields and harvesting crawfish from March through June. Areas overgrown with brush and trees are also being flooded and turned into crawfish farms; a sizable pond will yield anywhere from 1,000 to 2,000 pounds of crawfish per day. Commercial fishermen bring their catch to one of the many processing plants in the state where the crustaceans are washed, boiled with spices, peeled and packaged to be sold to restaurants and markets.

But the best way to get familiar with a crawfish—having first sampled a couple of the dishes it graces—is not to join the commercial fishermen but to go out on a Sunday with an Acadian family to some pond near Breaux Bridge. I went with a man whose first name is Achille (pronounced *ah-sheel,* his handsome, dark-haired, glowing-eyed wife Clea and their two young sons Theobald and Homer. (Greek names abound in Acadian homes, often the names of famous figures in Classical history or literature.) We drove a short distance out of town, then went a little farther on foot, to where the first ponds are seen and where the soil just begins to make a squishy noise underfoot. There Achille keeps a small boat, with a baited crawfish cage in it, tied under mossy lowering branches. He and his wife, who had come along politely in my honor, took me onto the skiff; from it Achille used a lift net with a piece of meat tied to the center, and also dropped the baited crawfish cage, in case the catch by hand was not so good. Theobald and Homer stayed on the banks, working furiously with just their hands and a small chunk of meat tied to a string.

By early afternoon, Achille was swearing softly in French; the lift net

had produced only a few crawfish and the cage hadn't done much better. But then he went back to it, raised it again with a shrug, and *hein! Laissez les bons temps rouler . . .* let the good times roll, his luck was with him at last. The cage had more than enough crawfish in it to justify his exertions. He held up the catch proudly to show his sons on the bank of the pond. The older one, Theobald, nodded. Homer, aged six, held up a basket with at least twice as many crawfish as their father had caught. Achille laughed and rowed toward shore.

The spring day began to wane, with a shimmering sun over the quiet pond. The flat boat glided smoothly over the water in a long restful sweep that seemed weightless to me only because I had not yet encountered the true master of marshland transportation, the pirogue—but that was to come later, in another place.

We came ashore and walked onto the bank. Clea had a surprise for me: from the car she took a black iron pot with some water and a box of matches. The boys scurried about to find enough dry sticks to build a fire. Clea rinsed a few of the crawfish, boiled the water, and with a certain vagueness dropped in some herbs and spices that she had been hiding in the pocket of her skirt—plus one more herb that she had seen growing over there by that bush. Then into the pot went the crawfish—only for a short time until they turned bright red. The water was spilled out and the boiled crawfish were laid on a plank to cool. Clea explained apologetically that they were not as good as when put in the icebox long enough to chill them, but these would do for a taste. She peeled one for me, her fingers moving as rapidly as a hummingbird's wings, so that the little red crawfish seemed held by magic in the air between her palms. But the real magic was in the flavor, for in no more than 20 minutes from start to finish, Clea had produced a food that was sweet and at the same time spice-hot, tender and fresh and salty. I tried to say that I wanted only a bit and was met with disbelieving smiles. The holder of the record for the annual crawfish-eating contest in Breaux Bridge consumed 33 pounds of them in one day, and the runners-up weren't far behind him.

A lone mosquito announcing the arrival of evening warned Achille that it was time to go home. Back at the house, Clea said she would now show me how crawfish was really done. I demurred. *Mais non,* Achille said, you can't insult an Acadian family by going home with them and then not eating. What did I catch all these *écrevisses* for? What do you mean, you've eaten . . . a day when you haven't had any rice, you haven't eaten. Just sit down and have a little blackberry wine, it makes a good apéritif, sweet and not too strong (his wife looked at him), no, not strong at all (his wife looked again), well, not *that* strong . . . a man needs something to give him an appetite, after all. While Clea cooked, Achille invited me to look around his small house. It was not one of the old-time Acadian houses; those are to be seen farther downstream on the Teche. But Acadian the house was—with a kind of simple grandeur that pervades most Acadian homes no matter where. The walls were white, the rooms immaculately clean but not overly decorated or frilly. A red cloth on a table and three bursting azaleas on the mantel stood out starkly and brilliantly. Television? Yes. Air conditioning too, though Clea person-

Opposite: In the rustic kitchen of the Acadian House Museum in St. Martinville, the makings for an Acadian breakfast of cane syrup and cornmeal mush called coush-coush *(Recipe Index)* stand ready on a table. Dating back to the 1760s, the house stands on the grounds of the Longfellow-Evangeline Memorial State Park, and is traditionally associated with the thwarted lovers whose story was celebrated by the poet Henry Wadsworth Longfellow.

The Crisp Confection That Acadians Call "Pig's Ears"

The pastries shown in the making on these and the following pages are twirled and partly folded as they fry, and long ago some unknown Acadian wit decided that the finished products looked porcine and dubbed them *oreilles de cochon*, or pig's ears. Despite their humble name, these old-time favorites of the Louisiana bayou country are an elegant sweet—and a tricky one to make. A master of the art, Mrs. Pline De Blanc *(left)*, who lives near St. Martinville, demonstrates the steps in these photographs. Mrs. De Blanc starts by preparing a batch of rich baking-powder dough. Then she breaks the dough into small pieces and rolls each of the pieces between her hands to make balls about 1 inch thick, like the ones shown at left.

Working on a lightly floured breadboard, Mrs. De Blanc maneuvers her rolling pin carefully to flatten each ball of dough into a paper-thin round 8 or 9 inches in diameter. As she completes the rounds she drapes them in a stack at the side of the board, overlapping them by about a half inch so that they can be peeled off separately without being torn when the oil in the kettle becomes hot enough for deep frying. Because of their size, pig's ears are fried and shaped one at a time, as pictured below.

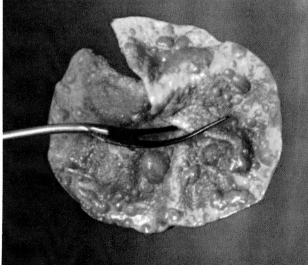

Mrs. De Blanc twists the tip of a long fork into the center of a frying round *(left)* to give it the pig's-ear shape shown at right.

After draining the shaped pig's ears briefly on paper towels, Mrs. De Blanc covers each of them with a few tablespoonfuls of cane syrup and chopped nuts, heated together just long enough to make the syrup thin and easily poured. The syrup gives the pig's ears a somewhat molasseslike flavor; the nuts add crunch to an already crisp confection.

ally doesn't like it; when she is alone in the house she always turns it off and opens the screened windows, for she prefers the warm damp breeze from the bayou.

The smells of her cooking arose as she prepared a *roux* in a black iron kettle on the stove, for in this Acadian home as in Creole kitchens a *roux* is the beginning of most dishes. Clea was making crawfish *étouffée,* possibly the best of all Acadian crawfish foods, and one that varies from cook to cook throughout the bayou country. This version combined crawfish tails with their fat, onions, bell peppers, green onion tops and parsley, all simmering with spices in the *roux* to make a thick stew that was ladled over white rice. We ate it by candlelight (another honor to a guest) and watched the velvety moths fluttering against the window screen like pieces of the night, while beyond them now and then we could see the flick of a bat's wings against a white moon. In the quietness, Achille talked of the Acadians who had been compelled to leave Canada in the *grand dérangement,* the diaspora of 1755 that separated them and sent them off in boats. Some 2,000 landed in Massachusetts, 700 in Connecticut, 300 in New York, 500 in Pennsylvania, 1,000 in Maryland, 1,200 in Virginia, 500 in North Carolina, 500 in South Carolina, 400 in Georgia and on and on. At the mercy of the British colonials, the Acadians were shipped to England or France, or kept and forced into contract labor as servants and prohibited from holding religious services. Those who eventually migrated to the bayou country of Louisiana were well trained in survival. The dangers of the swamps, the treachery of the weather were as nothing compared to what they had already endured, and they settled and prospered happily with their own customs, with a sense of joy in the land, and with an infinite ability to forget what is bad and to celebrate what is good wherever they were able to find it. A good crawfish *étouffée* is a culinary proof of that joy, for the mudbug of the bayous is turned into a rich dish that is a sort of taste salute to the swamp that yields up the crawfish as food.

At long last Achille announced that it was time for my first look at Bayou Teche. He explained, casually, that my senses were now prepared for it, and that this was the way I should first see it—at night, around 10 o'clock, when the light is silver. The moon looked wet and the water looked dry. Its black, seemingly motionless surface was like polished onyx, covered here and there with splotches of deep, shining green. One or two cypress trees bent over the stream, as if they had come to pray, their knotty knees jutting out of it; great oaks bowed, their branches filled with moss like pieces torn from clouds.

The word *teche* is said to come from an Indian word, *tenche,* meaning snake. Across the twisting waters of this bayou, great Creole plantations and modest Acadian dwellings—as well as the houses of Anglo-Saxons —have all confronted each other. Splendor has been here and poverty, storms and balmy days, yellow-fever epidemics and health. And dominating everything has been the bayou. Along its banks there are rows and arches, endless avenues and double avenues of spreading live oaks —"the emblem of the Teche." Moss swings over the clumps of motionless cane and over the fans of palmettos. A few water hyacinths float here and there on the water; in the past, they threatened to multiply until they choked all navigation and became a nightmare that had to be erased. There are orange trees and magnolias; everywhere on the banks tiny wild flowers bloom and glint, night and day, like sequins.

Follow the royal Teche downstream in the early morning to St. Martinville, once called the "Petit Paris" of this bayou, where titled émigrés lived a rococo life in supreme Creole elegance—giving fêtes and balls and dancing the minuet down to the water's edge. Their opulence is gone now, and St. Martinville is known not because of the Creoles but because it is the last resting place of an Acadian heroine who is revered almost as a saint, though some say she never really existed. Her name was Evangeline, and she is the symbol of all Acadiana. You had better listen to her story; you won't be allowed to leave Acadian country without hearing it. If you arrive at breakfast time, stop first and have a dish of coush-coush with some family along the road. Acadian hospitality makes all other Southern hospitality look meager and, if you speak French at all, you won't be allowed even to ask directions from a family here without sharing their food. Coush-coush, often served in the morning, is a fried cornmeal mush that may be eaten either with salt and pepper or with syrup or sugar and hot milk. I prefer it the second way—sweet on the tongue and energy-making in the stomach; it is to cereals what gumbo is to other soups. If you arrive later than breakfast, say around 11, the family may sit you down to a plate of *poulet aux gros oignons*—fine hot chicken cooked with onions, green peppers and other vegetables. With a little cold beer, this hearty dish will make you want to sit back for a story. Follow it with a cup of thick black Acadian coffee, which makes even Creole coffee look limpid, and any story is bound to seem real. . . .

Take, for instance, the story of Emmeline Labiche, an orphan girl who lived in the 18th Century in Acadie in French Canada. She was 16 when she became engaged to a young villager named Louis Arceneaux. The day before the wedding, the new British masters of Canada dealt the great blow—the forced exodus of the Acadians. The pair was separated and each put on a different boat, headed for different destinations. Emmeline hardly noticed where her boat docked; the hardships that followed were nothing to her. Wherever she was taken, she had only one goal, to be reunited with her lost love. In time she arrived in the bayou country, caring not at all for the lush new Eden, searching for one face. One day, walking in St. Martinville, she saw a man seated under a heavy oak tree in the park. She went pale, ran forward and reached out to him. Louis Arceneaux rose to meet her. There was a moment's silence, then he mumbled something about never having expected to see her again; and something else about being pledged to another woman. He turned abruptly and walked away.

Emmeline, the story goes, lost her mind and wandered daily along the banks of the Teche like an Acadian Ophelia, picking wild flowers and moss until at last her health gave way and she died. Her guardian, it was said, lived to be 103 and visited the girl's grave daily until she too died, in 1830. About 15 years later, in the distant North, the novelist Nathaniel Hawthorne retold the story, as he had heard it from a minister, to his friend Henry Longfellow. The poet began to read up on the history

Opposite: In Thibodaux, the largest town on Bayou Lafourche, everyone knows Lester Bourgeois as the *boudin,* or sausage man. Men of his family have been making *boudin* locally as long as anybody can remember, and the shop he inherited from his father is now the only one of its kind in town. In the picture he holds a chunk of *fromage de tête de cochon,* or headcheese; on the block before him, ranged clockwise from left foreground, are *boudin rouge* (blood sausage), *saucisse boucaner* (smoked pork sausage), a slab of the headcheese, several links of *boudin blanc* (a sausage made with pork shoulder), and *andouilles* (smoked sausages that are made with meat taken from the neck and stomach).

and geography, the flora and fauna of the bayou country and its people. In the long poem he produced, by now a classic, the heroine is named Evangeline and Louis is named Gabriel. The story deviates from the South Louisiana version, for Evangeline follows Gabriel much longer, and finds him only when he is dying in a hospital. But the Acadians have adopted Longfellow's Evangeline as their own folk heroine and are now convinced that she truly existed—that Evangeline and Emmeline are one. Today the area around St. Martinville is called "Evangeline country," and in the town you may visit the "Evangeline Oak" under whose broad branches Emmeline Labiche is said to have come upon Louis Arceneaux. In the graveyard of the St. Martinville Catholic Church, which still has part of its original chapel, built in 1765, there is a small grave topped by the life-sized figure of a young girl. This is the last resting place of Emmeline; but the tombstone also bears the name Evangeline. Some say that there are times when you can feel her presence in the town. And if you are a man who goes for a walk at night with an Acadian girl, past the grave or under the oak, she is more than likely to walk close to you; even the shyest girl may take your hand, to make sure that for that one second she is not alone. . . .

Yet even on the most beautiful bayou, all is not so romantic or so sweet. Life is a practical business in and around St. Martinville. Walk not far outside the town to a small group of Acadian homes where a *boucherie,* a cooperative butchering, is taking place. Family, neighbors and relatives have all gathered for the day-long affair. Very early in the morning fires are lit under two huge black iron pots, one filled with water, the other to be used to cook the cracklings. First the men go to butcher the pigs, whose squeals cut the air like knives. The skin is removed and the cracklings cook slowly until they are of a light amber hue, salty, crisp and yet so fragile they melt on the tongue. There is a holiday air to the proceedings as the women busy themselves throughout the day making two kinds of sausage, *boudin* and *andouille, chaudin* (stuffed *ponce, Recipe Index)* and *fromage de tête de cochon* (headcheese). The two sausages are garlicky and dark-flavored, the first slightly more pungent than the second, but both fire-making in one's insides. The *chaudin* is still richer, with the kind of taste that makes your ears feel as if they were glowing. The headcheese is light, with a delicate flavor. Best of all is the backbone stew *(Recipe Index)* that everyone will share toward the end of the day, a stew made of the pig's leftovers, including the backbone and the ribs. Ladled over the ever-present Acadian rice, backbone stew seems to absorb all the other flavors—delicate and rich, sweet and salt, spicy and smooth—in a way that makes you wonder why anybody ever bothers eating beef when there is pork around.

After you have eaten some of it, walk to the bayou's edge both for exercise, which you will need, and to observe the colors of the darkening sky mirrored on the water. It is a curious fact about the bayou that it never quite looks the same as when you last saw it. Bend over the glittering surface of the water and your own reflection will stare back as if it had always been secretly lurking there, waiting for you to arrive. The flowers and trees and the clouds, too, may be seen reflected in the water, like parts of an antimatter world glimpsed for an instant in cold clear silver before darkness comes. There is a strangeness about the Teche that has never quite been explained, and one feels it particularly in the evening.

There have in fact been many people who have sensed the mystery, and those who have lived here have often taken on strange and outlandish ways—or at least they have kept to the "old country" ways that seem strange and outlandish to other Americans. Elsewhere in the United States it would seem odd for funeral announcements to be tacked to town posts rather than printed in an obituary column, so that those who wish to learn about the *veillées,* or wakes, can do so by just taking a stroll. Elsewhere you do not find starkly simple things so harmoniously joined in space and time to things of great luxury. Not so far from where I visited the *boucherie,* there lived, in the 19th Century, a Creole planter named Charles Durand. He was a rich man even before he arrived from France to lay out one of the biggest plantations in the area. He did things in a big way, this Durand; if he decided to be surrounded by trees, there had to be an avenue of them three miles long, alternating pines with oaks. The ornaments of his carriages were made of gold. The banquets he gave were not just banquets, they were more like orgies, huge feasts of flavors that rose steaming from gumbos and jambalayas, bisques and *gâteaux,* of endless varieties of edibles from town and country, Acadian and Creole and European and African and Indian and West Indian dishes. The banquets became so famous that Durand was at a loss for something special to do when, a few years before the Civil War, his two daughters simultaneously accepted marriage proposals.

He had already served the best food anyone around had ever eaten, laid out in a more grandiose manner than anyone had ever seen. But Durand was a resourceful man. He imported a large load of enormous spiders, and a few days before the double wedding he set them loose in his trees. The spiders went to work spinning webs from branch to branch, leaf to leaf, top to top, connecting each tree with the next in a vast intricate filigree of lacework. The morning of the wedding, Durand had a great many bellows filled with gold and silver dust, and ordered the thousands of webs to be thoroughly sprayed. The dust stuck to the cobwebs and Durand's daughters were married, his guests wined and dined, beneath a three-mile canopy of glittering, wildly delicate silver and gold. Another host might have feared the tropical weather here; one short burst of rain would have ruined the décor. But Durand had no fear—and of course it didn't rain.

Always the Bayou Teche leads south, curling and recurling, down toward the Gulf. Here is a house, there a bank shaded only by oaks. Farther along, the oaks nearly meet overhead, and in the deepening green gloom there is a stillness broken only by the scream of crickets in the late afternoon. The light thickens; living things hardly move. A boy fishing looks like the far-reaching root of the tree he is standing next to; just his eyes move as you come near and even the line that hangs from his pole into the black water makes no ripples. You get a sense here of the jungle, where survival depends not so much on your ability to move quickly as on your ability to stand as motionless as wood. But you can talk to the

Continued on page 151

To start the *boucherie,* the Landreneau men douse the slaughtered pig with boiling water and scrape off its bristles.

Making the Most of a 100-Pound Hog at an Old-fashioned Acadian Boucherie

For Acadians, the butchering of a hog can become a social event with festive overtones. Years ago hog butcherings, called *boucheries,* were held everywhere in Acadian country, and always in winter, when cool weather gave farmers a little latitude for curing meat before it spoiled. Nowadays you must go deep into the back bayous to find a *boucherie,* and it may be held at almost any time of year, for modern refrigeration makes the weather irrelevant. These pictures show a *boucherie* in the countryside near Mamou, at the home of Alcée Landreneau. The time was spring, and the participants included practically every known relative of the Landreneau family. Starting early in the morning with a squealing 100-pound hog, the Landreneau clan proceeded to turn out headcheese, blood sausage, white sausage, cracklings, backbone stew and a variety of other tasty products, and ended with an enormous feast eaten under the trees and garnished with the music of an Acadian trio.

146

With Sady Courville *(left)* and Cyprien Landreneau on fiddles, and Preston Manuel playing guitar, music fills the spring air all through the afternoon. Meanwhile Mrs. Alice Fruge *(left, below)* and Mrs. Adam Landreneau busily stuff *boudin* (sausage meat) into hog intestine and commercial casings. Late in the day, when appetites have been sated, the trio will play waltzes and galops and the young folks will dance.

In well-seasoned iron pots, stews and cracklings cook over hardwood coals for the *boucherie* feast. The pot at left above contains *grattons,* or cracklings, fragments of pork skin fried to crispness in their own lard. Bubbling in the other pots are various parts of the pig, mostly such plebeian cuts as backbone and leftover scraps, although ribs are sometimes added for good measure. At right, Mrs. Fruge ladles cracklings into a bowl; in a moment they will be salted and served, still hot, as an hors d'oeuvre.

A finished dish at last: *chaudin,* stuffed pig's stomach, with a bowl of savory pork gravy to be spooned over it. A sort of Acadian haggis, the *chaudin* contains ground pork seasoned with onions, garlic, parsley and pepper.

The members of the clan gather around the laden table. Besides all the various pork dishes there are salad, rice dressing, yams and bread.

Having waited nearly all day for something, *anything,* to eat, Marcella Fruge helps herself to an overflowing plate of pork stew, rice dressing, green salad, baked sweet yam, cracklings, pork sausage and *boudin.* Later she went on to have seconds.

young fisherman and get a friendly reply. The basket behind him is half-filled with catfish, their long feelers waving like whiskers in the air. Behind that a short distance is the house where the boy lives; it is stark, made of cypress; the walls are daubed with mud and Spanish moss. There is a built-in porch and a high steep-pitched roof. The porch, or gallery, runs the width of the house and fronts on the bayou. The steep roof makes a spacious attic, called a *garçonnière,* where the boy and his brothers sleep now that they have grown too big for the trundle bed downstairs; the attic is reached by means of a staircase leading from the front porch, and the stairs also provide extra sitting places for family and visiting friends. Outside the kitchen window is a long *tablette,* a vital part of the home: a long, wide slab of wood on which the boy's mother can do everything from washing dishes to cleaning vegetables. Right now she is using it as a vantage point to keep an eye on her son and two of her chickens which are being teased by a neighbor dog, and as a flat surface to work on as she chops up some peppers in preparation for supper.

Lunch, which she calls dinner, is already made. She beckons and the boy seems to see her without turning. Go with him; his mother will welcome you to a dish of dark brown gravy and chopped chicken giblets cooked with rice until not a white grain can be seen. It is called dirty rice and it is another of the original soul foods—as good to the body and spirit as it is to the palate. The steam smells better than you thought steam could, and the taste is as rich and dark-stained as the rice. Whoever first said that rice should always be "fluffy and dry" is here disproved. It should often be soft and wet as the swamp air around you now or the ground under your feet. On one end of the *tablette* there is a platter of fried catfish from an earlier catch. The chunks of fish are golden and crisp on the outside, oily and smooth and hot within. There is a sweet taste to them that lingers even after they are eaten. The Acadians know how to fry plain catfish so well that they make it seem the most subtle of all seafoods. Beyond the plate, at the edge of the *tablette,* a yellow and black grasshopper hangs. It is bigger than any grasshopper you will find outside of the bayou country, and the boy sees it too. He goes on eating with one hand, and with the other he flicks it into a tin can, to be used later for bait. Then he finishes his meal and wanders back to the water's edge, and you take your leave.

Farther downstream is New Iberia, named by Spanish settlers. Long forced to take second place to the opulent "Petit Paris" of St. Martinville, New Iberia's strategic location on the Teche eventually made it a first-class city on its own—a center for fishermen and trappers, moss pickers and shippers of salt from the nearby mines. An excellent way to look around is to go first to one of the little restaurants in town and buy an order of stuffed Louisiana shrimp. Have them wrapped in a brown paper cone, and dip into it leisurely as you walk through the gardens of Shadows-on-the-Teche, a restored mansion that was once part of a great plantation. It is one of the handsomest houses on the bayou, with tall, slim, stately columns—an extraordinary example of European and other influences that combined to produce a new architectural style in the Louisiana country. In the gardens you hear the calls of Acadian boatmen passing on the bayou. Shadows was begun in 1830 by the owner of the plantation, David Weeks, and his master builder James Bedell. It took three years, and on the brink of its completion Weeks died. Later the Civil War, malaria, cholera plagues and capricious sugar and cotton prices all took their toll. Then, after World War I, the great-grandson of the original owner, Weeks Hall, took up residence and began the patient process of restoring the mansion to its old splendor. The interior is in the style of a French château; the columns are Tuscan; the deep porches are traditional bayou. As you wander through the gardens, with their statuary and their old camellia trees and oaks, you sense the elegant ease of the life that was lived here.

The waters of the Teche pass Shadows gracefully, nearing their journey's end in the Gulf. Before you follow the bayou to its last stop, take the time for a side trip to Avery Island, where hot peppers grow in a profusion of colors—crimson, yellow and green on the same bush—like vegetables that have soaked up almost too much richness from the earth. In the fall they are picked by employees of the McIlhenny Company, ground and fermented for three years and mixed with vinegar to produce a sauce once known only to South Louisiana cooks but now used all over the world —Tabasco. Thanks to Tabasco, the tastes of the old Creoles and Acadians affect the eating habits of people who know nothing of their cuisines. Oysters in Athens are enhanced, and hangovers in Hong Kong helped, by the flavor of Avery Island's vinegar-soaked red peppers. Walter McIlhenny, the current owner of the company, is himself a gourmet, a gentleman of the old school who knows more about peppers than anybody has a right to know, and who adds the flavor to his own food with the deft hand of a master artist.

Not far from Avery Island, visit Abbeville and the extensive fields of yellow cane that produce sugar and syrup for Louisiana kitchens. Walk through Steen's syrup mill; the smell of boiling cane syrup that swims up from the great vats is one of those smells that should be given to every child as a present in itself. Once you have sniffed it in your early years, it will haunt you for the rest of your life, like the memory of a tune. The very last of the boiled syrup becomes thick as taffy, the color of gold in amber. This final stage, the essence of syrup, is called *la cuite,* after the French for "cooking"; if you leave a fractious child alone with a very small can of it and a spoon, you will return to find him lamblike. Steen's *la cuite* has a taste so sweet it is wicked. Acadian youngsters dip balls of salty hot popcorn into it. The lightness of the corn with the heaviness of the syrup, the tang of the salt with the intensity of the sweet produce a taste that can best be described as an entire fiesta. Acadian grandmothers have another use for *la cuite:* they mix it with eggs, flour, salt, cinnamon, allspice, cloves, fruit juice, candied fruit peels, dates, candied pineapple, raisins and nuts to make the sort of fruitcake that explodes its flavor like the shattering of a lovely prism. Buy a slice of Acadian fruitcake at a local grocery to savor as you drive back to the bayou. But be careful to hold the cake with two fingers only—and careful not to touch the steering wheel with those two fingers, or your life for the next hour will make W. C. Fields' famous act with flypaper seem a mere rehearsal.

En route back to the bayou stop at the Rip Van Winkle Gardens, where the wet climate and fertile soil have produced a gardener's dream of grandeur. You are on Jefferson Island now, another of the five islands in this vicinity. The pirate Jean Laffite sought refuge here, and is rumored, inevitably, to have buried some treasure—a claim partly substantiated several decades ago when one treasure hunter turned up pots of Spanish, Mexican, French and American gold and silver coins. During the 19th Century the island was turned into a hunting and fishing preserve by the well-known actor Joseph Jefferson. The gardens are named for his most famous role, that of Rip Van Winkle, and they will do for your eye and nose what that fruitcake just did for your tongue. Crape myrtle, magnolias, yellow jasmine, oleanders and gardenias lie in a sweeping rainbow under mossy live oaks. Through the flowers, an immense black iron antique sugar kettle can be seen, in which cane juice was originally boiled over open fires. There are cascades of daffodils and narcissuses, sheets of camellias and azaleas and wisteria, glitterings of hollyhocks, bougainvilleas, forget-me-nots, hydrangeas . . . and more and still more, until the colors and the sweet aromas seem to have melded with the aftertaste of the fruitcake to make you dizzy.

From Jefferson Island, drive back to Bayou Teche and follow it the short distance south to Morgan City, where it empties into Berwick Bay, at the mouth of the Atchafalaya River. The water here is so deep that barges had to be sunk to provide a stable bottom for the bridge that spans the bay. The air is fresh, with a salt tinge to it. The accents are many, mostly French and Spanish and Italian. Oystermen and fishermen and trappers bring their catches to Morgan City, and along its waterfront the shrimp fleet is blessed once a year—on Sunday morning of Labor Day weekend —by a priest who sprinkles holy water over the gaily festooned boats before they set out. If you are lucky enough to be there that day, the finest way to watch is through the window of a small four-table restaurant, over a plate of fried shrimp. The shrimp will surely be the freshest you have ever eaten. They have been dipped in a seasoned batter and fried so fast that they come out like feathers; they make you wonder why people ever call fried food heavy when it is so clearly the opposite. Inside the shells of batter are the fresh, succulent, hot shrimp. On the tar-soaked docks, some Acadians are now cheering the priest as he invokes God's blessing for the shrimp trawlers. The holy water is sprinkled, the crowd roars, and the little boats, strung with multicolored flags, set out to trawl in the Gulf.

Before the day ends in a Gulf mist, you will want to visit a different kind of bayou setting—and even before that, you will want to experience an old Acadian custom as applicable to travel as it is to food: the custom of lagniappe—literally translated, "something extra." If you order a dozen cookies of one kind from an Acadian baker, you will find that you have been given 13—or 12 plus a couple of strange-looking cookies you never expected. The lagniappe cookies are the baker's way of saying that he hopes you will come back. Similarly, if you travel with an Acadian down Bayou Teche, he will not leave you when the trip is over. Instead, he will take some time off—two or three days if necessary—to show you a couple of other places in Acadiana not in any way connected to the bayou, places you did not expect to visit. There is always a little "something extra" to see in this part of the world, he will explain, no matter how much time or trouble it takes; there is always just one more taste.

West of the Teche is an area of many square miles, a place of smaller bayous and wooded "islets," of grasslands and rice fields, where not so very long ago Acadians were concentrated in their greatest number. As recently as World War II the automobile was hardly known in this area; people traveled by horse and buggy. In some places cattle graze in herds still tended by Acadian cowboys on horseback, for all the world like their Texas counterparts, except that they are smaller in build, dark, and speak a language that would give a Texas horse the hiccups.

Many of the old ways are also still to be seen at gatherings of local people. One such occasion is a *fais dodo,* originally a sort of Acadian hoedown; the name now seems a misnomer because *fais dodo* is translated literally as "go to sleep," and these festivities, eating as well as dancing, may well continue till dawn. A rich beef stew, sometimes called cow gumbo, may be served, darkly pungent, spice-hot, redolent with onions and fresh thyme, and for dancing there is an Acadian band—accordion, fiddle and "ting-a-ling," or triangle. Entire families may be present; certainly not one child has been left at home. There are no baby-sitters hereabouts, or if there are, they are the *nainaines,* the godmothers, or maybe the grandmothers—and they don't like being left at home either. At the old parties, one side of the room was allotted to the children and the *nainaines* who kept them quiet, preferably sleeping, while the band played on. Nowadays, a mother will hold her baby in her lap until she gets up to dance, and then will hand her charge to someone else. As the evening wears on, there will be coffee, and to complement its strong taste, crumbly Acadian sugar cakes and cookies so powdery sweet and light that they almost dissolve in the hand. Then to keep the infants sleeping, a song may be sung:

> *Fais dodo, Minette* . . .
> *Fais dodo, mon piti bébé,*
> *Quand quinze ans aura passé,*
> *Minette va so marier.*

> Go to sleep, my kitten . . .
> Go to sleep, my little baby,
> When fifteen years have fled,
> My kitten will be wed.

Marriage is in the air at all times in the backlands, and a proper Acadian wedding reception makes a *fais dodo* seem niggardly by comparison. Harnett Kane reports that in the late 1930s, he saw no fewer than a hundred horses and buggies flocking to one such reception, and it wasn't considered a very large one. Second in importance only to the bride and groom are the cakes, so many different kinds and in such profusion that they are uncountable. For days before the wedding, members of the bride's family are at work, making cakes of all sizes and colors; there can't be too many and too few would cause more than a few remarks from the guests

154

Continued on page 158

Bred from seeds imported from Mexico in 1848, pepper plants flourish on Avery Island. Only fully ripe red peppers go into Tabasco sauce. A pepper picker *(below)* earns from 12 to 14 cents per pound.

Salt below, Peppers above, on an Island That Isn't an Island

Rising some 150 feet above the lowlands 125 miles west of New Orleans, Avery Island is at once an agricultural marvel and a contradiction in terms. It is not an island, but an oversized hillock, surrounded by marshes and swampy thicket. It consists of a base of pure salt and—loosely speaking—a topping of peppers. The Avery and McIlhenny families, owners of the "island," mine salt and enjoy their exceptionally beautiful gardens while growing the peppers used to make Tabasco, the world's best-known hot sauce. Developed over 100 years ago, Tabasco sears mouths from Copenhagen to Hong Kong—and every drop still comes from the pepper fields of Avery.

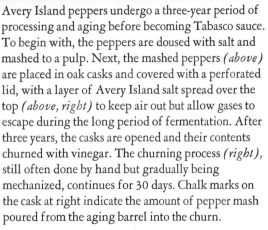

Avery Island peppers undergo a three-year period of processing and aging before becoming Tabasco sauce. To begin with, the peppers are doused with salt and mashed to a pulp. Next, the mashed peppers *(above)* are placed in oak casks and covered with a perforated lid, with a layer of Avery Island salt spread over the top *(above, right)* to keep air out but allow gases to escape during the long period of fermentation. After three years, the casks are opened and their contents churned with vinegar. The churning process *(right)*, still often done by hand but gradually being mechanized, continues for 30 days. Chalk marks on the cask at right indicate the amount of pepper mash poured from the aging barrel into the churn.

The vat at left contains an awe-inspiring quantity of pure, very hot Tabasco sauce—strained, filtered and ready for bottling. One last technological trick draws the liquid through the tiny nozzle hole of a Tabasco-sauce bottle: an ingenious machine sucks the air out of the bottle, creating a vacuum inside, and the sauce is automatically drawn in. Over 10 million bottles like the one below are dispatched from Avery Island every year.

as to the happiness in store for the newlyweds. In the homes of some brides, there is still a room designated as the Cake Room. On the wedding day it will be given over to cakes of every description; white and pink, beige and yellow and cherry red; plain and sugared; round and square and flat and raised; firm and flaky; brittle and crunchy; sweet and fruity and tart—and all wondrously good. There will be some other things to eat too, and drinks to toast with, but it is the cakes that give this happy event its fairy-tale quality.

There are other celebrations in the backlands for which no invitation is needed. In April, in the town of Mansura, there is a Cochon de Lait festival, and the smells of roast piglet singe the air for miles around. The 20- to 30-pound pigs are set in rows over blistering hot hickory fires, at just the right height to ensure that the excess fat will drain out, drip into the flames, and rise again as smoke to crisp and flavor each piglet's skin and turn it the color of dark honey. When done, the inside is tender and juicy, the outside is as brittle as well-cooked bacon. The Governor of Louisiana has granted Mansura the title of La Capitale du Cochon de Lait, and presiding over the fête each year is last year's queen, a slim young girl who carries her honor as proudly as if she were Miss America—only she is Miss Cochon de Lait, or Miss Suckling Pig. She abdicates daintily as this year's queen is chosen, and in the smoke-filled air the happily crunching crowds pause just long enough to murmur their approval.

There is one final bit of lagniappe for the traveler available in one or another of the smaller country towns between Mansura and Breaux Bridge where old-time barbecues are still held. A good slow Acadian barbecue can put the Cochon de Lait festival out of mind in short order. It generally takes place in the woods, where men dig a five-foot trench and line it with branches of aromatic leaves from bay, sassafras, hickory and pecan. Smoldering embers of oak as well as hickory and pecan are laid on top, to be followed by more leaves, layer upon layer up to the top of the trench; chicken wire is stretched over the whole. Great cuts of beef, pork and, sometimes, mutton are seasoned with salt and pepper and a sprinkle of sage and thyme. The meat is placed on the chicken-wire grill and basted from a boiling black iron pot that contains a sauce made of oil or lard, onion, garlic, shallots and herbs and spices. The meat cooks slowly—it stifles, rather, in the smoke from the wood and the leaves, until the red coals can be seen at the bottom of the trench. The smell hangs upon the air like a thundercloud; it makes all other cooking smells a little insipid. The flavor of the different meats, basted from the top and seared by the blend of aromatic smoke from the bottom, is both delicate and strong, rich and simple, and once it is tasted it will ruin you for other barbecues in other places. This is the way meat should always be cooked, saturated with tastes of earth and green and wood; and the way it should always be eaten, in country air that is polluted by nothing more than the sharp, challenging scents of food and wild flowers.

And now your lagniappe tour is done. You must leave the woods and go back to the water, for always water must be returned to in bayou country, like the reprise of a much-loved song. It is time now to see the life and sample the cooking in a very different kind of bayou.

Opposite: The whole world knows Tabasco, but only Louisianians know some of the other condiments used to brighten the products of Creole and Acadian kitchens. In the picture opposite, an array of Louisiana's favorite condiments and spices—jars of Creole mustard and filé powder, bottles of whole and chopped peppers, and freshly picked ripe peppers—is displayed on the back porch of the Acadian House Museum in St. Martinville.

CHAPTER V RECIPES

To serve 2

2 one-pound oven-ready squab
  pigeons
½ teaspoon ground hot red pepper
  (cayenne)
1 teaspoon salt
2 tablespoons butter
2 tablespoons vegetable oil
½ cup finely chopped onions
½ cup finely chopped celery
2 medium-sized carrots, scraped and
  thinly sliced
¼ cup finely chopped scallions,
  including 3 inches of the green
  tops
¼ cup flour
2 cups chicken stock, fresh or
  canned
½ cup dry red wine
¼ pound firm fresh mushrooms,
  trimmed, wiped with a dampened
  towel and cut lengthwise
  including the stems into ¼-inch-
  thick slices
½ cup fresh or thoroughly
  defrosted frozen Lima beans
2 tablespoons finely chopped fresh
  parsley, preferably the flat-leaf
  Italian variety

To serve 4

2 cups yellow cornmeal, preferably
  the water-ground variety
½ cup unsifted flour
1 tablespoon double-acting baking
  powder
2 teaspoons sugar
2 teaspoons salt
1½ cups water
8 tablespoons lard

Pigeon Casserole

Wash the pigeons briefly under cold running water and pat them completely dry, inside and out, with paper towels. Season the cavities and skin of the birds with ¼ teaspoon of the red pepper and ½ teaspoon of the salt, then truss them neatly.

In a heavy 4- to 5-quart casserole, melt the butter with the oil over moderate heat. When the foam begins to subside, place the pigeons in the casserole and brown them, turning the birds about with a spoon and regulating the heat so that they color richly and evenly on all sides without burning. Transfer the birds to a plate and set them aside.

Add the onions, celery, carrots and scallions to the fat remaining in the casserole and, stirring frequently, cook for 8 to 10 minutes, or until the vegetables are soft and delicately browned. Add the flour and mix well. Stirring constantly, pour in the chicken stock and the red wine in a slow, thin stream and cook over high heat until the sauce mixture comes to a boil and thickens lightly.

Stir in the mushrooms, Lima beans and the remaining ¼ teaspoon of red pepper and ½ teaspoon of salt. Return the pigeons and the liquid that has accumulated around them to the casserole and turn the birds about with a spoon to coat them evenly with the sauce and vegetables.

Reduce the heat to low and partially cover the casserole. Turning the birds from time to time, simmer for about 45 minutes, or until they are tender and a thigh shows no resistance when pierced deeply with the point of a small sharp knife.

Taste for seasoning, add the parsley and serve at once, directly from the casserole or from a large heated bowl.

Coush-Coush
FRIED CORNMEAL

Combine the cornmeal, flour, baking powder, sugar and salt in a deep bowl and stir with a wooden spoon until all the ingredients are thoroughly combined. Pour in the water and stir vigorously to make a smooth, thick paste.

In a heavy 9- to 10-inch cast-iron skillet, melt the lard over moderate heat until it is hot but not smoking. Add the cornmeal mixture and pat it flat in the skillet with the back of the spoon. Then increase the heat to high and fry the cornmeal cake for 10 to 12 minutes, or until it is brown and crusty on the bottom.

Stir the cornmeal mixture to distribute the bits of brown crust evenly through it. Reduce the heat to low, cover the skillet tightly, and cook the coush-coush for 15 minutes longer.

Spoon the coush-coush into heated individual bowls and serve at once, as a breakfast cereal.

Coush-coush is traditionally accompanied by milk and sugar, or by pure cane syrup *(see Glossary)*.

A hunter's well-earned reward lies in a hearty casserole of pigeon enhanced by onions, celery, carrots, mushrooms and Lima beans in a red-wine sauce.

To make about 3 dozen 1-inch balls

5 pounds live crawfish or ½ pound
   frozen crawfish meat, thoroughly
   defrosted and drained, and
   chopped into small bits
2 tablespoons butter
2 tablespoons flour
½ cup milk
¼ teaspoon ground hot red pepper
   (cayenne)
½ teaspoon salt
2 tablespoons finely chopped fresh
   parsley, preferably the flat-leaf
   Italian variety
2 tablespoons finely chopped
   scallions, including 3 inches of
   the green tops
3 eggs
3 cups soft fresh crumbs made from
   French- or Italian-type white
   bread, pulverized in a blender
Vegetable oil for deep frying

Crawfish Balls

*Crawfish are farmed commercially in Louisiana and are available there
most of the year. During the summer, live crawfish also may be found in
some Midwest and Pacific states, and purchased at gourmet fish markets
or stores that specialize in Scandinavian foods. Frozen crawfish meat may
be ordered from many fish dealers. Both live crawfish and the frozen
meat can be obtained by mail (see Shopping Guide, page 199).*

Soak the live crawfish in cold water for at least 10 minutes, then wash
them thoroughly under cold running water. In a heavy 8- to 10-quart
pot, bring 4 quarts of water to a boil over high heat. Using tongs, drop in
the crawfish and boil them briskly, uncovered, for 5 minutes.

Drain the crawfish in a large colander and, when they are cool enough
to handle, shell them one at a time in the following manner: With your
hands, break off the ridged tail, snap it in half lengthwise and lift out the
meat in one piece. If you like, you can snap off the large claws, break
them with a nutcracker and pick out the bits of claw meat.

Some or all of the yellow fat or "butter" from the body of the crawfish
may slide out when you break off the tail. If it does not, cut off the top of
the head just behind the eyes, scoop the body shell clean with the tip of
one thumb and pick out the yellow fat. Chop the crawfish meat into small
bits, and reserve the meat and fat (there will be about 2 cups). Discard
the shells, heads and intestinal matter. (Frozen crawfish meat needs only
to be defrosted and drained, then chopped into small bits.)

In a heavy 1- to 1½-quart saucepan, melt the butter over moderate
heat. Add the flour and mix well. Stirring constantly with a wire whisk,
pour in the milk in a slow, thin stream and cook over high heat until the
mixture comes to a boil, thickens heavily and is smooth. Reduce the heat
to low and simmer uncovered for 2 or 3 minutes.

Stir in the red pepper and salt and, with a rubber spatula, scrape the
entire contents of the pan into a deep bowl. Add the reserved crawfish
meat and fat, the parsley and scallions, and mix all the ingredients
together gently but thoroughly. Taste for seasoning.

Break the eggs into a shallow bowl and beat them to a froth with a
fork or wire whisk. Spread the bread crumbs on a plate or a piece of wax
paper. Scoop up about 1 tablespoonful of the crawfish mixture at a time
and, with your hands, pat and shape it into a ball about 1 inch in diameter. As you form each ball, roll it in the bread crumbs, immerse it in the
beaten eggs, then roll it in the crumbs again to coat it evenly. Arrange the
balls side by side on wax paper and refrigerate them for at least 30 minutes to firm the coating.

Preheat the oven to its lowest setting. Line a large shallow baking pan
with paper towels and place it in the middle of the oven.

Pour the oil into a deep fryer or large saucepan to a depth of 3 inches.
Heat the oil to a temperature of 350° on a deep-frying thermometer.

Deep-fry the crawfish balls, five or six at a time, turning them with a
slotted spoon for about 3 minutes, or until they are golden brown and
crisp on all sides. As they brown, transfer the balls to the lined pan and
keep them warm in the oven while you deep-fry the rest.

Serve the crawfish balls hot, as a first course or with drinks.

Boiled Crawfish

Combine the water, lemons, onions, celery, chili, garlic, shellfish boil and salt in a 10- to 12-quart enameled pot, and bring to a boil over high heat. Cover tightly, reduce the heat to low, and cook for 20 minutes.

Meanwhile, soak the live crawfish in a sinkful of cold water for at least 10 minutes, then wash them thoroughly—a small batch at a time—in a colander set under cold running water.

With tongs, drop about 5 pounds of the live crawfish into the pot and boil briskly, uncovered, for 5 minutes. Transfer the boiled crawfish to a heated platter, then drop about 5 more pounds of live crawfish into the stock remaining in the pot and boil them for 5 minutes. Repeat the entire procedure two more times and, when all of the crawfish have been boiled, serve them at once in their shells. (For directions on how to crack and eat crawfish, see page 132.) Because they are so highly spiced, they are eaten without any accompaniment except cold beer.

NOTE: In Louisiana, crabs and shrimp are boiled and served in the same fashion as crawfish. Substitute three dozen live blue crabs or 4 pounds of large shrimp in their shells for the crawfish, and boil them in one batch. Boil the crabs for 10 to 15 minutes, the shrimp 5 minutes.

To serve 4 to 6

6 to 8 quarts water
2 lemons, cut in half crosswise
4 medium-sized onions, with skins intact
2 celery stalks, including the leaves, cut into 3-inch lengths
1 dried hot red chili *(caution: see note, Recipe Booklet)*
4 garlic cloves, peeled and bruised with the flat of a cleaver or large heavy knife
1 cup shellfish boil *(below)*, or substitute 1 cup commercial shrimp spice or crab boil
2 tablespoons salt
20 pounds live crawfish

Shellfish Boil

In Louisiana, a "boil" is a mixture of dried spices used to flavor the stock in which crawfish, shrimp or blue crabs are boiled.

Mix the mustard, coriander, dill, allspice, cloves, chilies and bay leaves together in a jar, cover tightly and store the boil at room temperature.

To make about 1 cup

¼ cup mustard seeds
¼ cup coriander seeds
2 tablespoons dill seeds
2 tablespoons whole allspice
1 tablespoon ground cloves
4 dried hot red chilies, each about 1½ inches long, washed, stemmed and coarsely crumbled *(caution: see note, Recipe Booklet)*
3 medium-sized bay leaves, finely crumbled

Oreilles de Cochon
DEEP-FRIED PASTRIES SHAPED LIKE PIG'S EARS

Combine the flour, baking powder and salt, sift them together into a bowl and set aside. In a deep bowl, beat the eggs to a froth with a wire whisk or a fork. Beating constantly, gradually pour in the cooled melted butter. Then stir in the flour mixture ½ cup at a time. Divide the dough into 16 equal portions and shape each portion into a 1-inch ball. On a lightly floured surface, roll each ball into a paper-thin round about 8 inches in diameter.

Pour vegetable oil to a depth of about 1½ inches into a heavy skillet or casserole at least 10 inches in diameter and 2 inches deep. Heat the oil to a temperature of 350° on a deep-frying thermometer.

To make each pastry, slide a round of dough into the skillet. As soon as the round rises to the surface of the oil, pierce its center with the tines of a long-handled fork. Rotate the fork clockwise, flattening the tines against the dough, to simultaneously twist the center of the round and fold the far side over on itself. Turn the pastry and brown it for a minute. Then transfer it to paper towels to drain while you fry the rest.

While the pastries are still hot, combine the cane syrup and pecans in a small saucepan and stir over low heat until the syrup is warm and fluid. Then dribble about 2 tablespoons of the cane-syrup mixture over the top of each pastry. Serve the *oreilles de cochon* warm or at room temperature.

To make 16 eight-inch round pastries

2 cups unsifted flour
2 teaspoons double-acting baking powder
½ teaspoon salt
2 eggs
8 tablespoons butter, melted and cooled
Vegetable oil for deep frying
2 cups pure cane syrup *(see Glossary, page 198)*, or substitute 1⅓ cups dark corn syrup mixed with ⅔ cup dark molasses
1 cup coarsely chopped pecans

Stuffed *ponce,* or pig stomach, is in effect a king-sized sausage with a stuffing of ground pork, diced yam, green peppers and scallions.

To serve 6

A 1-pound pig's stomach *(ponce)*
3 thin slices homemade-type white
    bread, crusts removed
½ cup milk
2 tablespoons butter
¼ cup finely chopped onions
¼ cup finely chopped green
    peppers
¼ cup finely chopped scallions
1½ teaspoons finely chopped
    garlic
1½ pounds lean ground pork
2 medium-sized yams, peeled and
    cut into ¼-inch dice
1 egg
½ teaspoon ground hot red pepper
    (cayenne)
2 teaspoons salt
2 tablespoons vegetable oil
3 to 4 cups water

Stuffed Ponce

With your fingers, pick off and discard any bits of fat clinging to the lining or surface of the pig's stomach. Then place the stomach in a deep pot, pour in enough cold water to cover it by at least 1 inch and let it soak for about 2 hours. Rinse the stomach briefly under cold running water and pat it completely dry, inside and out, with paper towels.

Meanwhile, prepare the stuffing in the following manner: Combine the slices of bread and the milk in a bowl and let them stand at room temperature until all the liquid has been absorbed. Place the bread in a sieve and, with the back of a large spoon, press out any excess milk. Discard the milk and set the bread aside.

In a heavy 10-inch skillet, melt the butter over moderate heat. When the foam begins to subside, add the onions, green peppers, scallions and garlic and, stirring frequently, cook for about 5 minutes, or until the vegetables are soft but not brown. With a rubber spatula, scrape the entire contents of the skillet into a deep bowl and let the vegetables cool to room temperature.

When the vegetables are cool, add the reserved bread, the ground pork, yams, egg, red pepper and salt. Knead vigorously with both hands, then beat with a large spoon until the mixture is light and fluffy. Because the stuffing contains raw pork, fry a spoonful of it in a skillet before tasting it for seasoning. With a large needle and strong white thread, sew up one of the openings of the stomach. Then fill the stomach cavity with the stuffing and sew the other opening securely shut.

Heat the oil over moderate heat in a heavy casserole just large enough to hold the stomach comfortably. Add the stuffed *ponce* and turn it over with two wooden spoons until it is lightly browned on all sides. Pour in 1 cup of the water and, when it comes to a boil, cover the casserole tightly. Reduce the heat to moderate and steam the *ponce* for 3 hours, regulating the heat to keep the water at a simmer. Check the casserole every 20 minutes or so and add boiling water as necessary to keep the liquid at a depth of about ½ inch.

Transfer the stuffed *ponce* to a heated platter and let it rest for at least 10 minutes for easier carving. Meanwhile, boil the liquid remaining in the casserole until it is reduced to a thin gravy with the intensity of flavor you desire. Pour the gravy into a bowl and serve it separately. At the table, carve the *ponce* crosswise into ¼-inch-thick slices.

Crawfish Étouffée

Étouffée literally means "smothered," and in this dish the crawfish tails are blanketed with a rich, thick sauce.

Soak the live crawfish in cold water for at least 10 minutes, then wash them thoroughly under cold running water. In a heavy 8- to 10-quart pot, bring 4 quarts of water to a boil over high heat. Using tongs, drop in the crawfish and boil them briskly, uncovered, for 5 minutes.

Drain the crawfish into a large colander and, when they are cool enough to handle, shell them one at a time in the following manner: With your hands, break off the ridged tail, snap it in half lengthwise and lift out the meat in one piece. If you like, you can snap off the large claws, break them with a nutcracker and pick out the bits of claw meat.

Some or all of the yellow fat or "butter" from the body of the crawfish may slide out when you break off the tail. If it does not, scoop the shell clean with the tip of one thumb and pick out the yellow fat. Reserve the crawfish meat and fat (there will be about 2 cups). Discard the shells, heads and intestinal matter.

Bring the fish stock to a boil in a small saucepan set over high heat. Remove the pan from the heat and cover to keep the stock hot.

In a heavy 5- to 6-quart casserole, warm the brown *roux* over low heat for 2 or 3 minutes, stirring constantly with a spoon. Add the onions, scallions, celery and garlic and, stirring frequently, cook over moderate heat for about 5 minutes, or until the vegetables are soft. Then, stirring constantly, pour in the hot fish stock in a slow, thin stream and cook over high heat until the mixture comes to a boil and thickens lightly.

Add the tomatoes, Worcestershire, red pepper, black pepper and salt, and reduce the heat to low. Simmer partially covered for 30 minutes, then stir in the crawfish meat and fat and heat them through.

Taste for seasoning and ladle the crawfish *étouffée* into a heated bowl. Mound the rice in a separate bowl and serve at once.

To serve 4

5 pounds live crawfish
2 cups freshly made fish stock (*Recipe Booklet*)
4 tablespoons brown *roux* (page 66)
1 cup finely chopped onions
1 cup finely chopped scallions, including 3 inches of the green tops
½ cup finely chopped celery
1 teaspoon finely chopped garlic
A 1-pound can tomatoes, drained and finely chopped
1 tablespoon Worcestershire sauce
¼ teaspoon ground hot red pepper (cayenne)
1 teaspoon freshly ground black pepper
2 teaspoons salt
4 to 6 cups freshly cooked long-grain white rice

To serve 8 to 10

A 6-pound lean pork loin, including
    the bones, sawed into 2-inch
    chunks
¼ teaspoon ground hot red pepper
    (cayenne)
1 teaspoon salt
½ cup flour
½ cup vegetable oil
2 cups finely chopped onions
½ cup finely chopped celery plus
    ¼ cup finely chopped celery
    leaves
2 tablespoons finely chopped garlic
1 quart chicken stock, fresh or
    canned
2 fresh parsley sprigs, preferably the
    flat-leaf Italian variety

To make one 9-inch square cake

9 tablespoons butter, softened
2 tablespoons plus 2½ cups
    unsifted flour
1½ teaspoons double-acting
    baking powder
½ teaspoon baking soda
1 teaspoon ground ginger
1 teaspoon ground cinnamon
¼ teaspoon ground nutmeg,
    preferably freshly grated
¼ teaspoon ground cloves
½ teaspoon salt
½ cup coarsely chopped pecans
½ cup seedless raisins
1 cup pure cane syrup (see Glossary,
    page 198), or substitute ⅔ cup
    dark corn syrup mixed with ⅓
    cup dark molasses
1 cup boiling water
½ cup sugar
2 eggs

Backbone Stew

Pat the chunks of pork loin completely dry with paper towels and season them on all sides with the red pepper and salt. One at a time, roll the pork chunks in the flour to coat them lightly all over, and vigorously shake off the excess flour.

In a heavy 12-inch skillet, heat the oil over moderate heat until a light haze forms above it. Add the pork and brown the chunks, turning them frequently with kitchen tongs or a metal spatula and regulating the heat so that they color deeply and evenly without burning. Transfer the browned pork chunks to a heavy 8-quart casserole.

Discard all but about ½ cup of the fat remaining in the skillet, and add the onions, the chopped celery (but not the leaves) and the garlic. Stirring from time to time, cook over moderate heat for 8 to 10 minutes, or until the vegetables are lightly browned.

Pour in about ½ cup of the chicken stock and bring to a boil over high heat, meanwhile scraping in the brown particles that cling to the bottom and sides of the skillet.

Pour the entire contents of the skillet over the pork, add the remaining 3½ cups of chicken stock, the chopped celery leaves and the parsley and bring the casserole to a boil. Reduce the heat to low and simmer, partially covered, for 2 hours, or until the pork is tender and shows no resistance when pierced with the point of a small sharp knife.

With a large spoon, skim as much fat as possible from the surface of the stew. Taste for seasoning and serve the backbone stew at once, directly from the casserole or from a heated bowl.

Gâteau de Sirop
SYRUP CAKE

Preheat the oven to 350°. With a pastry brush, spread 1 tablespoon of the softened butter over the bottom and sides of a 9-by-9-by-2-inch baking pan. Add 1 tablespoon of the flour and tip the pan from side to side to distribute it evenly. Invert the pan and rap the bottom sharply to remove the excess flour.

Combine 2½ cups of the flour, the baking powder, baking soda, ginger, cinnamon, nutmeg, cloves and salt, and sift them together into a mixing bowl. In a separate bowl, mix the remaining tablespoon of flour with the chopped pecans and raisins. Pour the syrup and boiling water into another bowl and mix the liquids well.

In a deep bowl, cream the remaining 8 tablespoons of softened butter and the sugar together by beating and mashing them against the sides of the bowl with the back of a large spoon until the mixture is light and fluffy. Beat in the eggs, one at a time.

Add about ⅔ cup of flour-and-spice mixture and, when it is well incorporated, beat in ½ cup of the syrup mixture. Repeat three more times, alternating about ⅔ cup of the flour-and-spice mixture with ½ cup of the syrup mixture, and beating well after each addition. Add the floured pecans and the raisins and, with a rubber spatula, fold them in gently but thoroughly.

Pour the batter into the prepared pan, spreading it evenly and smoothing the top with the spatula. Bake the syrup cake in the middle of the oven for 50 to 60 minutes, or until a toothpick or cake tester inserted in the center comes out clean.

Cool and serve the syrup cake from the pan or, if you prefer, turn it out on a wire rack to cool and serve the cake from a plate.

Headcheese

On the farms of South Louisiana, this savory jellied meat is made from the head of a hog. The following recipe uses instead fresh pig's feet, tongue and heart, because these ingredients are more readily available from most retail butchers.

Place the pig's feet, heart and tongue in an 8- to 10-quart enameled or stainless-steel pot and add the water, ¼ cup of the salt, the vinegar and 1 tablespoon of the lemon juice. Bring to a boil over high heat, meanwhile skimming off the foam and scum as they rise to the surface. Then reduce the heat to low, cover partially, and simmer for about 4 hours, or until all the meats are tender and show no resistance when pierced deeply with the point of a sharp knife.

With tongs, transfer the tongue, feet and heart to a cutting board. Measure and reserve 3½ cups of the cooking liquid. While it is still warm, skin the tongue with a small sharp knife, cutting away the fat, bones and gristle at its base. Cut or pull off the meat from the pig's feet and discard the bones, skin, gristle and fat. Slice the pig's heart lengthwise into quarters and cut away the arteries and veins and any pieces of fat. Cut all the meats into small chunks and put them through the coarsest blade of a food grinder. There should be about 5½ cups of ground meat.

In a heavy 12-inch skillet, melt the butter over moderate heat. Add the onions and, stirring frequently, cook for about 5 minutes, or until they are soft and translucent but not brown.

Pour in ½ cup of the reserved cooking liquid and, stirring from time to time, simmer over low heat for 15 to 20 minutes, until almost all of the liquid has evaporated.

Stir in the ground meat, the remaining 3 cups of cooking liquid, 3 tablespoons of lemon juice and 2 teaspoons of salt. Add the bay leaf, sage, mace and red and black pepper, and bring to a boil over high heat. Reduce the heat to low and simmer, partially covered, for 10 minutes longer.

Remove the skillet from the heat, stir in the parsley and scallions, and taste for seasoning. With a rubber spatula, transfer the entire contents of the skillet to a 9-by-9-by-2-inch baking dish and smooth the top with the spatula. Cool to room temperature, then cover with foil or plastic wrap and refrigerate for at least 4 hours, or until the headcheese is thoroughly chilled and firm to the touch.

To unmold and serve the headcheese, run a thin-bladed knife around the edges of the dish to loosen the sides and dip the bottom briefly into hot water. Place an inverted platter on top of the dish and, grasping the platter and dish together firmly, turn them over. The headcheese should slide out of the dish easily.

Slice the headcheese thin and serve it with crackers or toast.

To make one 9-by-9-by-2-inch loaf

4½ pounds fresh pig's feet
2 pounds fresh pig's heart, trimmed of excess fat and thoroughly washed
1 pound fresh pig's tongue, trimmed of excess fat
4 quarts water
¼ cup plus 2 teaspoons salt
1 tablespoon cider vinegar
4 tablespoons (¼ cup) strained fresh lemon juice
2 tablespoons butter
1 cup finely chopped onions
1 medium-sized bay leaf, finely crumbled
1 teaspoon ground sage
¼ teaspoon ground mace
½ teaspoon ground hot red pepper (cayenne)
1 teaspoon freshly ground black pepper
1 cup finely chopped fresh parsley, preferably the flat-leaf Italian variety
1 cup finely chopped scallions, including 3 inches of the green tops

2 dozen large individual frogs' legs
(about 4 pounds), thoroughly
defrosted if frozen

1 teaspoon ground hot red pepper
(cayenne)

1½ teaspoons salt

½ cup vegetable oil

4 tablespoons brown *roux (page
66)*

½ cup finely chopped onions

2 tablespoons finely chopped green
pepper

2 tablespoons finely chopped celery

A 1-pound can tomatoes, drained
and coarsely chopped, with all the
liquid reserved

2 teaspoons finely chopped garlic

2 tablespoons finely chopped scallions

2 tablespoons finely chopped fresh
parsley, preferably the flat-leaf
Italian variety

1 lemon, thinly sliced

To make 3 sausages, each about 30
inches long

3 three-foot lengths hog sausage
casing

3 pounds boneless lean pork,
trimmed of excess fat and cut into
1½-inch chunks

4 cups coarsely chopped onions

1 medium-sized bay leaf, crumbled

6 whole black peppercorns

5 teaspoons salt

1 cup coarsely chopped green
pepper

1 cup coarsely chopped fresh
parsley, preferably the flat-leaf
Italian variety

½ cup coarsely chopped scallions

1 tablespoon finely chopped garlic

2½ cups freshly cooked white rice

1 tablespoon dried sage leaves

2½ teaspoons ground hot red
pepper (cayenne)

½ teaspoon freshly ground black
pepper

Frogs' Legs Sauce Piquante

Pat the frogs' legs completely dry with paper towels and season them
evenly on all sides with the red pepper and 1 teaspoon of the salt.

In a heavy 12-inch skillet (preferably one with a nonstick cooking surface) heat ¼ cup of the vegetable oil over moderate heat until a light
haze forms above it. Add 12 of the frogs' legs and fry them for 4 or 5 minutes, turning them once or twice with tongs or a large metal spatula and
regulating the heat so that they color richly and evenly without burning.
As they are cooked, transfer the frogs' legs to a platter. Pour the remaining ¼ cup of vegetable oil into the skillet and, when it is hot, fry
the other dozen frogs' legs in the same fashion.

Stirring constantly, add the brown *roux* to the fat remaining in the
skillet. Drop in the onions, green pepper and celery and, stirring frequently, cook over moderate heat for about 5 minutes, or until the vegetables are soft. Stir in the tomatoes and their liquid, add the garlic and the
remaining ½ teaspoon of salt and boil briskly, uncovered, for about 5
minutes longer. When the vegetable-sauce mixture is thick enough to hold
its shape almost solidly in the spoon, return the frogs' legs and the liquid
that has accumulated around them to the skillet.

Stirring and basting the frogs' legs with the sauce, cook for a minute
or so longer to heat the legs through. Then mix in the scallions and
parsley and taste for seasoning. *(Piquante* means "pungent," and the
sauce should be distinctly peppery.)

With tongs or a slotted spoon, arrange the frogs' legs attractively on a
large heated platter. Pour the *sauce piquante* over the frogs' legs, garnish
the platter with the lemon slices, and serve at once.

NOTE: Louisiana cooks also use *sauce piquante* with turtle meat, shrimp,
crawfish, fish and wild or domestic birds of every kind.

Boudin Blanc

*Boudin is the French term for the blood sausage, or "pudding," made
with the blood of the pig. Boudin blanc is a white sausage made with
pork but no blood. This Louisiana version adds rice and is even whiter.*

Place the sausage casing in a bowl, pour in enough warm water to cover
it, and soak for 2 or 3 hours, until the casing is soft and pliable.

Meanwhile, put the pork in a heavy 4- to 5-quart casserole and add
enough water to cover it by 1 inch. Bring to a boil over high heat and
skim off the foam and scum that rise to the surface. Add 2 cups of onions,
the bay leaf, peppercorns and 1 teaspoon of the salt. Reduce the heat to
low and simmer, partially covered, for 1½ hours.

With a slotted spoon, transfer the chunks of pork to a plate. (Discard
the cooking liquid and seasonings.) Put the pork, the remaining 2 cups
of onions, the green pepper, parsley, scallions and garlic through the
medium blade of a food grinder and place the mixture in a deep bowl.
Add the rice, sage, red and black pepper, and the remaining 4 teaspoons
of salt. Knead vigorously with both hands, then beat with a wooden spoon
until the mixture is smooth and fluffy. Taste for seasoning.

Wash each sausage casing under cold running water to remove all

Frogs' legs *sauce piquante* are simmered to succulence in a peppery Creole blend of brown *roux* and garden-fresh vegetables.

traces of the salt in which it is preserved. Hold one end securely around the faucet and let the water run through to clean the inside of the casing.

To make each sausage, tie a knot 3 inches from one end of a length of the casing. Fit the open end over the funnel (or "horn") on the sausage-making attachment of a meat grinder. Then ease the rest of the casing onto the funnel, squeezing it up like the folds of an accordion.

Spoon the meat mixture into the mouth of the grinder and, with a wooden pestle, push it through into the casing. As you fill it, the casing will inflate and gradually ease away from the funnel in a ropelike coil. Fill the casing to within an inch or so of the funnel end but do not try to stuff it too tightly, or it may burst. Slip the casing off the funnel and knot the open end. You may cook the sausages immediately or refrigerate them safely for five or six days.

Before cooking a sausage, prick the casing in five or six places with a skewer or the point of a small sharp knife. Melt 2 tablespoons of butter with 1 tablespoon of vegetable oil in a heavy 12-inch skillet set over moderate heat. When the foam begins to subside, place the sausage in the skillet, coiling it in concentric circles. Turning the sausage with tongs, cook uncovered for about 10 minutes, or until it is brown on both sides.

VI

Acadian Life in Hurricane Country

Long before the Acadians settled in the bayous of Louisiana, they were fishermen—in Nova Scotia centuries ago, and in Brittany before that. Throughout their history, they have also been devout Catholics, and they still adhere to such ancient nautical rituals as the blessing of their fishing boats. At left Father Allen Roy, standing on a wharf on the Robinson Canal on Bayou Petit Caillou, sprinkles holy water and offers a prayer for an Acadian shrimp boat embarking on a three-week voyage in the Gulf of Mexico.

Running roughly north to south like Bayou Teche, but a bit nearer to New Orleans, is another bayou that might compare with any Main Street U.S.A., except that it is made of water rather than asphalt. Bayou Lafourche, which flows 120 miles from its start at Donaldsonville to its end in the Gulf of Mexico, has been called "the longest village street in the world." It forms a front yard for the houses on its banks. The houses mostly face the bayou, for the people who live in them like to shape their lives that way, their backs turned on the noises and eruptions of the outside world. Though it lacks the lushness and past glamor of Bayou Teche, Bayou Lafourche has another quality that is, in its own way, even more dramatic: the quality of everyday, humdrum, middle-class life, Acadian style—but lived on the brink of disaster.

For the lower Lafourche is in a dangerous part of hurricane country. The Acadian homes on its banks stand like sturdy sentinels; yet no matter how well the houses are constructed, few can withstand the fury of a full hurricane that happens to pass directly overhead. Through the years these houses have been razed, and razed again. There is a watchfulness in the eyes of the people who live on Bayou Lafourche that can only be called the look of survival. Their way of life, their homes, their cooking have all been affected by the will to survive, for only by emphasizing the simplest and most basic fundamentals of existence can they hope to confront true danger. Those few houses that have been spared by water and wind over the years are plain, and much like the one belonging to the boy we saw fishing on the Teche, except that on the Lafourche, the kitchen is a

separate room, often built outside the house (a wise arrangement in a warm climate), and the *tablette* at which the woman of the house works has another vital purpose beyond the washing of dishes or the preparation of food. It serves as a kind of instant megaphone: a woman can receive news from one side of her house, run to the other side and relay the information over the *tablette* at her kitchen window.

In earlier days every house had its kitchen garden fronting on the bayou, and there were fish and crabs and shrimp to be caught in the water; behind the house were cows and pigs and chickens, and beyond that wild game—a fine arrangement, if you have to cope with the fury of the skies during hurricane season and want to make things down on earth as simple as possible for the rest of the year. In the old days, too, everybody knew just about everybody else on Bayou Lafourche, and that phenomenon has not entirely faded, for a man who lives upstream is likely to have aunts and uncles on both banks, and cousins all the way down to the Gulf. Even a good friend is called a "cousin"; and some habits and customs on much of this middle-class bayou are not so different now from what they were 20 or 50 or in some cases even 100 years ago.

There is, for instance, the Acadian custom called charivari. In hurricane country, you sometimes need a kind of merriment and gaiety as a release: life is too serious to be taken always too seriously. Imagine that you have been visiting with the family of a man named Jean: he has accepted

you as a sort of honorary member of his clan, for you are learning the ways of his people. One day a certain Monsieur Suisse, a rich widower of 50 who lives downstream a few miles, marries a lovely girl who is about 30 years his junior. Yes, this is plenty of reason for a charivari. After dark on the wedding night, you and Jean and several of his friends gather; you all get into boats and travel downstream noiselessly, gathering other boatloads of people as you go. By the time you have arrived *chez* Monsieur Suisse, there are 30 or 40 of you standing silently on his front lawn in the darkness. But the silence will not last. Some of the men carry pots and pans, others spoons or metal bars. Aristide over there has brought a metal washboard and a stone to scrape it with. His brother holds some cowbells. Another man has a trumpet, somebody else a pair of cymbals, and there are many horns. At a given signal the instruments are all simultaneously put into use, and a din arises from the lawn that defies any decibel count. The beating of iron on tin, the screech of metal, the braying of the trumpet and horns and the clash of the cymbals join the cowbells to make a cacophony that seems to burst out of the bayou itself, as if all the devils in hell had come together to confer.

Despite the clamor, the house of Monsieur Suisse remains dark for 45 minutes. Then, at last, a light flickers in a window and the crowd roars. The front door opens and Monsieur Suisse appears in nightshirt and slippers. He does not seem too terribly pleased; but on the other hand he can-

At dawn on a September morning Marcel Bienvenu sets out decoys for teal in a flooded rice pond near Gueydan, Louisiana. This part of South Louisiana is prime duck-hunting country and the teal season runs a month each fall, with a daily limit of four birds per hunter. Bienvenu and the five other hunters in his party bagged their limit before nightfall, then headed for their lodge and a roast-duck dinner.

173

Duck-and-sausage gumbo *(Recipe Index)* is a stick-to-the-ribs stew that is spiced with freshly chopped onions, scallions, celery and green pepper and fired with generous dollops of red pepper and Tabasco. The gumbo is thickened during the last stage of its preparation with a few spoonfuls of filé powder.

not afford to appear *dis*pleased. The rules are that if he refuses to make you welcome, the charivari will be repeated tomorrow night—and the next night, and every night after that, for 30 nights in a row—until he has found a way to mind his manners. No, even if his face shatters, he must force a smile and invite all of you in for wine and food.

This is possibly the ultimate test of a host's ability to be gracious in the face of disaster. If, while he wines and dines his unwanted guests, Monsieur Suisse allows himself the indulgence of a single rude remark to even one of them, all of them will be back tomorrow night, and the chances are there won't be 40 people, but 80, for the promise of a sequential charivari would make people who have never heard of Monsieur Suisse rub their palms in glee. Monsieur Suisse knows this. He turns on the light in his kitchen, contorts his face muscles into a grimace that is meant to convey pleasure, says "Bienvenus, mes amis," and in you come. You, too, are polite, and you pretend not to notice the glare behind his eyes. Chairs are pulled out, some people sit on the floor, and now the young bride joins the party to put out the food.

There is cheese with the wine, and some good *boudin,* or sausage. Begin with that. If her mother has taught her anything at all, the bride will also throw a few ingredients together and produce some sort of dish within an hour, say, to feed the crowd which is by now toasting the newlyweds in slightly drunken gaiety. The bride gets busy; there is some chopped meat, some vegetables and red peppers, and a platter of fresh-killed chicken she was planning to cook for her own family on their traditional call the next afternoon. All that is enough to make an Acadian chicken *sauce piquante,* and she sets to work, giggling at one or two of the bawdy remarks passed back and forth among the guests within her hearing. But she must not giggle too hard, or her husband will lose the silent battle he is fighting with himself and let his temper fly. Her arms move quickly over the stove, and the dish is soon finished: seasoned pieces of chicken that have been browned and then cooked with onions, bell peppers, garlic, celery, tomato paste, mushrooms, red wine and fiercely hot red pepper. Ladled over rice in plates and gumbo bowls, the rich red sauce has a zing to it that tastes as if it has been touched by lightning, and some of the guests add Tabasco to make it even hotter. The white rice holds it and cools it; more wine flows as the night gets later and later. Finally, even Monsieur Suisse's eyes look grudgingly happy, a look fused by the heat from the food, the red wine and the merriment in the room —a merriment that softens now as dawn approaches over the quiet bayou.

Much of living seems a celebration on Bayou Lafourche if you are staying with your Acadian friend Jean in the soft air of late fall. September is past; hurricane season has come and gone; and, barring a flood, the house is safe for another year. You sit on the long half-outdoor gallery in the afternoons with family and friends and neighbors, talking and watching the light change, sipping coffee in small cups, for the Acadians drink coffee literally all day long, and no more than a taste is required at any given time. The smell of wet is in the air, crickets call out, and there is a splash from a garfish on the water; the flowers on the bushes on the lawn are "red-red" or "white-white" in the deepening orange sun. Acadians, you will find, when they speak English do not bother much with words like "very"—or with any adjective unless it radically changes the meaning of something. To them, a "green-green" leaf is somehow more intense than just a very green one—and in much the same way a single pot containing everything becomes more intensely pleasing than several courses of food and sauce served separately.

"Tonight we are expecting some cousins from upstream," Jean's wife will say; "there are a lot-and-a-lot of them, so we'll have a lot-and-a-lot of food." As she speaks, a chugging on the road back of the house announces the arrival of an odd-looking truck. One side of it is covered only by canvas, which is soon raised to show the wares inside. This is the *marchand-charette,* or traveling store, a tradition among Acadians that has never been broken: the cart from which goods were purveyed long ago in provincial France has become a truck on wheels here, and everything from soap to rolling pins or spices may be found in it. A family that is low on cash may pay for the goods with freshly laid eggs or even live chickens. Bartering is expected, and when it is over, the man on the truck will stay to repeat gossip he has heard upstream, for among his other duties he serves as a kind of mobile gazette. He will pick up a bit of gossip here too, before the truck goes chugging off again down the road and Jean's wife comes slowly back to the house with her new-bought goods to prepare for the company meal.

Pain perdu (Recipe Index) is a form of French toast frugally based on day-old bread. Topped with powdered sugar and served here with sausages, it is kept warm on a 19th Century plate equipped with an inner compartment for boiling water. Labeled pots hold coffee and warm milk for *café au lait*.

But the word company is rarely used here the way it is in other parts of America. Among the Acadians, the business of paying calls on another family—or another part of your own family—is a kind of ritual that has been maintained happily down through two centuries. Clemence is coming tonight, you will hear; that's Jean's third cousin twice removed (or is it his second cousin three times removed?). Anyway, he is bringing his family and two of his wife's cousins who are staying with him, as well as some in-laws he will pick up on the way downstream. There should be no more than 10 or 12 in all, counting the children—unless Jean's wife's Aunt Clarisse, who lives farther downstream, decides to join the group. The man on the truck had said that Clarisse had mentioned to him yesterday something about her coming over tonight . . . or did he say tomorrow night? *Eh bien,* you never know—that's the point—and because you never know, you are always prepared. Other hostesses in other places, worrying about an extra guest turning up at the last moment, would do well to take a lesson from the Acadian housewives along Lafourche, who do not consider that six or even eight extra guests are anything out of the ordinary, and who cook accordingly.

Many of the best Acadian dishes are designed with this in mind. Among the finest, and certainly the most famous, is jambalaya. Jean's wife takes the large black iron pot and sautés some onions in butter and a little oil. After a few minutes, she adds some fresh thyme, bay leaves, parsley and garlic. Her hand circles over the mixture for a while, stirring it; then she puts in a red pepper and some tomatoes, chopped with their juices. When all that is done, she takes the pot off the flame and sets it on the back of the stove until she knows how many people she is going to have to feed. As night comes on, they begin to arrive—those from upstream and those from down, for it turns out that it was tonight, after all, that Clarisse has sent word she will come. (She could have telephoned? Yes, but why? You never know when the phone lines will be blown down—the older ways are always better.) So, now, let's see, that's 11, 12, 14 . . . 16 in all, with the babies. That's fine, for the mixture Jean's wife has already prepared would have taken care of 20 as easily as 16; she could always make a little more of it if needed. People are sitting all over the gallery now. Some are drinking beer, the children are playing, stories are being told; the evening, like the air, is soft and easy.

When people begin to glance expectantly toward the kitchen, Jean's wife gets up and goes in to finish cooking. She pours some dark beef stock into the mixture she has made, stirs and heats it all together, and then, when it is simmering, puts in several pounds of shrimp that she has already peeled and deveined. The shrimp simmer until they begin to turn pink. Then she adds several handfuls of rice, without measuring them, for she knows by the look of the liquid how much rice it will take—just as she knew from glancing at the number of guests on the gallery how much stock to pour. She covers the pot, turns the fire down, and simmers the dish until the rice is done. She does not need any kind of timer; she herself is a timer. When you have cooked rice twice a day all your life, your own instinct tells you, better than a clock, when it is ready.

Soon the lid comes off, and the steaming shrimp jambalaya is spooned onto plates that are passed one by one to the people on the gallery. The guests taste it and compliment Jean's wife on her cooking, for though jambalaya is a common dish in these parts, no two recipes for it are exactly alike. Each cook varies it slightly—and each is right (for one good version see the shrimp-and-ham jambalaya listed in the Recipe Index). There is also chicken jambalaya, often made with the addition of smoked sausage; and there are beef jambalaya and crawfish jambalaya *(Recipe Index)* as well as others. Sometimes ham or shellfish is added to one or another of them, sometimes not. Like the Spanish *paella* that is its ancestor, jambalaya is simply rice with whatever kind of meat or poultry or seafood you happen to have available, in whatever combination your taste buds tell you is right. And like *paella,* it can be cooked over a wood fire outdoors; if that is not done along the Lafourche, the choice is due more to the wetness of the earth and the weather than to a preference for indoor cooking. Besides, you can always take your plate and go outside with it. The taste of a good shrimp jambalaya is sharp and full; flavors of beef stock and fresh vegetables and shrimp have been absorbed together into the rice to produce the kind of meal that sharpens any party, almost as if the different personalities of the guests had meshed in perfect harmony. The fresh wet smells of green growth along the Lafourche are in the air around you as you eat, and they intensify the flavor of the food.

As fall turns to winter, Jean will now and then make a trip into the swamps to shoot wild duck and geese. Go along with him once, and glide through the flat dark waters in a pirogue—that tricky means of transportation inherited from the Indians, and used by the Acadians in a way that seems supernaturally skillful. A pirogue is simply a hollowed-out cypress log. It may be large or small, depending on the size of the tree; a very small one seats one person alone, a large one will take a family. But whatever the size, the pirogue responds to the movements of the man with the paddle as if it were an extension of his body. The trick to sitting in a pirogue is perfect balance; a man who has never been in one will turn it over almost instantaneously, and for a long time thereafter, whenever he gets into one again, he will find himself sitting stiffly upright and trying not to breathe. You would not think that plain breathing could overturn a cypress log, but it can (this writer knows from experience). Still Jean, or any other Acadian in the area, can sit relaxed, move from side to side, and even shoot a gun from a pirogue without overturning it; his body automatically compensates for its own movements and makes its own balance, much as a man on a unicycle manages to stay upright.

Watch Jean manipulate this pirogue, and you will understand, at last, what the Acadians mean when they claim a pirogue can "ride on a heavy dew." A clump of grass thrusts out of the swamp water and Jean glides over it as if it were not there. The pirogue cuts silently between the trees, leaving only a slim trail behind it, like a crease in the water. No one speaks. There is always a strange stillness in a cypress swamp, like the stillness in a hurricane's eye. Nothing seems to move, yet it is as if you can hear plants growing. The air is so thick you can feel the shadows that pass over you as the pirogue moves. The knobby knees of the cypress trees jut out around you; the heavy gray moss hangs overhead as though

Mrs. Olga Fandal brings up two submerged crab boxes. She will tow them to a nearby platform on piles to inspect their contents.

A Wet but Worthwhile Wait
for a Crab to Leave Its Shell

As practiced by the Fandal family of Mandeville on Lake Pontchartrain, crabbing is a cross between fishing and farming, but wetter, trickier and more arduous than either of them. The Fandals specialize in soft-shell crabs. The term soft-shell refers not to a kind of crab, but to a specific point in the crab life cycle. All crabs periodically outgrow their shells and live for a few hours in a soft-shell state before the new shell begins to harden. An otherwise ordinary crab commands a far higher price at market during this brief period; the trick is to pick the crab at the right moment. The way the Fandals manage it is to catch hard-shell crabs in the lake, then segregate these crabs in underwater boxes near the shore according to the imminence of their molt, when they shed their shells. The boxes must be checked regularly (four times a day for "busters," as crabs about to molt are called) until the shells split and the crabs creep out. Then it's off to the city—and a meal for some epicure.

180

Mrs. Fandal's son Fred *(left)* checks out a box of "peelers"—crabs that will shed their shells in a day or two. If the shell cracks when pressed at the sides, the crab is classified as a "buster" and moved to another box. Below, having shed their shells, soft-shell crabs are packed for sale by the Fandals.

it were waiting. You have a sense that everything here is waiting—always waiting—but for what? The answer looms over and under you, behind and ahead of you, suspended in the quiet.

Jean glides to a place where there is grassy earth above the water, and ties the pirogue to a tree. You step out gingerly and follow him with care, stepping where he steps, for a change in the color of the grass may mean quicksand, and a harmless-looking twig may be a snake. You are both wearing high boots, and you walk along without talking, respecting the silence, not so much for the sake of any game that might be lurking as for the reverence that is appropriate in an old church. Something in the swamp demands that respect, and you give it without question. Soon you are out of the deepest part of the swamp, walking in the marshes. Jean has stopped, frozen in his tracks. Even as you wonder what has caught his eye, he raises his rifle. A shot rings out, then another. Though you have seen nothing move, he nods, satisfied, and begins to walk again.

Later, back at Jean's house, the duck, geese, deer—whatever he has shot —must be divided and brought as gifts, before nightfall tomorrow, to relatives and friends up and down the bayou. If he has not bagged enough for both his own family and the others, it is his family that will do without. His cousins will do likewise when they go hunting, so in the long run he will not suffer; the bayou country sets as much store by manners as do the most elegant Parisian drawing rooms. By late December, enough people have gone hunting to guarantee Jean's family roast wild goose for Christmas. When the day arrives, his wife makes a highly seasoned stuffing containing the giblets, fresh oysters, bread crumbs, red pepper, onion, garlic, thyme and green pepper—and, so that it won't be too bland, a little black pepper too. The geese are placed in the usual black iron kettle (called a Dutch oven elsewhere) and slipped into the oven to roast; every now and then they are basted with a mysterious dark sauce that thickens as the cooking progresses. The pungent smell fills the house and wafts out to the bayou, where it blends with other cooking odors wafting out from other houses and over the water. No words can accurately describe the taste of Acadian roast wild goose with oyster stuffing. It is rich and stinging and sweet, gamy and juicy and crisp—and has one thing more: a special, nameless flavor, the taste of Christmas. After the roast goose there is coffee, and dessert will be homemade ice cream and oatmeal cookies with a sugar crystal topping. And so the Christmas meal ends with a sparkle and a smooth, quiet sweetness.

South of Bayou Lafourche is the marshland that borders the Gulf Coast. There is a marked change in the look of the earth around and under you, and a corresponding change in the lives of the people here. They have a name for the marshland—*la prairie tremblante,* the trembling prairie. The distinction between earth and water is at best a shaky one, and shaky in the literal sense of the word. If you are not native to these parts, never walk alone. And if you are inclined to daydream, do not walk at all; in the marshland you must definitely look where you are going. Here what appears to be dry is dry only on top; if you step on it, you will find yourself up to the waist in a mixture of slime and water. You do best to stay in the small flat boat with your new host Alcibiade, who has lived all his

Opposite: A crab chop can fool the eye with its uncanny resemblance to a breaded veal or pork chop—which has led some authorities to suggest that crab prepared this way was originally devised as a special dish for meatless Fridays and the Lenten days of abstinence. A favorite with both Acadian home cooks and professional chefs, the dish is displayed here on an antique restaurant plate with menu items and their prices printed around the rim. To prepare the chops *(Recipe Index),* bits of crabmeat are bound together with a thick white sauce, patted into flat teardrop shapes, then coated with egg and bread crumbs and browned in butter.

life hereabouts. He knows the difference between salt cane, cattails, oyster grass and the other forms of vegetation; an almost imperceptible change in the color of the surface matter can tell him more than an encyclopedia about what lies underneath. He and his brother and a cousin all live within a relatively small area. One is an oysterman; the other two are crabbers, with one of them doubling as a muskrat trapper. All three men and their families eat what is provided for them by the water and watery earth of the marshland.

Glide on the water through the grass that grows higher than the boat, past long mounds of dry earth that rise high enough to support one or two oaks on their shell-filled banks. These mounds are called *chênières,* after the oaks that clutch and grip the soil above the brackish water whose salt would kill them. Some of the *chênières* are big enough to hold a house or two; here and there, cows nibble at the grass that edges a *chênière,* and from time to time you will see a houseboat moored to the bank. The water around you is turning lighter; the sea is beginning to encroach on the land. In some places, salt- and fresh-water fish mingle and swim past each other; birds of every species imaginable screech through the air.

Alcibiade guides you expertly, using not a paddle but a pole; the boat turns around a clump of high grass, and you see a shack built on stilts above the water. Beyond it is another shack and beyond that a third. In one of them Alcibiade lives with his family. He will take you there, but first he has work to do. It is spring, and he must attend to his nets, for the best crabbing starts now and will continue through summer. The nets are baited and sunk into the water, with pieces of wood floating to mark the place of each. Alcibiade continues to pole the boat until he reaches a grass-enclosed lake. There he takes the boat from net to net, emptying the contents of each at his feet. The hard crabs swirl and bump together around your ankles; you must raise your legs to avoid being nipped or bitten by their strong pincers. The crabs are blue, of many different sizes, and if you look closely, you will see that some of the shells are cracked, as though they had been broken by falling into the boat. Alcibiade will tell you that this is not the case—the crabs are only shedding their shells, as they must about once a month during their first year, less often after that, until they achieve full growth. After each shedding the crab must live without its shell, defenseless, for a few hours or so while its new shell begins to toughen in the water. The soft-shell crab, a gourmet treat that will bring the highest price of all, is not to be found in these nets, for blue crabs are cannibalistic, and during the time a crab is unprotected, he can't afford to associate with his own kind. You must look for him elsewhere, as Alcibiade now demonstrates. He knows where the crabs go to hide while they are minus their shells.

When he has finished emptying the nets, he poles the boat to the lake's edge. Here he has no need for markers. Small bushes protrude from the water—not bushes of natural growth but thick branches he himself has planted. He stoops over, quickly raises one of the branches and shakes it into a box in the boat. Several soft-shell crabs fall out, and he replaces the branch in the water to attract others.

Only when Alcibiade has gone through every branch is it time to return to his house on stilts. Here, before he does anything else, he must separate the crabs into boxes for shipment to the markets and restaurants of New Orleans. He flips them in one by one according to size—and, more important, according to the stage of development of the shell. He cannot put a soft-shell in with the hard-shell crabs or soon there won't be anything left of it. The "busters"—the ones that are just beginning to break through their shells—go into one box; the soft-shells into another; the hard-shells into a third. He takes several busters now, deftly cracks and discards the shells that remain, and carries the crabs to his wife, who is waiting to show you how they are cooked.

The restaurants of New Orleans as well as the other cities and towns in South Louisiana feature soft-shell crabs on their menus as soon as they are in season; but connoisseurs ask specifically for the busters, which are far more tender than the "paper-shells," which have begun to harden again in the water. Alcibiade's wife cleans the busters, dips them in a mixture of butter and lemon juice, rolls them in flour that has been seasoned with cayenne and other spices, and places them on the broiler rack of her oven. In 10 minutes they are on your plate, sizzling hot and crisp, juicy and crunchy and sweet. The taste has a tang and a freshness to it that few restaurants can reproduce, for there is something of the marshland in it—something that rides on the air.

Spend the night here cushioned in marsh breezes; at this time of year they are soft, though they can quickly turn treacherous when hurricanes are in season. In the morning, before you continue your tour through this fringe of the earth, breakfast on hot black coffee and *pain perdu (Recipe Index),* made especially to give you a proper send-off. The literal translation of the name of this dish is "lost bread"; other parts of the country call it French toast, and it is made by both Creole and Acadian cooks. To prepare it Alcibiade's wife lightly beats a few eggs, adds some sugar, beats a little more and then puts in a splash of brandy that she has been saving since last Christmas. A dash of orange-flower water is added and, in this mixture, while she is melting lard in an iron skillet, she soaks some slices from a loaf of bread that has gone stale. The bread softens somewhat and is then transferred to the skillet where it browns slowly, giving off a wonderful breakfast smell. It is served hot, sprinkled with powdered sugar and accompanied by a pitcher of cane syrup and another of Louisiana honey that has been mixed with melted butter. Everyone at the table digs in. Because stale bread has been used, there is no heaviness to this *pain perdu;* it is light, and it has a sweet richness that makes it as good without syrup as with. Add a bit of the warm buttery honey and you will never want to get up to any other food in the morning.

Now Alcibiade will take you to see other members of his family. There is his brother who traps muskrats not many miles from here. On the way, you stop to visit a cousin who "seeds" and harvests oysters, for the brackish mixture of waters in the coastal marsh, not as salty as the water of the open Gulf yet not sweet either, breeds the best of the oysters you have enjoyed eating in New Orleans. Alcibiade's cousin owns his own oyster lugger. He is worth watching, for he knows more about an oyster than an oyster does; he knows, for instance, that each oyster may change its sex

Just off the ragged shoreline of Bay Tambour, some 60 miles south of New Orleans, Leon Cognevich's oyster boat lies at anchor. Here, on 500 leased acres of brackish shallows, Cognevich runs an oyster "farm." He creates an artificial oyster bed by depositing old oyster shells or actual oysters on the floor of the bay; "spats," as the young floating oysters are called, attach themselves to this artificial bed.

twice during its life span; this protects the species against extinction, for once a male oyster is anchored on the bottom of a lake, he is there for life, and there is no guarantee that a female will be conveniently nearby. The two, in fact, do not come together at all; each secretes a substance in the water, and it is only the sperm and the egg that meet. The female lays 60 million eggs, just a few of which will ever reach maturity. The baby oysters swim free until they find a place where they may attach themselves and grow. Here Alcibiade's cousin lends a helping hand, for what is called seeding is merely the dropping of old, discarded oyster shells into the lake bottom so that the infant mollusks may find and grow on them. Then, in about a year and a half, he must rake them up and take them to another place he knows, nearer the Gulf, where the salt content of the water is higher. There he drops them in again to mature; and there he will reap the harvest when it is ready for the city market. Let him shuck an oyster now for you to taste. Even if you have grown up eating them, you will think you have never had one before. The breezes of the marsh and of the open Gulf seem to meet inside the flavor, and the oyster liquor has an incredible delicacy to it.

Your next stop with Alcibiade is his brother's houseboat. From there you accompany the two men into another part of the marshes where muskrats run. Alcibiade's brother makes a good living trapping and selling the muskrats for their fur. He knows the special look of the grass where they

build their houses, and there he has laid his traps. Muskrats are nocturnal animals, and the morning is a good time to take them. You and Alcibiade help his brother empty each of his traps and bring the catch back to the houseboat. En route back, you are more than ever seduced by the quiet beauty of the marshes, the thickly waving grasses, the muted colors reflected in the flat shivering water. You pass Alcibiade's cousin, now busy using a net to scoop up, with deft grace, a diamond-back terrapin he has spotted; it is big enough to make a meal that will amply satisfy all the brothers, their wives, their children and guests. There are turtle farms that breed terrapin especially for Louisiana consumption, but there is no need to buy one if you can net it in your own back yard.

While the men and children attend to skinning and stretching the muskrat hides, on the houseboat Alcibiade's sister-in-law goes about preparing turtle soup *(Recipe Index)*. She makes a *roux* of butter and flour and lets it cook to a thick russet color. Then she adds chopped celery, onions, garlic, tomatoes, bell peppers and a couple of red peppers. While all this boils, she adds green onions. Then she puts in cloves and allspice and bay leaf and thyme and lemon slices. The houseboat tips and rocks under her as another boat passes. She adds the turtle meat, which she has diced and rolled in red and black pepper and salt. The soup simmers for two hours. It is stirred only by the rocking of the houseboat, and as it slides around slowly in the pot, the always unpredictable winds and cur-

Using a pair of old-fashioned scissorslike tongs, Cognevich harvests oysters he planted years earlier. The method is laborious, but he prefers it to the power dredging done by large commercial oystermen. A dredge would wreck the oyster beds he has gone to so much trouble to build, and the tongs permit him to choose full-grown oysters and return the undersized ones to the beds to grow some more.

As long ago as 1734 a writer traveling through Louisiana ate some Lake Pontchartrain oysters and pronounced them "very well tasted." His observation still holds good. Today the true purists among local oyster lovers frequent oyster bars like Casamento's, on Magazine Street. Casamento's oysters *(right)*, freshly opened and served on the half shell, are accompanied by a variety of condiments—horseradish, ketchup, hot sauce, Tabasco peppers in vinegar—with which customers can prepare their own sauce. At far right, Joseph Casamento and his son Joseph Jr. shuck oysters briskly to keep up with their customers.

rents from the Gulf seem to have decided to lend a hand with the cooking. The aroma from the pot is marvelous; it mixes with the marsh air until you are dizzy with hunger. Then, a few minutes before serving, the cook adds the whole turtle eggs, and after them the yolks of some hard-boiled chicken eggs that she has mashed with a fork, seasoned with salt and pepper, splashed with sherry and stirred into a paste.

You sit at the table in the main room of the houseboat, near the stove, and a deep bowl of the stew is set in front of you. Thin slices of lemon lie on top, and for you, the guest, they have been sprinkled with paprika, parsley and the minutely chopped tops of green onions. There is a loaf of hot French bread in the center of the table and, again in your honor, a bottle of red wine. This is a meal that could not be bettered by Escoffier with 20 assistants. There is a kind of dark arrogance to the taste of the stew that makes any other stew seem bland and pallid. It is highly spiced yet subtle in flavor; wildly pungent, but easy on the tongue. The essence of the marshland lies in the tang of this dish, born of the water and rocked by the wind. You will want to dunk crusts of bread into the last of the dark gravy, and swallow them with a sip of the wine, whose warm taste matches the burning glow of the stew. Afterward you sit near an open screened window on the houseboat as the last odors of the food mingle with the wet marsh smell and the drifting Gulf wind.

The next morning you will be ready to visit the strings of islands that

streak along the Gulf coast like oddly shaped fish running close to shore. They have interesting and sometimes strange names—among them, Grand Isle, Timbalier Island, Wine Island, the Isles Dernières (or Last Islands), and in the distance leading west to the Texas border, Marsh Island and Pecan Island. In the past, some of the islands were luxurious resorts where Creole planters spent their summers. Today some are bird sanctuaries, some are wildlife reservations, and some are just big uninhabited sandbars. Like the Gulf coast mainland, all of them through the years have been ravaged by hurricane after hurricane, flattened by vicious winds and covered by high waves.

The storms have been innumerable; a few of the more devastating hurricanes, such as those of 1856 and 1893 and 1965, are still talked about. Thousands of people have met a violent death; gala parties have turned into nightmares, with ballrooms and entire hotels swept away, leaving only a few survivors clinging to trees or found floating on broken branches or slats of wood. After each hurricane, it is said that no one will ever live here again. And still, after each hurricane, the people slowly begin to rebuild here and there on the sand and the flat shining earth. As time passes, a house appears, followed by another and after it a hotel and an oyster bar and a little restaurant; then a boat dock and a summer cottage. Life goes on. If you ask the residents why, they will tell you it is because they happen to live here; if you ask them why they happen to live here, they

189

will say it is because this is where they live. One year an island may be an empty, lonely-looking place where children come to dig for buried pirate treasure, and in a year or two or three it will be built up again. One day it will look more or less the same as it always looked before. And one day after that, the bruise-colored sky will darken; the bird cries will take on a strange ring; the air will grow heavy and still. Then the sky will explode, lashing the earth with whips of rain and wind, growing until great seas rise from the Gulf to meet the clouds.

In its day, Grand Isle contained orange groves and sugar cane. At its center wild orchids once grew riotously; there was lush vegetation, banana plants, oleander in a profusion of colors. Where yesterday fishermen's shacks stood on the shore, today fiddler crabs skitter over flat sands barely above sea level. A few trees, their tops flat and sheared by strong wind, still remain in the soil, holding the earth together. There are motels now, and private homes are being built; people come here to fish and swim. Sunday on the beach, a family gathers to clean and fillet some fish they have caught. They have brought along some plates and a deep skillet, a couple of lemons, some oil and garlic and salt, a little cornmeal and a bucket of ice filled with cold beer. The fish fillets are left to lie for an hour or so swathed in a blanket of fresh-squeezed lemon juice and crushed garlic, while the children rollick on the sand and the parents sip beer and build a fire of twigs and branches. The oil is heated in the skillet until it is blistering hot; the fillets are dipped in the cornmeal and dropped in. The garlic-fried fish comes out crisp and light and too hot to eat; it is allowed to cool a few moments in the sea air. The children come running and the family eats, as the day begins to end. The sharp lemon-garlic taste of the fish balances the softness of the quiet air. Nothing seems to stir, for the weather goes to extremes here: fury of wind is often followed by long days of calm and gentle skies.

As on the other islands and on the mainland marshes, everything happens here or nothing does. More people will come next summer to fish from the beaches or go out in boats in search of tarpon and tuna and marlin. By then the lushness of the vegetation will show again. Herds of cows will graze in the new grass. New paths will lead through the palmettos to new houses with wide porches for sleeping and beds covered by mosquito nets. The houses will have thermometers and barometers on the walls, to give fair warning of the next disaster. In the mornings, men will be seen on the beaches with large nets, throwing them out and drawing them in, seining for hours. Others will go out in boats to fish in the deeper waters. Women will stand on the sand, casting long lines that will bring in enough to feed their families during the day. The coastal islands will grow again into small communities—until the next hurricane.

Travel back to the mainland beaches, and in some places you will see stark reminders of the last hurricane. Gutted shells of houses stand next to a naked row of twisted stools that was once an oyster bar. For mile after mile along the coast the devastation has been all but complete. One house that was partially spared has been turned into a small restaurant. Business is slower than slow; only the fishermen and the men who run the shrimp boats eat here. Stop and have a bowl of redfish courtbouillon, a dish that is to the bayous and marshes and Gulf coast what a hamburger is to the Midwest. A rich brown *roux* has been made and combined with tomato purée, onions, shallots, garlic, celery and bell pepper. Bay leaves and allspice and red pepper and other spices have been added, and a dash of Tabasco. Redfish meat and a bit of claret have been put in and simmered gently for an hour, and the courtbouillon is served in a gumbo bowl with rice. It is red and thick and searing, and just one taste of it makes you imagine you can stand up even to the weather.

At dawn, in the first gray sheath of light when the water and the sky are the same color, go out on one of the shrimp boats. Take a covered basket of fried frogs' legs *(Recipe Index)* with you and a bottle of wine; as any Creole or Acadian will tell you, Louisiana frogs' legs are better than even France knows about. The shrimp trawler slides past reed-banked channels into the open Gulf mist. For a time the land disappears. Then you see another ghostly ship like yours nearby, and another. The little shrimp-boat fleet rides together as the day opens. The fog burns off slowly and you begin to see outlines of the coast, deserted and invitingly white in the morning sun. One of the men on your boat stands motionless looking down at the water. Suddenly he frowns. You follow his line of vision, but you see nothing—only the blue-gray surface of the sea. Still, he has noticed something; don't ask him what, for he won't quite know himself. He has a sense of what is swimming underneath, he has learned it by year after year of watching; he just knows, that's all. A trawl is dropped from the boat and dragged slowly along through the water. After a while it is raised and dumped on the deck. A quivering mass of marine life rolls out, silver and pink and translucent, flipping and wriggling and crawling over itself. Yes, there were shrimp running down there, thousands of them. There were a few fish too, and sting rays and jellyfish and turtles and other things, as if the core of the sea had been scooped up. The men get busy with wooden rakes, separating the shrimp so that they can be transferred to another boat that operates as a carrier, taking the catch back to shore; the trawlers themselves stay out to work. The other fish are thrown back, the trawl is dropped again, and the men rest for a while. Share your meal with them. The frogs' legs have a good, fresh taste and the meat under the crisp-fried skin is opaque and more tender than fried chicken. It is fitting that you should have frogs' legs here, for they taste better in the salt sea spray, and you wash them down with sun-warmed red wine. Now at the end of your travels, this is the last of the flavors of the coast. Here Creoles and Acadians have swapped tastes down through the years, surviving on rivers and lakes and bayous and marshes, living on the harvests of their waters, and on those of the open sea.

Ask the old fisherman hunched next to you about the coast. The desolation won't last, he says. That last hurricane was terrible, but one day the people will come back. *Mais oui,* they will build it up again. Look there at the Isles Dernières; there was once a fine resort over there, you know. There is nothing much there now, but there will be.

He goes on talking, and in his voice there is a hopeful ring of the future. The shrimp trawler moves slowly along in the rising wind.

Strawberry Ice Cream

Pick over the berries carefully, removing the stems and hulls and discarding any fruit that is badly bruised or shows signs of mold. Wash the fruit briefly in a large sieve or colander set under cold running water, then spread the strawberries on paper towels to drain and pat them completely dry with fresh paper towels. Quarter the berries, dropping them into a deep bowl as you proceed.

In a heavy 2- to 3-quart saucepan, heat 1 cup of the cream, the sugar and the salt over low heat, stirring until the sugar is dissolved; do not let the mixture come to a boil. Pour the mixture into a deep bowl, stir in the remaining 3 cups of cream, the vanilla extract and 2 cups of the quartered berries, and refrigerate until the mixture is chilled. Cover the remaining strawberries tightly with foil or plastic wrap and refrigerate until you are ready to use them.

Pack a 2-quart ice-cream freezer with layers of finely crushed or cracked ice and coarse rock salt in the proportions recommended by the freezer manufacturer. Add cold water if the manufacturer advises it. Then ladle the chilled cream mixture into the ice-cream can and cover it.

If you have a hand ice-cream maker, fill it with the chilled cream mixture and let it stand for 3 or 4 minutes before beginning to turn the handle. Then, slowly at first, crank continuously for about 5 minutes. Stir in the reserved strawberries and the liquid that has accumulated around them and crank for 10 to 15 minutes more. Do not stop turning at any time or the ice cream may be lumpy.

When the handle can barely be moved, the ice cream is ready to serve. If you wish to keep it for an hour or two, remove the lid and dasher. Scrape the ice cream off the dasher and pack it firmly into the container with a spoon. Cover securely, pour off any water in the bucket and repack the ice and salt solidly around it.

If you have an electric ice-cream maker, fill the can with the chilled cream mixture, cover it, turn on the switch and let the mixture churn for about 5 minutes. Stir in the reserved strawberries and their liquid, cover again and continue to churn for about 10 to 15 minutes more, or until the motor slows or actually stops. Serve the ice cream immediately or follow the procedure above to keep it for an hour or two.

Lacking an ice-cream maker, stir the reserved berries and liquid into the chilled cream mixture and pour the mixture into four ice-cube trays from which the dividers have been removed. Spread the ice cream evenly and smooth the top with a rubber spatula. Freeze for 3 to 4 hours, stirring every 30 minutes or so and scraping into the ice cream the ice particles that form around the edges of the tray.

Tightly covered, the strawberry ice cream may safely be kept in the freezer or the freezing compartment of the refrigerator for several weeks. Before serving it, place the ice cream in the refrigerator for 20 to 30 minutes to let it soften slightly.

To make about 2 quarts

2 quarts firm ripe fresh strawberries
1 quart heavy cream
1 cup sugar
1/8 teaspoon salt
1 tablespoon vanilla extract

At the Rienzi plantation on Bayou Lafourche, now the residence of Mr. and Mrs. Lawrence Levert, an alfresco table offers a diversity of summer fare: strawberry ice cream, lemonade, fruit-filled watermelon and pecan pie.

To serve 6 to 8

1 pound *chaurice (Recipe Booklet)* or other hot sausage, skinned and sliced into ½-inch-thick rounds
Vegetable oil, if needed
2 five-pound ducks, each cut into 8 pieces
4 teaspoons salt
Freshly ground black pepper
½ cup flour
6 tablespoons brown *roux (page 66)*
1 cup finely chopped onions
½ cup finely chopped scallions
1 cup finely chopped celery
1 cup finely chopped green peppers
3 quarts warm water
½ teaspoon Tabasco sauce
1½ teaspoons ground hot red pepper (cayenne)
¼ cup finely chopped fresh parsley, preferably the flat-leaf Italian variety
Filé powder *(see Glossary, page 198)*
6 to 8 cups freshly cooked long-grain white rice

To serve 6

6 tablespoons brown *roux (page 66)*
½ cup finely chopped onions
½ cup finely chopped celery
½ cup finely chopped scallions
2 teaspoons finely chopped garlic
3 cups coarsely chopped drained canned tomatoes
1 cup canned tomato purée
1 cup finely chopped green peppers
1 cup fish stock *(Recipe Booklet)*
½ cup dry red wine
1 large bay leaf
½ teaspoon crumbled dried thyme
¼ teaspoon crumbled dried marjoram
¼ teaspoon ground allspice
2½ pounds redfish or red-snapper fillets, skinned and cut into 3-by-1-inch strips
2 tablespoons fresh lemon juice
½ teaspoon ground hot red pepper (cayenne)

Duck-and-Sausage Gumbo

In a heavy ungreased 12-inch skillet, fry the sausage over low heat, turning the slices frequently with a slotted spatula until the bottom of the pan is filmed with fat. Increase the heat to moderate and, turning the slices occasionally, continue to fry until the sausage is richly browned. Transfer the sausage slices to paper towels to drain. There should be about ½ cup of fat in the skillet; if not, add vegetable oil to make up that amount.

Pat the pieces of duck completely dry with paper towels and remove any large pieces of fat. Season the birds with 2 teaspoons of the salt and a few grindings of black pepper. Roll the ducks in the flour to coat the pieces on all sides and vigorously shake off the excess flour.

Brown the ducks, five or six pieces at a time, in the hot fat remaining in the skillet. Turn the pieces frequently with tongs and regulate the heat so that they color deeply and evenly without burning. As they brown, transfer the pieces of duck to paper towels to drain.

Warm the *roux* over low heat in a heavy 12-quart enameled or cast-iron pot. When the *roux* is smooth and fluid, stir in the onions, scallions and celery. Stirring frequently, cook over moderate heat for about 5 minutes, or until the vegetables are soft. Mix in the green peppers. Then, stirring constantly, pour in the warm water in a slow, thin stream and bring to a boil over high heat.

Add the sausage slices, the pieces of duck, the remaining 2 teaspoons of salt, the Tabasco and the red pepper. When the mixture returns to a boil, reduce the heat to low and cover the pot partially. Simmer the gumbo for 2 hours. Remove the pot from the heat and, with a large spoon, skim as much fat from the surface as possible. Stir in the parsley and 2 teaspoons of filé powder, and taste for seasoning. The gumbo should be hotly spiced and may require more Tabasco and/or red pepper.

Ladle the gumbo into a heated tureen and serve at once, accompanied by the rice in a separate bowl. Traditionally, a cupful of the rice is mounded in a heated soup plate and the gumbo spooned around it. Present additional filé powder for those who like gumbo with a stronger flavor.

Redfish Courtbouillon

In a heavy 4- to 5-quart casserole, warm the brown *roux* over low heat for 2 or 3 minutes, stirring constantly. Add the onions, celery, scallions and garlic and, stirring occasionally, cook for about 5 minutes, or until the vegetables are soft.

Add the tomatoes, tomato purée, green peppers, fish stock, wine, bay leaf, thyme, marjoram and allspice and, stirring from time to time, cook briskly, uncovered, until the mixture is thick enough to hold its shape almost solidly in the spoon.

Drop in the strips of fish and turn them about with a spoon to coat them evenly. Stir in the lemon juice and red pepper, reduce the heat to low, and simmer tightly covered for 20 to 25 minutes, or until the fish flakes easily when prodded gently with a fork.

Remove and discard the bay leaf and taste the sauce for seasoning. Serve the redfish courtbouillon at once, directly from the casserole or from a heated serving bowl.

Crab Chops

In a heavy 1- to 1½-quart saucepan, melt 4 tablespoons of the butter over moderate heat. Add the flour and mix well. Stirring constantly with a wire whisk, pour in the milk in a slow, thin stream and cook over high heat until the mixture comes to a boil, thickens heavily and is smooth. Reduce the heat to low and simmer uncovered for 2 or 3 minutes.

Stir in the red pepper and salt and, with a rubber spatula, scrape the entire contents of the pan into a deep bowl. Add the crabmeat, chopped parsley and scallions, and mix all the ingredients gently but thoroughly. Taste for seasoning. Cover the bowl with foil or plastic wrap and refrigerate for at least 2 hours, or until the crab mixture is somewhat firm.

Break the eggs into a shallow bowl and beat them to a froth with a fork or wire whisk. Spread the bread crumbs on a platter or a piece of wax paper. Divide the crab mixture into six equal portions and, with your hand, pat each portion into a teardrop-shaped "chop" about 5 inches long and ½ inch thick. As you form each chop, place it in the bread crumbs and turn it carefully to coat both sides. Immerse the chop in the beaten eggs and then turn it over in the crumbs again to bread it evenly. As you proceed, arrange the crab chops side by side in a large pan lined with wax paper. Refrigerate them for at least 30 minutes to firm the coating.

In a heavy 12-inch skillet, melt the remaining 6 tablespoons of butter with the oil over moderate heat. When the foam begins to subside, add the crab chops and, turning them once with a metal spatula, fry them for about 10 minutes, or until they are delicately browned on both sides.

Arrange the crab chops on a heated platter or individual plates and, if you wish, insert a crab claw at the narrow end of each chop *(photograph, page 182)*. Garnish with the lemon wedges and parsley sprigs, and serve the crab chops at once, accompanied by a bowl of Creole tartar sauce.

To serve 6

10 tablespoons butter
¼ cup flour
1 cup milk
½ teaspoon ground hot red pepper (cayenne)
1 teaspoon salt
1 pound (about 3 cups) fresh, frozen or canned crabmeat, thoroughly drained and picked over to remove all bits of shell and cartilage
¼ cup finely chopped fresh parsley plus fresh parsley sprigs for garnish, both preferably the flat-leaf Italian variety
¼ cup finely chopped scallions, including 3 inches of the green tops
3 eggs
3 cups soft fresh crumbs made from French- or Italian-type bread, pulverized in a blender
2 tablespoons vegetable oil
6 cooked blue-crab claws, in their shells (optional)
1 lemon, cut lengthwise into 6 wedges
Creole tartar sauce *(Recipe Booklet)*

Pecan Lace Cookies

Preheat the oven to 400°. With a pastry brush, spread 2 tablespoons of the softened butter over two large baking sheets. Sprinkle each baking sheet with 1 tablespoon of the flour and tip the pan from side to side to distribute the flour evenly. Invert the baking sheet and rap it sharply to remove the excess flour. Combine ½ cup of the flour, the baking powder and the salt, and sift them together into a bowl. Set aside.

In a deep bowl, cream 2 tablespoons of softened butter by beating and mashing it against the sides of the bowl with the back of a spoon until it is light and fluffy. Add the sugar, beat in the eggs and the vanilla extract, and stir the flour mixture into the batter. Then add the pecans.

Drop the batter by the heaping teaspoonful onto the prepared baking sheets, spacing the cookies about 3 inches apart. Bake in the middle of the oven for 5 minutes, or until the cookies have spread into lacelike 4-inch rounds and have turned golden brown. Let the cookies cool for a minute or so, then transfer them to wire racks to cool completely.

Let the baking sheets cool completely, then coat them with the remaining 2 tablespoons of softened butter and 2 tablespoons of flour, and bake the remaining cookies in the preheated oven. In a tightly covered jar or box, the cookies can safely be kept for a week or so.

To make about 30 four-inch round cookies

6 tablespoons butter, softened
4 tablespoons plus ½ cup unsifted flour
1 teaspoon double-acting baking powder
A pinch of salt
2 cups sugar
2 eggs, well beaten
1 teaspoon vanilla extract
2 cups coarsely chopped pecans

To serve 4

Two 1½-pound oven-ready pintail
  ducks, with the necks, gizzards
  and hearts reserved
1 teaspoon salt
¼ teaspoon freshly ground black
  pepper
2 tablespoons flour
6 slices lean bacon
2 medium-sized onions, peeled and
  sliced crosswise into ¼-inch-
  thick rounds
½ cup dry red wine
½ cup chicken stock, fresh or
  canned
4 medium-sized carrots, scraped and
  sliced crosswise into ¼-inch-
  thick rounds
¼ teaspoon crumbled dried sage
  leaves
¼ teaspoon finely grated fresh
  lemon peel
⅛ teaspoon crumbled dried thyme

Braised Pintail Duck

Wash the ducks and giblets (the necks, gizzards and hearts) under cold running water and pat them completely dry with paper towels. Season the cavities of the birds with the salt and pepper and rub the flour into their skin. Truss the ducks neatly.

In a heavy 10-inch skillet, fry the bacon over moderate heat, turning the slices frequently with tongs until they are crisp and brown and have rendered all their fat. Transfer the bacon to paper towels to drain, crumble the slices into small bits, and set them aside.

Add the duck necks, gizzards and hearts to the fat remaining in the pan and, turning them frequently, fry over moderate heat until they are richly browned. With a slotted spoon, transfer the giblets to a heavy 6- to 7-quart casserole.

Then brown the ducks in the bacon fat, turning them with tongs or a spoon and regulating the heat so that they color deeply and evenly without burning. Transfer the birds to the casserole and add the onions to the fat remaining in the skillet. Stirring occasionally, cook over moderate heat for 8 to 10 minutes, or until the onions are soft and brown. With a slotted spoon, add the onions to the ducks.

Pour off the fat remaining in the skillet, add the wine and stock, and bring to a boil over high heat, meanwhile scraping in the brown particles that cling to the bottom and sides of the pan. Stir in the carrots, sage, lemon peel and thyme, and pour the entire contents of the skillet over the ducks. Scatter the reserved bacon bits on top.

Bring the casserole to a boil over high heat, reduce the heat to low, and simmer tightly covered for 1 hour, or until the birds are tender and a thigh shows no resistance when pierced with the point of a small sharp knife.

Taste for seasoning and serve at once, directly from the casserole. Or, if you prefer, arrange the ducks side by side on a deep heated platter and ladle the carrots, onions and cooking liquid over them.

To serve 4

5 eggs
½ cup granulated sugar
3 tablespoons brandy
2 tablespoons orange-flower water
1 teaspoon finely grated fresh lemon
  peel
8 half-inch-thick slices of day-old
  French- or Italian-type bread
1 pound lard
Confectioners' sugar

Pain Perdu

The name pain perdu, which literally means "lost bread," refers to the fact that the dish is made with stale bread that might otherwise be discarded. Even in this rather elaborate version of the recipe, it is clear that pain perdu is related to our familiar French toast.

In a large, deep bowl, beat the eggs and granulated sugar with a wire whisk or a rotary or electric beater until they are frothy and well combined. Beat in the brandy, orange-flower water and lemon peel, then add the bread slices and turn them about in the egg mixture to moisten them evenly. Let the bread soak at room temperature for at least 30 minutes.

In a heavy 12-inch skillet, melt the lard over moderate heat until it is very hot but not smoking. Fry the bread, three or four slices at a time, for 2 minutes on each side, turning the slices carefully with a wide metal spatula and regulating the heat so that they brown richly and evenly without burning. As they brown, transfer the bread slices to paper towels to drain.

Sprinkle the *pain perdu* with confectioners' sugar and serve at once, accompanied if you like by a pitcher or pure cane syrup *(see Glossary)*.

Tourtes Douces
BLACKBERRY TURNOVERS

To make 2 dozen 8-inch turnovers

5 cups unsifted flour
2 teaspoons double-acting baking
  powder
1 teaspoon salt
1 teaspoon vanilla extract
¾ cup milk
10 tablespoons butter, softened
8 tablespoons vegetable shortening,
  softened
1½ cups granulated sugar
2 eggs
5 cups blackberry jam *(below)*
Confectioners' sugar

Combine the flour, baking powder and salt and sift them into a bowl. Add the vanilla extract to the milk and set the mixture aside.

In a deep bowl, cream 8 tablespoons of the softened butter, the vegetable shortening and granulated sugar together by beating and mashing them against the sides of the bowl with the back of a large spoon until the mixture is light and fluffy. Beat in the eggs, one at a time. Add about 1½ cups of the flour mixture and, when it is well incorporated, beat in about ¼ cup of the milk mixture. Repeat two more times, alternating about 1½ cups of the flour with ¼ cup of the milk and beating well after each addition.

Divide the dough into 24 equal portions and pat and shape each portion into a ball. Arrange the balls in one layer in a shallow dish, drape wax paper over them, and refrigerate for about 1 hour for easier rolling.

Meanwhile, warm the blackberry jam in a small saucepan, stirring frequently until it is fluid. Pour the jam through a fine sieve set over a bowl to strain out the seeds, then let the jam cool to room temperature.

Preheat the oven to 375°. With a pastry brush, spread the remaining 2 tablespoons of softened butter evenly over two large baking sheets. To shape each turnover, place one ball of dough at a time on a lightly floured surface and roll it into a circle about 8 inches in diameter. Spoon about 3 tablespoons of the blackberry jam onto the center of each circle and spread it evenly, leaving at least ½ inch of dough exposed around it.

Moisten the exposed dough with a finger dipped in water and fold the circle over to make a half-moon shape. With the tines of a fork, crimp the curved edges tightly together and pierce the top of the turnover in two or three places. As you proceed, arrange the turnovers side by side on the buttered baking sheets.

Bake in the middle of the oven for 20 minutes, or until the *tourtes douces* are delicately browned. With a spatula, transfer them to wire racks to cool to room temperature. Just before serving, sprinkle the turnovers lightly with confectioners' sugar.

Blackberry Jam

To make about 5 cups

6 cups fresh ripe blackberries
½ cup water
4 cups sugar

Pick over the berries carefully, removing any stems and discarding fruit that is badly bruised or shows signs of mold. Do not discard any under-ripe berries; although tarter than ripe ones, they contain more pectin —the substance that jells the fruit.

Wash the blackberries briefly in a large sieve or colander set under cold running water and drop them into a heavy 4- to 6-quart enameled casserole. Add the water and sugar, and bring to a boil over high heat, stirring until the sugar dissolves. Reduce the heat to moderate and, stirring from time to time, cook uncovered until the jam reaches a temperature of 221° (or 9° above the boiling point of water in your locality) on a jelly, candy or deep-frying thermometer.

Remove the pan from the heat. With a large spoon, carefully skim off the foam from the surface and ladle the blackberry jam into hot sterilized jars. For canning and sealing directions see the Recipe Index.

Glossary

ABSINTHE: Bitter anise-flavored green liqueur composed of aromatic plants and high-proof spirit. Because it contains the dangerous oils of wormwood, which are said to drive people mad or make them suicidal, the sale of true absinthe is prohibited in most countries. The sale of the liqueur itself was banned in the United States in 1912. To take the place of absinthe in mixed drinks, there are sweeter anise-flavored liqueurs such as Herbsaint, Ojen and Pernod.

ANDOUILLE: Smoked Creole-Acadian sausage stuffed with cubed lean pork and flavored with such seasonings as vinegar, garlic, red pepper and salt.

BEANS, SMALL RED: Flat oval-shaped dried beans, smaller than the familiar red kidney beans and darker in color than pinto beans. In South Louisiana small red beans are the preferred variety for the traditional dish of red beans and rice. They are available at most groceries, but dried red kidney beans can be substituted.

BOUDIN (literally, "pudding"): In South Louisiana, as in France, the name for blood sausage.

BOUDIN BLANC: Fresh Creole-Acadian sausage, made with lean and fat pork, rice, seasonings.

BOUDIN ROUGE: Fully cooked and smoked Creole-Acadian sausage, made with lean pork, calf's blood and rice, and sometimes pig's liver, heart and tongue as well. The sausage is flavored with such seasonings as onions, parsley, red pepper and salt.

BROKEN RICE: *See* Rice, broken.

CALA: Sweet, deep-fried breakfast cake, made from a rich rice dough, shaped in balls.

CANE SYRUP, PURE (ribbon cane syrup): Sweet dark-brown sugar-cane syrup, with a flavor somewhat like that of dark-brown sugar. To make it, the juice extracted from sugar cane is boiled, filtered and boiled again until it reaches the consistency of heavy maple syrup. (With further boiling, it would become *la cuite*.) Like maple syrup, the cane variety is used on breakfast cakes or in desserts. Available in Louisiana or by mail (*Shopping Guide*) in 12-, 24-, 45- and 90-fluid-ounce cans. As a substitute, combine two parts dark corn syrup with one part dark molasses.

CHAURICE: Highly spiced fresh sausage made of ground veal, beef and pork, and flavored with such seasonings as thyme, cloves, bay leaf, nutmeg, mace, garlic, red pepper and white pepper. It is an old-time Louisiana sausage, still especially popular for barbecues.

CHICORY ROOT: White root of a special variety of chicory (not the kind grown for salad greens), which is dried, roasted and ground to a desired fineness. When brewed with coffee, it gives the beverage a distinctive flavor. *See also* Creole coffee.

CORN FLOUR: Yellow or white corn, milled to the texture of wheat flour. It tastes like cornmeal and in South Louisiana is often used to coat seafood and vegetables for deep frying. Available in Louisiana groceries, elsewhere in health-food stores.

CRAWFISH (crayfish): Fresh-water crustacean, related to the lobster and resembling a miniature version of it. Found in rivers, lakes and bayous of South Louisiana, and highly valued for the sweet white meat. Available fresh in Louisiana and some Midwestern and Pacific states, the meat is also sold frozen by some fish dealers (*Shopping Guide*).

CREOLE COFFEE: The standard brew of both the Creole and the Acadian cuisines, made from a darker-than-normal roast coffee and usually mixed with ground roast chicory root. The beverage is always prepared in drip pots and is very strong.

CREOLE CREAM CHEESE: Thick, white, smooth-textured fresh cheese, with the sweet flavor of whole cream. The cheese is made from skim milk that is clabbered, then ladled into perforated molds to drain overnight. When packaged in the typical 12-ounce container, 5 ounces of the drained curds are topped with 7 ounces of a thin light fresh cream. Creole cream cheese is a unique South Louisiana product—softer, more delicately flavored and much more perishable than the familiar Philadelphia-type cream cheese. It is usually eaten at breakfast or lunch with sugar and fruit, although some people prefer it with salt and pepper.

CREOLE MUSTARD: Pungent prepared mustard made from the spicy brown mustard seeds rather than the more familiar, but somewhat blander, yellow seeds. The seeds are steeped in distilled white vinegar, then coarsely ground and left to marinate for up to 12 hours longer before packing. The finished product is available throughout Louisiana, at fine food stores elsewhere in the United States or by mail (*Shopping Guide*) in 5¾-ounce jars. Creole mustard should be refrigerated after it is opened. As a substitute, use any strong-flavored prepared brown mustard.

CUITE, LA: Pure cane syrup cooked to the consistency of taffy. (The term *la cuite,* derived from the French word *cuire,* "to cook," is used in the sugar-refining industry to refer to a boiling process.) Though it may be poured over breakfast cakes, like maple syrup, *la cuite* is so sweet that it is generally eaten in very small quantities. In Louisiana, children wrap *la cuite* on a stick and dip it in chopped walnuts or pecans to make a lollipop. Packed in 12-ounce cans; available in some groceries in Louisiana or by mail (*Shopping Guide*).

FILÉ POWDER: Ground dried sassafras leaves from trees that grow wild along the coast of the Gulf of Mexico. First used as a seasoning by the Choctaw Indians, it is popular today for flavoring and thickening gumbo. Filé becomes stringy when boiled and should be added to a gumbo only after the gumbo pot is taken off the stove. Filé is available wherever fine herbs are sold.

GUMBO: Spicy, thick Creole soup composed of fish or shellfish, poultry, game, meats and vegetables in any of a great variety of combinations. Gumbo is thickened with either okra or filé powder and is served ladled over rice. The name is probably derived through the Portuguese *quingombo* from *quillobo,* an African word for okra.

GUMBO Z'HERBES (or *gumbo aux herbes*): Thick Creole soup originally composed of fresh greens and seasonings. Developed as a Lenten dish, it was traditionally prepared on Good Friday with seven herbs to ensure good luck. It is now served the year round, and modern recipes often include meats.

HERBSAINT: Greenish-amber liqueur flavored with a blend of spices and herbs in which anise predominates. First marketed under this name in New Orleans by an apothecary, J. Marion Legendre, in 1934, it is based on a recipe for a wormwood-free absinthe that Legendre's father had learned in southern France.

JAMBALAYA: Highly seasoned stew, composed of any of several combinations of seafood, meat, poultry and vegetables, and cooked with white rice. The dish was brought to New Orleans by the Spaniards in the late 1700s, and the name is probably derived from the Spanish *jamón,* or "ham." Originally made only with ham, it was later modified to include the variety of meats or shellfish used today.

JERUSALEM ARTICHOKE: Edible tuber of a variety of sunflower native to the United States. On the outside the tubers look like small rough-skinned sweet potatoes, but their flesh is white. Cultivated by the Indians before the arrival of Columbus, they were introduced into Europe in the 17th Century. The tuber tastes like the heart of the globe, or French, artichoke —whence its name. The use of the word Jerusalem in the name may be a corruption of the Italian *girasole,* meaning sunflower.

MIRLITON (vegetable pear, mango squash, chayote, *christophene,* chocho): Tropical squash, round or pear-shaped, ranging from white to dark green in color, and from 3 to 8 inches long. It may be either smooth or corrugated and is sometimes covered with soft spines. The firm, crisp flesh surrounds a single flat seed and tastes more delicate than summer squash. Mirliton squash are available in the Louisiana area in early fall, and in some Latin American markets elsewhere the year round. It will keep for about a week in the refrigerator. (*Photograph, page 97.*)

MUSTARD, CREOLE: *See* Creole mustard.

OJEN: Anise-flavored 84-proof liqueur made in Jerez, Spain. It is another of the "absinthe" drinks and, like Herbsaint and Pernod, turns cloudy when mixed with water.

ORANGE-FLOWER WATER: A subtle and fragrant flavoring made from orange-tree blossoms steeped in water. It is available at fine food stores everywhere.

ORGEAT: A flavoring syrup prepared from powdered dried blanched almonds and sweetened with sugar. It is available at fine food stores everywhere.

PARSLEY, FLAT-LEAF: In South Louisiana, the most commonly used parsley (known elsewhere as Italian parsley). The blander curly parsley is used primarily for garnishes.

PERNOD: Anise-flavored apéritif, made in France. It is another of the "absinthe" drinks and, like Herbsaint and Ojen, turns cloudy when mixed with water.

PEYCHAUD BITTERS: Spicy red flavoring introduced to New Orleans in the 1790s by A. A. Peychaud, an apothecary. Peychaud is also sometimes credited with inventing the cocktail because he blended his bitters with cognac in an egg cup, or *coquetier,* to produce one of America's earliest mixed drinks. Despite differences in flavor, other kinds of bitters may be substituted for Peychaud.

PONCE: From the French word *panse,* meaning paunch, or stomach. In Louisiana, pig's stomach is filled with a spicy meat-and-yam mixture and steamed to produce an oversized sausage called a stuffed *ponce.*

REDFISH (red drum, channel bass): Copper- or bronze-colored salt-water inshore fish with a distinctive black spot at the base of the tail. It is an important commercial fish of the Gulf and South Atlantic Coasts, and a favorite with sports fishermen.

RICE, BROKEN: In the Louisiana area a name sometimes used for short-grain rice, which produces a stickier jambalaya than the long-grain variety. Many cooks pound short-grain rice to make it even starchier. If this type of rice is not available, pound the long-grain variety with a mortar and pestle or put it through a food grinder. If you prefer a nonsticky jambalaya, use long-grain rice.

RIVER SHRIMP: Tiny fresh-water shrimp found in the Mississippi and other Louisiana rivers and available only in that area. Unlike Gulf shrimp, river shrimp are always sold with the heads on. They are about 1½ to 2 inches long (with the heads) and run at least 60 to 70 to the pound. They are caught in traps, often baited with cornmeal, and are sweet and delicately flavored, but rare (the commercial catch of river shrimp is about 5,000 pounds, compared to over 230 million pounds of Gulf shrimp).

ROUX: A mixture of flour and fat used as a thickening agent for sauces, soups and gravies. Although the term *roux* is familiar in French cooking, the kind of brown *roux* used in Louisiana is unique. In both Creole and Acadian cuisines, the flour and fat (usually vegetable oil) are cooked very slowly until the mixture is brown and has a nutlike aroma and taste. This *roux* then serves as the base for bisques, gumbos and other soups, as well as for gravies and stews.

SAUTERNE: A white domestic table wine. The sauterne called for in some of the recipes in this book should be American-made, as used in South Louisiana, not the French Sauternes.

SCALLION: A pencil-thin onion with a white base and a long green top. The term is used for three members of the onion family: the young green shoots of any white globe onion; the bunching onions, which grow in clusters on enlarged root crowns; and the young green shallot.

SHALLOT: A member of the onion family, which grows in clusters on a large root, somewhat like the bunching onion. The young green shoots are the most common scallion in Louisiana. If left in the field to develop and dry, the shoots become the brown or reddish dried shallot cloves used in classic French cooking.

TROUT, SPECKLED: Louisiana name for the spotted sea trout, a blue-gray salt-water inshore game fish that is heavily marked on the upper parts of its sides with round black spots or speckles. The fish is abundant in the Gulf of Mexico and also occurs from New York to Florida along the Atlantic Coast. It is related to the weakfish or gray sea trout, which may be used as a substitute for it in cooking. (Confusingly, the term speckled trout is also used for the brook trout in some parts of the Northeastern U.S. and Canada.)

YAM: In Louisiana and most Southern states, the preferred sweet potato is the orange-fleshed moist variety commonly called a yam. Following this local custom, the recipes in this book use the term yam for the orange sweet potato. The true yam belongs to a wholly different botanical family and is a large tropical tuberous vegetable with a thick, somewhat hairy skin and white, yellow or red sweet-tasting flesh.

Most of the ingredients and utensils called for in this book's recipes can be found at any grocery or supermarket, or in a housewares shop. Even such distinctively Creole and Acadian products as crawfish and filé powder are sometimes available at fine food stores. For information about sources for Herbsaint or Peychaud bitters in your area, you may write to Sazerac Co., Inc., 328 N. Cortez St., P.O. Box 52821, New Orleans, La. 70150. The following places accept mail orders for the products specified, but—because policies differ and managements change —it is best to write to them before ordering to determine what they have in stock:

*Pure ribbon cane syrup and
La Cuite*
C. S. Steen Syrup Mill, Inc.
P.O. Box 339
Abbeville, La. 70510

Smoked sausage
Bourgeois Meat Market
519 Schriever Highway
Thibodaux, La. 70301

Creole cream cheese
Borden, Inc.
P.O. Box 10098
New Orleans, La. 70121

Live crawfish, frozen crawfish meat, redfish and speckled trout
Battistella's Sea Foods, Inc.
910 Touro St.
New Orleans, La. 70116

Food-coloring paste
Wilton Enterprises, Inc.
833 West 115 St.
Chicago, Ill. 60643

Creole drip coffeepots, cast-iron cooking pots
La Nasa Hardware Co., Inc.
1027 Decatur St.
New Orleans, La. 70116

Peychaud bitters, dark roast and chicory coffee, filé powder, Creole mustard, orange-flower water, orgeat syrup, pecans
Gourmet Shop
D. H. Holmes Co., Ltd.
819 Canal St.
New Orleans, La. 70112

Dried red beans, corn flour, dark roast and chicory coffee, filé powder, Creole mustard, short-grain rice, smoked sausages, Steen's pure ribbon cane syrup and La Cuite
Frank A. Von der Haar
4238 Magazine St.
New Orleans, La. 70115

Recipe Index

NOTE: An R preceding a page refers to the Recipe Booklet. Size, weight and material are specified for pans in the recipes because they affect cooking results. A pan should be just large enough to hold its contents comfortably. Heavy pans heat slowly and cook food at a constant rate. Aluminum and cast iron conduct heat well but may discolor foods containing egg yolks, wine, vinegar or lemon. Enamelware is a fairly poor conductor of heat. Many recipes therefore recommend stainless steel or enameled cast iron, which do not have these faults.

Credits and Acknowledgments

The sources for the illustrations that appear in this book are shown below. Credits for the pictures from left to right are separated by commas, from top to bottom by dashes. Photographs by Richard Jeffery—Cover, pages 12, 13, 26, 30, 31, 36, 40, 41, 44, 61, 65, 68, 72, 84, 85, 88, 89, 93, 94, 98, 101, 102, 104, 107, 108, 109, 111, 114, 115, 117, 119, 121, 125, 132, 133, 161, 164, 169, 174, 176, 177, 182. Photographs by Anthony Blake—pages 9, 15, 16, 17, 20, 21, 22, 23, 32, 34, 56, 57, 58, 59, 81, 82, 97, 105, 106, 110, 128, 130, 131, 136, 138, 139, 140, 143, 146, 147, 148, 149, 150, 159, 170, 172, 173, 180, 181, 186, 187, 188, 189, 192. Other photographs—page 4—Ken Heyman, Richard Henry, Charles Phillips—Monica Suder, Philip Dowell, Calvin Bleu. 6—Drawings by Mary Farnberg. 46 through 52—Richard Meek. 76, 77—Anthony Donna courtesy New York Public Library. 83—Courtesy Chicorée Leroux. 155, 156, 157—Elliott Erwitt © 1970 Magnum Photos.

For help and advice in the production of the book, the editors thank the following: *in New Orleans:* Angelo Alciatore, Henri A. Alciatore, Roy Alciatore, Antoine's Restaurant; Albert Aschaffenburg, Lysle Aschaffenburg, Douglas Leman, Jeff Schaffer, Pontchartrain Hotel; Earl Bartlett Sr., Earl Bartlett Jr., Marie Di Betta, The French Market Coffee Co.; Adam Bealer, Vaucresson Café Creole; Mr. and Mrs. Thomas N. Bernard; Edward Berns; Joseph L. Billiot, McFadden Duffy, Dr. Ted Ford, Louisiana Wild Life and Fisheries Commission; Phil Brady, New Orleans Tourist and Convention Commission; Mrs. Ella Brennan Martin, Mr. and Mrs. Owen Brennan Jr., Mr. and Mrs. Richard Brennan, Betty Hoffman, Mrs. Jill Rouse, Brennan's French Restaurant; Perry Brown Jr.; Buster Holmes Restaurant; Mr. and Mrs. Benjamin Caldwell; Joe Casamento, Casamento's Restaurant; Angelo Chetta; Bill Cullison, Special Collections Division, Tulane University Library; Mrs. Carrie W. Dean; Richard Dixon, Municipal Auditorium; Earle Dow; Charles Estes, Borden Inc.; Justin Galatoire, Mrs. Yvonne Wynne, Chris Ansel, Galatoire's Restaurant; Reagan Garrett, Reising Bakery, Inc.; Don Hessemer, New Orleans Chamber of Commerce; Mr. and Mrs. Alden Laborde; Louisiana Tourist Development Commission; James T. Maxcy, Maxcy's Coffee Pot Restaurant; Mrs. Edward P. Munson; Father Nicolas, St. Louis Cathedral; Willis Otto; Harlon Pearce, Battistella's Sea Foods, Inc.; Alvin Pierce, Bon Ton Café; James Plauché, Corinne Dunbar's Restaurant; Mrs. Helen DeJean Pollock, Chez Helene; Mrs. Margaret Porpora, The Gumbo Shop; Mr. and Mrs. Ivan H. Purinton; Stanley Schwam, Sazerac Co., Inc.; Mr. and Mrs. Herbert W. Stamps; Dr. and Mrs. Roy T. Staub; Mary Taylor; Judge and Mrs. John M. Wisdom; Mr. and Mrs. William Walker Young Jr.; *in St. Martinville:* Mr. and Mrs. Marcel M. Bienvenu; Grace Broussard; Weston Champagne; Mrs. Pline DeBlanc; Mrs. Leona Martin Guirard, Acadian House Museum, Longfellow-Evangeline State Park; Mr. and Mrs. J. Burton Willis; *elsewhere in Louisiana:* Frank Melebeck, C. S. Steen Syrup Mill, Inc., Abbeville; Paul C. P. McIlhenny, Ned Simmons, McIlhenny Company, Avery Island; Gus Cranow, Joyce Yeldell, Tourist Development Commission, Baton Rouge; A. C. Moreau, Louisiana Cooperative Extension Service, Baton Rouge; Milton Andrepont, St. Martin Parish County Agent, Breaux Bridge; Mr. and Mrs. Sidney Champagne, Breaux Bridge Bakery, Breaux Bridge; Dr. and Mrs. Earnest Young, Breaux Bridge; Leon Cognevich, Buras; Father Allen Roy, St. Joseph Benedictine High School, Chauvin; Mrs. Chloe

Anderson, Mrs. Henrietta Rouse, Zaterain's, Gretna; J. D. Hanks, Hanks and Cormier Flying Service, Kaplan; John W. Lewis Jr., Lafayette; Mr. and Mrs. Alcée Landreneau, Mamou; Revon Reed, Mamou; Fred Fandal, Mrs. Olga Fandal, Mandeville; Mrs. J. A. Winkle, New Iberia; Lester Bourgeois, Bourgeois Meat Market, Thibodaux; Mrs. Rea Gilbert, LaFourche Parish Home Demonstration Agent, Thibodaux; Mr. and Mrs. Lawrence Levert, Rienzi Plantation, Thibodaux; *in Mississippi:* E. Moret Smith, National Marine Fisheries Service, Pascagoula; *in New York City:* Kate Titus Yutzy, Dudley-Anderson-Yutzy; *in Washington, D.C.:* Mrs. Helen Duprey Bullock, National Trust for Historic Preservation.

The following shops and galleries supplied antiques, tableware and other objects used in the studio photography in this book: *in Massachusetts:* Henry Coger, Antiques, Ashley Falls; *in New York:* James Abbe Jr., Oyster Bay; *in New York City:* Ancien Régime; Ann-Morris II; Baccarat Crystal; Bardith, Ltd.; Barley Twist, Antiques; David Barrett, Antiques; Boussac of France, Inc.; George Cothran, Flowers; Deacon Furniture; Hammacher Schlemmer; James II Galleries; H. J. Kratzer, Antiques; La Cuisinière; Herbert Lanning, Ltd.; Le Vieux Monde; Les Vieux Métiers de France; Mayhew; Past & Present; Paulette's Place; Raphaelian Rug Co., Inc.; Scalamandré Silks; Edward Sporar, Antiques; Tablerie; Window Shop, Inc.; Isobel Worsley; 1066 A.D. Antiques.

Sources consulted in the production of this book include: "Absinthe," Maurice Zolotow, *Playboy; A Book of Famous Old New Orleans Recipes,* Peerless Printing Co.; *Brennan's New Orleans Cookbook,* Hermann B. Deutsch; *Cajun Country Cookin',* John and Glenna Uhler; *Creole!,* Deirdre Stanforth; *Creole City, Its Past and Its People,* Edward Larocque Tinker; *Creole Cook Book,* Lafcadio Hearn; *Don's Secrets,* Avis M. Rupert; *Evangeline,* Henry Wadsworth Longfellow; *Fabulous New Orleans,* Lyle Saxon; *First —You Make a Roux,* Les Vingt-Quatre Club; *Gourmet's Guide to New Orleans,* Natalie Scott and Caroline Merrick Jones; *Gulf Coast Gourmet,* Jane S. Coleman; *Gumbo Ya-Ya,* Lyle Saxon; *History of the Acadians,* Bona Arsenault; *It's An Old New Orleans Custom,* Lura Robinson; *Louisiana,* American Guide Series, Federal Writers Project; *Louisiana Cookery,* Mary Land; *Louisiana's Fabulous Foods,* Lady Helen Henriques Hardy and Raymond J. Martinez; *Maylie's Table d'Hôte Recipes,* Anna May Maylie; *Mrs. Simms' Fun Cooking Guide,* Myrtle Landry Simms; *New Orleans Carnival Cook Book,* Women's Republican Publications; *New Orleans City Guide,* American Guide Series, Federal Writers Project; *New Orleans Cook Book,* Lena Richard; *New Orleans Creole Recipes,* Mary Moore Bremer; *New Orleans Cuisine,* Mary Land; *New Orleans Restaurant Cookbook,* Deirdre Stanforth; *New Orleans Sketches,* William Faulkner; *Queen New Orleans,* Harnett T. Kane; *Quelque Chose Douce* and *Quelque Chose Piquante,* Mercedes Vidrine; *Recettes du Petit Paris de l'Amérique,* Carmen Bulliard Montegut; *River Road Recipes,* The Junior League of Baton Rouge; *Talk About Good!,* Service League of Lafayette; *The Art of Creole Cookery,* William I. Kaufman and Sister Mary Ursula Cooper, O.P.; *The Bayous of Louisiana,* Harnett T. Kane; *The Complete Works of Kate Chopin,* edited by Per Seyersted; *The Grandissimes,* George W. Cable; *The Original Picayune Creole Cook Book,* The Times-Picayune Publishing Co.; *The Romantic New Orleanians,* Robert Tallant; *The World from Jackson Square,* Etolia S. Basso.

❎ Printed in U.S.A.